Toe Jam Days

Toe Jam Days

M. David Myerholtz

authorHOUSE®

AuthorHouse™
1663 Liberty Drive
Bloomington, IN 47403
www.authorhouse.com
Phone: 1-800-839-8640

First published by AuthorHouse   10/21/2011

ISBN: 978-1-4670-4240-6 (sc)
ISBN: 978-1-4670-4239-0 (ebk)

Library of Congress Control Number: 2011917599

Printed in the United States of America

DEDICATED TO

Our son Alan

whose story ended too early

PREFACE

Growing up in the 1940s and 1950s was certainly different from growing up today. Outdoor plumbing, the strong influence of farm life, walking to get just about anywhere, and the general innocence of that particular time, all helped shape my childhood. My parents and grandparents were the products of the Great Depression and World War II, so my childhood was influenced by those events and the effect of those events on my family. It is my hope that through this writing, my children and grandchildren will come away with a better understanding of what it was like for me as a child.

Throughout my life I interacted with family, childhood friends, teachers, clergy, coaches, and others who became a part of my life if even for a very short period of time. I took on some of their qualities without even knowing that they were an influence on me. I continued to change throughout my life as I had new experiences and was exposed to new people. Writing about my life has helped me to understand myself, who I am, and how I came to be where I am in life.

I will describe individuals and tell about the life experiences that we shared, but I will not tell their stories. Since I have not seen many of them in years, my views and remembrances are often based on memories made by a young child. I can only relate what I feel and remember of that particular time. I will add information that is necessary to make the situation understandable and include details that will help explain my personal relationships with parents, brothers and sisters, and the many aunts, uncles, cousins and other relatives that were a part of my early years. At times I will include family lore. Again, I will do this to explain the situation or my relationship with the individual that is the subject of my writing.

My memories are filled with my immediate family: Mom and Pa; my sisters Louise, Janet, and Caroline; and my brothers Ray, Dan and Art. My siblings will be introduced as they entered my life and became a part of my story. However, one conclusion I have come to is that most of my brothers and sisters had different relationships with our parents, grandparents, aunts, uncles and cousins than I did. Their perception of events and people are not the same as mine. I believe this is in part because of the twelve year age difference between my youngest sibling and me.

My memories are also filled with many not-so-immediate family members. I am one of fifty-three first cousins on the Myerholtz side of the family, and I am one of ten cousins on the Dickerson side, excluding the double-cousins.

I always called my mother, Mom, and my dad, Pa, so I will continue to write of them in this way. I will also write as if I am speaking and telling an oral history, so proper composition English may occasionally suffer as a result.

Today, I feel very good about my life and what it has been. That is not to say that it has been perfect and that there have not been tough times and difficult problems. I have experienced sorrows, losses, and bad decisions. However, good and bad, the past has made me who and what I am at this moment. I cannot go back and change this; nor would I want to.

PROLOGUE

**Mom and Pa on Their Wedding Day
October 28, 1938**

To set the stage for my life, I will begin with a brief history of my parents. Pa was the fourth of eleven children born to Harmon Henry Myerholtz and Anna Amelia Lehman. Nine of the eleven children survived birth to adulthood. Pa had two older sisters, Carrie and Augusta, and one older brother, Esta (Esty). He had three younger sisters: Irene, Anna May, and Lois, and two younger brothers, Harmon (Harmie) and Robert (Bob). Virgil and Kathryn were the two children who did not survive infancy.

Pa was born on January 7, 1918 in Stony Ridge, Ohio, during a blizzard which closed all of the roads. He was born at home and was probably premature because he only weighed about three pounds. From Grandma Myerholtz, I learned that he slept at night in the top drawer of the dresser by her bed. During the day, she put him in a shoe box and set the box on the open oven door of the wood cook stove to keep him warm. He had red hair which he inherited from his grandmother, Mary Spada Myerholtz. Pa was named Myron John Myerholtz. The John was after his great-great-grandfather who was the first Myerholtz of this family to come to America from Germany in the early 1830s. I don't know where the name Myron came from, but it didn't matter because everyone except Mom called him Red. I think that Mom was the only one that always called him Myron. Pa grew up in Woodville and at an early age, about nine or ten, he was farmed out as a helper to another farming family. He lived with the other family during the week and came home on the weekends. He was paid $8.00 a month for his work, but $7.50 went to his dad; Pa was allowed to keep fifty cents. He went to school at Woodville until the ninth grade, and then he quit school and got a full time job.

Mom was the fourth of eight children born to Charles Raymond Dickerson and Helen Louise Godsey. Seven of the eight children survived to adulthood. Mom had two older brothers, Richard and Frank, and one older sister, Kathryn (Kate). Mom had two younger brothers, Charles and William, and two younger sisters, Juanita and Shirley. William died when he was about thirteen months old. The story about his death was that William walked out onto a newly varnished floor and fell down, getting varnish over most of his body. He developed a high fever shortly after that and soon died. Richard also developed a high fever when he was young. He ended up being mentally challenged for the rest of his life. He had a mental capacity about equal to a sixth grader. He could read and write, but he did not have social skills, and he mostly liked to be alone in his room.

Mom was born on August 25, 1923 in Detroit, Michigan. Grandma and Grandpa Dickerson were living in a three-story row house along with Grandpa's parents, Grandma and Grandpa Polly, and Grandpa's sisters, Freda and Clarice. It was a very hot summer, and Great Grandpa Polly owned a vacant lot on a lake in the outskirts of Detroit. The family had set up a tent on the property, and they were spending a couple of weeks camping there to get out of the heat of the city. Mom was born in the tent during this time.

Mom grew up in Toledo, and while she attended a number of schools in the Toledo area and enjoyed school, she never did graduate. When she met Pa, he was living in Woodville, and she was living with her parents who were renting a house from a local farmer just south of Toledo. The house had a shed that Grandpa Dickerson used as a garage, and the second floor of the shed was used to store grain. One day two young men were shoveling wheat out of the shed, and Mom and her sister, Kate, went out to talk with them. One of the men, Don Steel, asked Mom if she would go out on a date with him the next day. Since Mom was barely fourteen, her mother hesitated, but finally agreed. The next day, Don arrived with another young man. He explained that he had gotten into trouble at home, and his parents were punishing him by not allowing him to go on the date. However, his father did give him permission to come over long enough to explain to Mom why he wouldn't be taking her out. Then Don introduced her to the young man who was with him and said that he had come along to take her on the date in his place. That person turned out to be Pa.

Mom and Pa started dating regularly. Pa would catch the trolley from Woodville to Toledo to see Mom, but he sometimes stayed too late to catch the last trolley back to Woodville. When this happened, he would try to hitchhike home, and when a ride wasn't available, he would walk the fifteen to eighteen miles back.

Mom had turned fifteen years old on August 25 and Pa would not turn twenty-one until January 7 when they were married on October 28, 1938. They eloped and married in Indiana where Mom could marry without her parents' consent. Grandma Dickerson did not want her to marry at fifteen, but Mom knew that she was pregnant, and Mom and Pa wanted very much to be married.

My sister, Louise, was born on June 26, 1939, and about this time Pa got quite sick with rheumatic fever. The doctor told him that he had permanent heart damage which would keep him from doing physical labor for the rest of his life. Pa didn't pay attention to what he was told with regard to taking it easy. He continued to work and pressed himself to do whatever was necessary at that time to keep his job driving a semi-truck. He often told us that the muscles in his leg became quite weak, and for awhile afterwards he would have to lift his leg with his hand to switch from the accelerator to the brake pedal in order to be able to drive his truck. I cannot recall a single time in his life when the rheumatic fever stood in the way of Pa physically doing what he wanted to do or what he had to do to provide for his family, although it did keep him out of the war. Pa was never without a job as long as he lived, including his retirement, maintaining some kind of part time job even then.

Having said all of this I will begin . . .

CHAPTER 1

EARLIEST MEMORIES

Me with Pa's Lunch Box

My first continuous memories center on the farm in Woodville. However, for as long as I can remember, I have had bits and pieces of memories of four distinct events that happened early in my life. I am not sure of the timing of three of these events, but they are real memories and according to my mother they happened when I was three or four years old while we were living in Toledo. Her memory of the exact time is a little fuzzy, too, but we both know that the events took place before we moved back to Woodville, Ohio. I say back to Woodville because Woodville is where I was born.

I was born on August 12, 1940 in the home of Grandpa and Grandma Myerholtz and Dr. Egger of Woodville was in attendance. Mom and Pa were living with my grandparents in a farmhouse on what is now Oak Street which runs off to the west from Route 105. The farmhouse has long been torn down. In fact, the ground where the house sat no longer exists. It was excavated away many years ago by the Woodville Lime Plant quarry operation, and a large open quarry is all that remains of my birthplace. I was named Myron David Myerholtz, Myron for my father and David was for my great-grandfather. But from day one, I was David. Shortly after my birth, my family moved to Toledo where we lived in houses on Huron and Superior Streets. Janet was born there on January 19, 1942, and Caroline was born on September 15, 1944.

As I previously stated, I have four distinct memories of this time. I have a memory of being in a room with my sister, Louise. The door to the room is closed, and there is a bed, a dresser, and nothing more that I can remember. The windows of the room are covered with newspaper, so the room is darkened, and a small light bulb in the ceiling light provides the only lighting. My sister and I are on the bed and we are talking. I can't remember what we are talking about, but we are the only ones in the room, and we are just talking.

When as a teenager I asked my mother about this memory, she explained that Louise and I had measles at the same time and that it was a common practice to isolate the individuals in a closed room. It was also a common practice to cover the windows with newspaper to cut down on the bright sunlight as it was thought that bright light during exposure to the measles could cause permanent eye damage. I guess we spent about a week in the room together with nothing to do but talk. We were not allowed to get up and play or move around much.

My second memory is of being in a room with Louise and Mom, who is holding my baby sister, Janet. The walls of the room are concrete and so is the floor. There is a round opening in the floor with a circular stairway coming up through the opening from below. Suddenly, Pa walks up the stairway and Mom, Pa, Janet, Louise and I leave the room. I finally shared this memory with Louise, shortly before her death, and she told me that we had gone down to get Pa out of jail. I later asked Mom about it and she told me the following story.

At the time this happened, Pa was working for the Gallant Coal and Lumber Company in Toledo, Mom was pregnant with Caroline, and we were living in the house on Huron Street. Some friends of Mom and Pa were having financial problems, and it was winter, and the friends were in need of some coal to heat their house. Pa made arrangements with the bookkeeper at Gallant Coal Company to buy a ton of coal for his friend and to have the cost of the coal deducted from his weekly pay check. He delivered the ton of coal to his friend's house. At the end of the day, the foreman noticed that the ton of coal delivered by Pa had not been paid for and accused Pa of stealing the coal. He called the police and had Pa arrested. The next day when all had been checked out with the bookkeeper, Pa was released from jail. Mom took Louise, Janet, and me on a bus to the Toledo police station to pickup Pa and so my memory of the concrete room and the circular stairway had taken place there. Pa was given his job back, and he continued to work at Gallant until we moved back to Woodville.

In the third early memory, I am outside and the ground is shaking from bombs that are exploding as airplanes fly low overhead. The noise is deafening, but there is a large crowd of people clapping and shouting. Again, when I finally asked Mom about this memory, she told me that at one point while we were living in Toledo, a war bond drive was held at Riverside Park. The Army put on a mock air attack to demonstrate our fighting force abilities which included dropping non-destructive, but noisy explosives.

My final early memory took place shortly before Caroline was born. We were living in Toledo in a house on Huron street. I can't remember exactly what happened. I only remember that Mom tried to catch or close the front door of the house, and she put her arm through the glass window. I remember that she cut her hand quite badly, and there was a lot of blood. This probably took place in July or August of 1944.

CHAPTER 2

THE WOODVILLE FARM

1945-1947

Courtesy of Sarah Rewoldt (abt. 2005)

Cow barn on Woodville Farm

Sometime in early 1945 we moved back to Woodville, Ohio. Pa hired on as a tenant farmer, and we moved onto the farm owned by Art Sanders. The Sanders farm was located on Route 20, Fremont Pike, about a mile west of the Village of Woodville. The farmland was situated on both sides of Route 20 and included a total of 500 hundred acres, three sets of houses and barns, and housing for a migrant family. Art Sanders, his wife, and son, Howard, lived in a large house located on the north side of Route 20, just east of what is now County Road 16. Their farm included a number of barns, and the main cattle barn was located by their house. It was very large and sat up on a raised area to allow cattle to enter the lower section of the barn from grade level. The main floor to the barn was accessible from an inclined drive up to the first floor level.

My main memory of this barn involves a time when I helped Pa clean out the cattle pens. It was winter and the temperature was below freezing. We used pitch forks to clean the floor of the pens and load the manure and straw bedding into a manure spreader. I remember being very puzzled about the fact that each pitchfork full of manure and straw was steaming as we lifted it from the floor and tossed it into the spreader, and that the whole manure spreader was steaming, even though it was so cold outside. I could not figure it out at that time, but I learned later that decomposing straw and manure generates heat.

About a quarter of a mile east of the Sanders place and also on the north side of Route 20 was the second house with a single barn. This house was occupied by Otto Krumnow and his wife, an older German couple. In my youth, I always thought that their name was Comenow; I guess I got this impression from the way Pa pronounced it. Later in life, I learned the correct pronunciation, and I also learned that we shared a common relative. Krumnows were also descendents of John Myerholtz who came to the United States from Germany. Otto was a tenant farm worker, and he and Pa worked together on the Sanders farm. Each morning he would come over to our house to get ready for the day's work because the horses were in the barn there.

About half way between the Sanders place and the Krumnow house, there was a small three room house that served as a home for migrant workers. We all called this place the 'beet shanty,' because the house was usually only occupied when migrant workers were needed, and this was during the sugar beet season. At the time that we lived on the farm, Mr. Sanders had a Mexican family, the Ramirezes, living fulltime in this house. The Ramirez family consisted of the parents, Hercules and Pauline, Raymond, the oldest son, Ruben, the youngest son, and their daughter, Rosa. They worked for the Sanders family during the growing and harvest seasons, and Hercules worked at the Woodville Lime plant during the winter months.

Directly across Route 20 from the Krumnow house and on the south side of the road was the house that we lived in. It was a large house with two large barns, a chicken coop, and a cattle pen, and as with every farm at that time, an outhouse. One of the barns, the one just to the east of the house, was the cow barn, and the other barn was the horse barn. Mr. Sanders had two horses that were used on a daily basis for farm-related work. One horse was totally black and was the larger of the two animals; his name was Bob. The second horse was a brown horse with a couple of white feet, and his name was Bill. We will learn more of Bill later.

Our house faced Route 20, with a drive on the east side of the house that led back to a turn-around area in front of the cow barn. An access lane continued past the cow barn on the east side, and passed through a gate into the cattle pen, then continued south past the horse barn to the pasture field, and finally ended in a small wooded area south of the barns. The cattle pen, lane, and pasture field were enclosed with a fence which allowed the cows and the horses to wander and feed in the pasture. In the center of the cattle pen was a large, circular, concrete water trough. The water trough was about three feet high and about ten feet in diameter. The chicken coop was on the south side of the house and to the west of the cow barn. The outhouse was just west of the coop. There was a concrete walk running from the side porch to the drive area, with a second walk south to the outhouse area. At the intersection of the walks was a hand pump that provided water for the farm.

The house was a two story structure with a cellar. There was a front door in the living room that we seldom used. We normally came and went through the kitchen door on the east side of the house that opened onto a porch and faced the drive. Off the kitchen was a storage room with a stairway to the cellar. The cellar had a concrete basin for storing milk and other perishables. There was also a door that went into the dining room where the stairway to the upstairs was located. The living room and another room that we used as a bedroom completed the downstairs. Mom and Pa's bedroom was set up in what was supposed to be the living room with a couple of beds in the bedroom for us kids. The upstairs had four bedrooms. I remember that we lived only on the first floor of the house, probably because quite often we had one of our aunts and uncles living upstairs. The house was heated by coal stoves, and there was a wood stove in the kitchen for cooking.

We had an icebox in the kitchen that did a good job of keeping things cold as long as there was ice. The ice was sold at grocery stores, and most small towns had an ice house that only sold ice. It could also be obtained from a delivery truck that came around about twice a week. Each customer was given a card about a foot square that was usually a bright color so it could easily be seen. The card had two large numbers written on each side. The card had 25 and 50 on one side and 75 and 100 on the other.

One number on each side was right side up, and the other number was inverted. The customer placed the card in the front window of the house and positioned it to indicate how many pounds of ice were needed, and that way the delivery man knew not only that ice was needed but also how much, and he only had to make one trip to the house.

As a tenant farmer Pa received a wage plus housing. We had a garden area, and Mr. Sanders allowed us to have a milk cow in the barn with some of his cattle. The cow we had was a Brown Swiss named Petunia. She belonged to Mr. Sanders, but she was ours to milk. We were also allowed to have some pigs in the pens and chickens in the coop.

The Sanders farm was operated as a large truck farm. There were the normal crops of corn, oats, hay and wheat for feeding livestock and selling grain. There were also crops of peas, tomatoes, sweet corn and sugar beets to be sold to the Heinz and Libby canning plants in Fremont, Ohio. It was possible to plant peas early in the year, harvest the crop, and replant the fields with sugar beets, and still get the beets out of the field before a hard freeze. Pa, along with Otto, Mr. Sanders, his son Howard, and whatever migrant workers were needed, farmed the fields. They used a steel-wheeled John Deere tractor as the main source of power for farming equipment. They also had a newer Silver King tractor with rubber tires and a three point hydraulic hitch. The team of horses was used on a daily basis for the farming work. Often, especially in the fall when it was rainy, the horses did most of the field work.

One of the benefits of living on a truck farm was that during the harvesting of the various crops, I could look forward to having some of the fresh-picked vegetables for supper. The peas were harvested in early summer, followed by the sweet corn and then the tomatoes. I liked them all, except when Mom cooked the tomatoes along with broken up pieces of bread and called it tomato pudding. I never liked that dish, and I could never understand why it was called tomato pudding since there was no pudding to it. It was just stewed tomatoes and soggy bread.

Mr. Sanders had two Diamond T semi-truck and trailer rigs that were used to haul farm products to the grain elevator and to the Heinz and Libby plants. In the winter, and whenever it was profitable, he used the semi-trucks to contract-haul bagged lime from the Woodville Lime Plant to various places in Ohio and neighboring states. One of Pa's jobs was to drive the semi-truck for delivery of the lime products to these various places. Whenever he hauled lime, Mr. Saunders would contract to pick up a return load of something to make the trip more profitable. Pa always enjoyed driving truck, and he particularly enjoyed driving Route 250 from Ohio into West Virginia. Pa said that Route 250 was the most challenging road to drive due to the steep grade and the sharp curves on the road as it wound its way up from the Ohio River. Whenever Pa had a run to Wheeling, we knew that we were going to hear another story about driving Route 250.

As I mentioned, we moved to the Woodville farm sometime in early 1945. I do not have a specific memory to tie this down, but I do remember certain things about this time related to the war. It was common practice to save all tin cans for the scrap metal drives. After Mom would open a tin can of soup or vegetables, it was my job to wash out the can and cut out the bottom of the can, place the top and bottom in the can, and then stomp on the can to flatten it out. We kept the flattened cans in a bin in the spare room. I can't remember if we took the cans somewhere, or if they were picked up by someone, but every so often the bin was emptied.

One other job that Louise and I shared was kneading the oleo. Butter was one of the foods that was rationed, and since we only milked one cow, we did not have enough cream to make butter so we bought oleo. At that time oleo came in a plastic bag that was sealed on both ends. The oleo was white and looked like lard. In the center of the plastic bag was a small bubble that was filled with yellow die. We had to pinch the bubble until it broke, releasing the yellow die into the bag with the white oleo. Then we would squeeze and knead the bag until the yellow die was thoroughly mixed into the oleo and the whole package was a buttery shade of yellow.

I have a number of short snapshot memories of the war. I remember that we would shop at the Red and White grocery store in Woodville, and we needed to have ration stamps to purchase items such as sugar and beef. We also needed ration stamps to buy gas for the car and shoes. One time Louise and I played with the ration stamps and lost some of them. We were in real trouble.

During the war it was common practice for the military to pass out cardboard squares imprinted with a large star to the parents or family of a serviceman. These stars were displayed in the front windows of the homes of the servicemen. Whenever we went somewhere in the car, Louise and I played a game where we each counted the stars that we saw on our side of the road to see who could find the most stars.

I remember the talk of uncles who were in the war. Pa had two sisters whose husbands were in the army. His older sister, Augusta, was married to Melvin Schwartzwalder, and Pa's younger sister, Irene, was married to Luther Archie (Slim) Covert. Slim was overseas in France and Germany while Melvin was stationed in France. Pa's younger brother, Harmon (Harmie), lied about his age and joined the Marines shortly before his seventeenth birthday. Harmie was in the artillery division and landed on Iwo Jima the second day of the invasion. Eventually, he took part in the occupation of Japan. Pa's younger sister, Anna May, had a boyfriend, Bill McDole, in the Navy in the Pacific Ocean. Mom's older brother, Frank, was in the Merchant Marines on the Atlantic Ocean.

I also remember all the talk when the war was over. I can't remember anything specific, except that it was over, and the uncles were coming home, and that Pa's sister, Anna May, got married to Bill McDole soon after he was discharged at the end of the war.

Melvin was transferred home from the army before the end of the war, and eventually he was sent to school in Fremont under the GI Bill. He and Aunt Augusta moved into the upstairs part of the Woodville farm house with us for about six months while Melvin was in school. My Aunt Augusta had two nicknames. People called her either 'Gusty' or 'Dutch.' I called her Aunt Gusty, but I would often refer to the couple as Dutch and Melvin. Aunt Gusty was the first woman that I can remember who wore pants most of the time, and I can only remember seeing her in a dress at a wedding or a funeral.

At this time Dutch and Melvin had four children: Shirley, Carl, Linda, and Betty. Each of their children was slightly older than the kids in our family, but it worked out well because each of us had a cousin about our own age to play with. Carl was about my age and we were the only boys. Although I can't remember exactly when Dutch and Melvin moved in except that it was sometime near the end of the war, and before I started school in September of 1946. Shirley and Carl never went to school in Woodville while I was in school there, so my best guess is that they lived with us during the late spring and summer of 1946.

CHAPTER 3

FINE-FEATHERED FRIENDS

Mom and Janet and Rhode Island White Chickens

Since we had a chicken coop, it was only natural that we would have chickens. Pa decided that if we had enough chickens, we could eventually sell the eggs and have some extra money. Late in the spring of 1946, we went to the Pemberville Grain Elevator and Pa bought 100 baby chicks. We brought them home in cardboard boxes in the backseat of the car that we had at that time, a 1933 Chevy. We put the baby chicks in the chicken coop with an electric brooder to keep them warm.

That spring, there was a late ice-storm which took down the electrical wires to the farm, and the brooder quit working. It was getting colder and the chicks were at risk. Pa decided that the only thing that we could do to save the chicks was to bring them all into the house. We carried the chicks in baskets, aprons, and whatever else we could use to quickly move 100 chicks into the spare room off the kitchen. Aunt Gusty and Uncle Melvin were living with us at the time, and Aunt Gusty was helping. She accidently stepped on one of the baby chicks and killed it, and Louise, who had witnessed the event, was so upset that she cried for at least an hour. We had the chicks in the house a little over a day before the electricity was back on, and we moved them back to the coop.

Once the chickens were old enough to begin laying, Louise and I had the job of daily gathering the eggs which Mom sold at the farm or gave away to our neighbors. A certain number of the chickens were roosters and one particular rooster made Louise's and my life miserable. He would get behind us and when we were not looking he would fly up and peck us on the back of the head. He wouldn't do it every time, but whenever we went out to the coop, we were afraid that we would be attacked by that rooster. If we ran directly at him, he would run away, but then he would sneak back among the other chickens and get behind us and all at once there he would be, flying at us and pecking again.

One day Louise and I were playing in the yard when we saw Pa coming in from hoeing weeds in the cornfield. We both started running toward him and suddenly the rooster was in the air, pecking Louise on the head. Whenever Pa hoed weeds, he always sharpened the hoe to a fine edge to cut through the weed stalk just below ground level. That day, I watched Pa in one quick instant slap at the rooster with his hand to get it away from Louise, and then swing that hoe like a golf club, slicing off the head of the rooster. The head went flying through the air like a nine iron shot. Needless to say, we had chicken for dinner that night.

Actually, we had chicken for dinner quite often at this time because we did have chickens, and chicken was Pa's favorite meal.

Pa told me, "You learn how to do something by watching others do it, and then doing it yourself." He was always showing me how to do things and encouraging me to try. One of the first things that he showed me was how to use a hatchet to chop kindling for the kitchen stove. It soon became my job to ensure that the wood box had a good supply of kindling to start the cook stove every morning. He also taught me how to raise chickens. I started learning at an early age how to pluck a chicken, clean a chicken, and eventually how to kill a chicken.

First, Pa showed me how to dip the already dead chicken in hot water and soak all of the feathers to loosen the skin around the feather quills. He showed me how to grab a handful of feathers, pull down firmly, and continue doing this till almost all of the feathers were removed. There were always a few of the very fine feathers that couldn't be pulled out. At this point, I learned to take the chicken to the cook stove, open one of the burner lids, hold the chicken over the open flame, and burn off the remaining feathers. I became aware quickly that this process produces a very distinctive odor. I also learned this was a good way to burn my hands and fingers if I wasn't careful.

The next thing I learned was how to clean a chicken. Pa showed me how to cut the chicken open, beginning at the bottom of the rib cage at the base of the breast bone and cutting down to the tail. He would then reach into the cavity of the chicken and remove the innards. He taught me that there are a lot of goodies inside the chicken that need to be saved in the cleaning process. The heart, the gizzard and the liver were always saved because they were good eating on their own. To this day, one of my favorite foods is fried chicken livers. When cooking soup, these innards made the soup all the better. In cleaning a hen, Pa taught me to look for chicken eggs in various stages of development from soft-shelled eggs to pea-sized egg yolks. The eggs were also quite good in soup.

The last lesson related to chickens that Pa taught me was how to kill a chicken. Chickens are strange birds in many ways. If a chicken is held on its back with its head down, it becomes disoriented and very calm. Pa used to say that it was hypnotized. I later learned that in actuality, the pressure of the a chicken's innards pressing against his lungs slowed his breathing down and caused him to become very slow to react. Knowing this about chickens is helpful when it comes time to kill one. Killing a chicken can be done in one of two ways. The first is by laying the chicken across a log and chopping the chicken's head off with an ax. The second is by grabbing the chicken by the head, letting the chicken's body hang down, and then using a quick cranking motion of the arm. The weight of the spinning chicken will separate the chicken's head from its body. The cranking motion was the way Pa normally killed a chicken, and it was also the way I saw Grandma Myerholtz kill many a chicken. It was a little more difficult for me to do this since I was small and too close to the ground for the cranking motion to work well. Also, I did not weigh much, so I had to brace my feet and hold the chicken up high. Eventually, after I got older, I learned the technique.

One other important fact to prepare for when killing a chicken was that once the head was off, the body of the chicken ran and flopped around the yard for a short period of time. This always caused any small sisters in the area to run screaming into the house. Once the chicken stopped flopping around, I had to hang it up by its feet on the clothesline to bleed out before plucking and gutting the chicken. Both Pa and Grandma had a special little wire attached to the end of the clothes line for hanging chickens by their feet.

At that time most grains for chicken feed came in cloth bags. Besides the normal burlap, there were bags made of a heavy grade cotton fabric which quite often had a flower print. It was common practice to take these feed bags and rip out the seams and then use the cloth to make clothes. Mom made dresses out of these bags for herself, as well as for my three sisters. I recall an old family photograph that shows Mom with my sisters Louise, Janet, and Caroline all wearing dresses with the same flowered pattern, all made from feed sack cloth.

The last thing that I will pass on about chickens is something that Grandma Myerholtz told me whenever it rained. She said that by watching the chickens, a person can tell if the rain will last all day, or if it will be only a short rain shower. If the chickens come in out of the rain, it is a sign that it will not rain for long. If the chickens stay out in the rain and keep looking for food, then it is going to rain all day. I don't know if this is true or not, but Grandma believed it.

At some point Mom decided that it would be a good idea to raise some ducks so Pa bought some baby ducklings. I can't remember how many ducks we had, but it runs in my mind that it was twenty-five. I am sure there was a good reason for wanting the ducks, but this is something that I never understood.

I found that ducks look like they are always smiling with their bills curled up at the sides of their head, and that they can be very entertaining, especially when they are swimming in the cattle water trough. However, this caused problems. The ducks began to fowl the water which was not good for the cattle so Pa decided that he would fix up a spot for the ducks to swim.

I have mentioned that there was a pump off the side walk on the east side of the house, and next to the pump was a large concrete water basin which at one time had been used to keep cans of milk cool. Pa filled the basin with water and set a wooden plank on the edge of the basin. It didn't take long for the ducks to learn that by walking up the plank they could get into the water. The problem was that the basin would not hold twenty-five ducks at the same time so there were always ducks jumping out of the basin because it was too crowded. Once a duck was out of the basin, he would walk back up the plank to get into the water again, and this would cause one of the other ducks to jump out of the basin and repeat the process. It was great fun to sit and watch this duck version of a Chinese Fire Drill.

One night we had a thunderstorm and some of the ducks got out of their pen and ended up on Route 20 in front of the house. We were not sure what happened exactly, but in the morning, five of the ducks lay dead on the road. Pa and I went out with scoop shovels and cleaned up the mess.

CHAPTER 4

HORSES, FISH HOOKS, AND OTHER DANGERS

Cathy, Louise and Me at the Woodville Farm

I have mentioned that at one point Aunt Gusty and Uncle Melvin were living upstairs with their four children, one of the children being my cousin, Carl. Although he was slightly older than me, Carl was my best friend, and the cousin that I spent the most time with while we were growing up. Carl had had a mild case of polio when he was three or four years old and was left with one leg shorter than the other so he had a slight limp, but it did not keep him from running or doing all of the things that a young boy does. Carl and I always found new and exciting things to do on the farm.

The two horses that we had on the farm were always an interest to us and eventually got us into some trouble. The horse named Bill was blind in one eye which made him a little skittish when approached from his blind side. In fact, he was always difficult to harness because of this. Bill often chased Otto Krumnow out of the barn when he tried to harness him, and Pa usually was the one who would settle Bill down and get him into harness.

After a hard day in the fields, it was common for Pa to clean the horses with a curry comb and brush, and both Carl and I had seen Pa do this a number of times. One afternoon in the summer of 1946, we decided that we would clean the horses even though they had not been out in the field that day. Pa was out on a lime delivery with the semi-truck, and Mom had gone along with Pa. Melvin was at school, leaving my Aunt Gusty with Carl and me and the rest of the kids.

Carl and I went out to the barn and got the curry comb and brush and walked out to the fenced in area behind the barn where the horses were grazing. Carl was going to brush Bob, and I was going to use the curry comb on Bill. As I walked behind Bill, I reached up and patted him on the hind leg, not even thinking that I was on his blind side. Bill's reaction was to kick back as I patted him. His hoof caught me in the middle of the forehead and sent me flying out behind him. As I looked up from the ground, I could see Carl climbing the fence and running toward the house yelling.

I finally got up and started to follow Carl. I was met by my Aunt Gusty and Carl coming back to the barn, and they helped me up to the house where my aunt made me lie down on the couch while she washed off my face. The hoof did not cut the skin, but it did scrape the skin enough to cause it to bleed, and I had a very large goose egg forming on my forehead. Since the icebox did not have much ice in it that day, my aunt took a large butcher's knife and lay it on the ice to cool it. She then put the knife on the bump forming on my head, and she kept repeating this process the rest of the day. I eventually went to sleep.

Mom and Pa arrived home well after dark, and I guess I was quite a sight. By that time my eyes were swollen shut, and my face was black and blue from my hair line down to my upper lip. Mom and Pa took me into Woodville to Doctor Drossel's house. He checked me out and decided that I was either very hard-headed or very lucky because I did not have any serious injury. He said that it was a good thing that the horse was unshod, or I would probably have been injured seriously. I used to kid about the fact that I had an excuse for being the way I was because I had been kicked in the head by a horse.

Bill and I had one other encounter later that year. Corn-pickers in those days were less than efficient. The picker was a device that attached to the side of the tractor and picked the ears off the cornstalks one or two rows at a time. The only problem was that the picker did not pick all of the ears. It was common practice to send workers into the field after the corn-picker to hand-pick the ears of corn that had been missed. One day Pa and Otto were scheduled to take the team of horses, Bill and Bob, and a wagon into the field to hand-pick any corn missed by the picker. They decided the job would go quicker if both of them could be on the ground picking corn with me in the driver's seat on the wagon to move the team and the wagon forward as they both picked.

Pa and Otto each wore a corn husker, a device strapped to their hand with a small hook positioned in the palm of their right hand. They would grab an ear of corn from the stalk with their left hand, jab the hook of the husker into the cornhusk, rip the husk off the ear, and then toss the husked ear into the wagon. Once they had picked all of the ears in the immediate area, they would move ahead of the team, and I would move the team and the wagon ahead to the place where they were then picking. This worked well for awhile.

When a corn picker goes through a field, it knocks down most all of the standing corn stalks. So when someone is hand-picking the missed ears, it is usually from stalks that are down on the ground which have to be picked-up to get to the ear. As Pa reached for one such corn stalk, a pheasant, hiding under the stalk, took to flight with its usual loud, raspy call. Unfortunately, this happened on Bill's blind side, and his reaction was to rear up on his hind legs and then bolt and run, taking Bob, the wagon, and me along for the ride. I had hold of the reins and tried to get the team to stop, but my tugging efforts on the reins did not overcome Bill's desire to get out of there. Soon I was just holding on for dear life. I think that Bob eventually decided that he had run enough, and the team slowed down and then stopped altogether. Pa caught up with us and was as angry as I have ever seen him at that time. He grabbed Bill by the bridle and actually punched the horse in the side of the head. I was happy to follow Pa's advice to walk back to the house and leave the moving of the team to Otto.

Carl and I had another adventure that caused me additional pain and a doctor's visit later that summer. I have previously mentioned that there was a concrete water trough in the cattle pen that was about ten feet in diameter and three feet deep. Sometimes when Pa would go fishing and catch small bull-heads, he would bring the fish home and put them in the water trough. One day when we had nothing better to do, Carl and I decided that we would go fishing in the water trough. All we needed was some fishing line, a couple of hooks, and some worms. The worms were easy. We just lifted up a few large rocks and we had plenty of bait. We were able to find some fishing line in Pa's fishing stuff, but the only hook that we could find was attached to a wad of entangled fishing line. We decided to cut the hook off the old tangle of line and tie it to the new line that we had found. I agreed to hold onto the hook while Carl cut the hook off.

Carl was using an old pocket knife that was less than sharp. He sawed away on the line for a bit, and then he gave the line a jerk to pull it off the hook. All he really did was set the hook firmly into the index finger of my right hand. We tried to pull the hook out, but it was a barbed hook and did not move; it just made my finger hurt even more. We went up to the house and Mom put some ice on my finger to help stop the bleeding. She got Pa out of the field, and they took me to Doctor Drossel's office where he cut the hook out with a scalpel without any anesthetic, telling me, "This will only hurt a little bit." I left his office wondering what, "This will hurt a lot," might have meant. I still have a small V-shaped scar on my right hand index finger as a reminder of that day.

Another experience I encountered that summer did not involve Carl. It involved his dad, Melvin. My Uncle Melvin was a source of a number of family stories over the years, usually dealing with things that he should not have done or said. Melvin was born as Carl Melvin Clark, and he was adopted as a child by the Schwartzwalder family. It was rumored that his birth father was a member of the Pretty Boy Floyd Gang, and that Melvin was adopted out when his father went to prison. Melvin was drafted into the army when the war broke out and eventually ended up in France. He was walking guard duty one night and managed to slip and fall off the wall that he was standing on, and he ruptured his appendix. He spent time in the Army hospital and then was sent back to the United States. He never saw combat, but he told everyone that he was wounded in the war, and that he received the Purple Heart for his wounds. He also told people that the first time he jumped into a fox hole, there were still foxes in the hole. Melvin was quite short and had a bit of a Napoleon complex which caused him to strut around like a banty rooster when he walked, especially if he had been drinking. He would also get very argumentative when he was drinking, and his cursing increased, to the point that every other word was a swear word. When Melvin was in an argument, he would punctuate each statement with a quick downward snap of his head as if he were spitting out the last word.

It was late in the summer and to help cool down the house, Pa opened the cellar windows to let air into the cellar at night. One morning Pa was out on a truck trip and Mom was fixing breakfast in the kitchen. We kept the milk in the cellar as there was a concrete trough there to hold water for cooling and keeping our milk. When she went down to get the milk, we heard her yell that there was a skunk, and she came running up the stairs as fast as she could.

Apparently, the skunk had crawled into one of the open windows and had either fallen or jumped down to the cellar floor and could not get out. To get the skunk out, Mom told me to go outside and open the grade level door on the outdoor stairway which led to the cellar. As I started to do as Mom had told me, Uncle Melvin entered the room. He quickly said that he would handle this, and he went into the storage room where Pa kept his rifle.

Melvin loaded the single-shot rifle and headed down the cellar stairs. By this time all of us kids were awake and aware that there was a skunk in the cellar. Eight kids, all under the age of eight, amassed at the top of the cellar stairs, each trying to get a glimpse of what was happening. We heard the rifle shot, followed by Melvin yelling, "Son of a bitch!" This was followed by the unmistakable smell of a skunk doing his worst.

It turned out that Melvin was not the best shot in the world, and the first shot from that single-shot rifle did little more than aggravate the skunk. By the time Melvin was able to reload and get off a killing shot, the skunk had done his business and eight kids were running out of the house through any open door they could find.

We spent many hours cleaning the cellar by washing down the walls and the floor with tomato juice which was supposed to neutralize the odor and using various cleaners. We finally got most of the smell out of the house about the same time that Aunt Gusty and Uncle Melvin moved to Blissfield, Michigan. Later in the fall, when it got cold enough to fire up the coal stoves, we found that the odor was not totally gone. However, it did eventually leave, and I still have the single shot rifle that Uncle Melvin used that day to save us all from the skunk.

CHAPTER 5

SPEAKING OF SKUNKS . . .

**Mom with Skunky in Her Arms in Woodville
Our '33 Chevy in the Background**

About the time I turned six, a small stray dog entered our lives. He showed up one morning and seemed to immediately adopt us as his family. Pa suspected that someone had dropped him off in front of the farm, hoping that we would take him in. As I said, he was small, with longish hair, and was black and white, so naturally we named him Skunky.

Skunky was a lot of fun for all of us kids. He would take off running in circles around us, coming just close enough for us to reach out and try and catch him but staying just out of reach. Soon everyone was running after him and the yard was full of kids running in all directions being led by a little black and white dog. He was also a brave little guy. It was not uncommon for stray dogs to show up in the yard from time to time, but no matter the size of the stray, Skunky would go into attack mode and end up chasing the stray out of the yard and down Route 20 a ways. Then he would come strutting back into the yard to be rewarded with petting and praise from everyone. We often wondered if the other dogs thought that Skunky was really a skunk because they all seemed to be frightened by him.

Skunky was the first dog we ever had as a family, and he was the first dog we ever had to bury. He, like the ducks before him, wandered out onto Route 20 one night, and was hit by a car or a truck and killed. We buried him at the edge of the garden behind the outhouse.

CHAPTER 6

FUN ON THE FARM

Pa and Me on the John Deere Tractor in Woodville

Once summer arrived, it was time to quit wearing shoes. Shoes were for winter and for going to school, but not for the summer months. At that time our shoes were rationed, and it was a common practice for Mom and Pa to buy us kids new shoes only in the fall before school started. So by summer our shoes were worn-out and did not fit all that well; they were just something that slowed us down.

We all spent the bulk of the summer shoeless. When we first took off our shoes and went outside, we avoided the stone driveway and stayed mainly in the grassy areas and in the dirt. I have to say, there was something very soothing about running bare-foot through a freshly plowed field of dirt, or when it grew hot in the summer, stepping into a freshly cultivated field and feeling the coolness on the soles of my feet. By continuing to go shoeless, our feet took on a whole new level of durability and toughness, and by the end of summer, we could run across the stone driveway with barely a break in our stride. Being shoeless meant that we suffered a few foot injuries, including stubbed toes and cuts from broken glass and old pieces of metal that we sometimes found with our feet while running through the grass and the weeds.

The truth about going shoeless is, that unless we washed our feet daily, the dirt, grass clippings, and various other tiny particles of whatever we may have stepped in or on that day became entrapped in the spaces between our toes and between the balls of our toes and the soles of our feet. When this mixture of matter combined with the moisture of the sweat or the dampness that we had picked up from the dew on the grass, it became almost jelly-like and lingered for days in these tiny spaces. This shoeless phenomenon was known as 'toe jam.' At this age and at this time, there were very few kids who did not carry a little toe jam around during the day. Many an evening, the last thing I would do before going into the house for the night, was rinse my feet off at the pump in the side yard. While this did not remove all of the collected toe jam, it at least got rid of the most obvious. So unless Mom took a long hard look at my feet, I did not have to get out the soap and water.

I think that my cousin Jerry Reyome was the undisputed, 'King of the Toe Jam,' within our family of cousins. It seemed that he took pride in being able to collect the largest amount of it between his toes, and whenever I saw him in the summer, one of the first things that he would show me was his feet and his current collection of toe jam.

The best part of a barn for a kid is the haymow, and the horse barn had the best ones. This barn had a Gambrel roof with a haymow on each side of the barn, and the center section of the barn was open from grade to the roof line. The mows were up about fifteen feet from the floor, and the roof was about another twenty feet above the mow floor. There was plenty of room above the haymow for the ropes and pulleys that hung from the roof rafters. We used to swing on the ropes from one side of the barn to the other, leaving from one mow and landing in the other mow. Games of tag took on a whole new challenge when players were able to avoid someone by grabbing a rope and swinging to the other side of the barn.

We also built tunnels using bales of hay. We laid two rows of bales about two feet apart, and then bridged those bales with other bales on top to close off the opening. We made the tunnel somewhat like a maze with dead ends and turns, so that when we were in the tunnel, we had to feel our way along the walls to eventually find the end. At one time, we even built a tunnel over a stall feeder opening in the mow floor. If someone took the wrong turn in the tunnel, he could end up dropping through the feeder which opened into the manger below.

Playing hide and seek in the barn was also great fun as there were so many places to hide, not only in the haymow, but in the lower areas in the stalls and feed bins. My favorite hiding place was under the feed box in Bill's stall, since everyone else was afraid of Bill and would not go into his stall.

The other great place for kids to play was the small woods at the end of the cow pasture. Louise, Janet, and Caroline and whatever cousins that might have been living with us or just visiting, would walk down the lane to the woods and spend a good part of a summer day playing in the woods. We sometimes took along sandwiches or cookies and had a little picnic. We could pick wild strawberries, raspberries, and hickory nuts depending on the time of year, and there were trees to climb and neat places to build forts out of old dead branches. One day when we were walking back to the woods, we invented a game that somehow never quite caught on as a popular childhood game.

Before I explain the game, I need to give some background information. The lane we walked to the woods also served as the lane that the cows walked to the pasture field, so of course, there were cow pies, round, brown, pie-shaped piles of excrement left behind by the cows. They were at various stages of aging. Some were quite moist and fresh, while others were days to weeks old. As a cow pie ages, it dries out and becomes very firm, to the point of being almost wood-like.

As I have mentioned, it was quite normal for all of us kids to be barefooted for most of the summer, and it generally was in the summertime that we walked to the woods. Walking down the lane, barefoot, amidst the cow pies, we invented the game. It was really quite simple. The point was for each of us to take a turn in order, and as we walked out to the woods, the person with the first turn had to touch his big toe to the first cow pie that we encountered. The second person had to touch the second cow pie and so on down the line. The person with the most fresh cow pies was the loser, and the person with the most aged and more firm cow pies was the winner. The loser was easily identified at the end of the walk, and I still wonder why this game never caught on.

Another source of real fun that I remember about the summers on the Woodville farm was playing in the rain. We did not have indoor plumbing at the farmhouse and baths were taken in a round galvanized tub on the kitchen floor. Mom would heat up the water on the kitchen stove, fill the tub, and then one by one us kids would take a bath using the same water. Mom usually started with the youngest, Caroline, followed by Janet and Louise, and I was last. This usually happened once a week. The rest of the time we washed whatever needed to be washed in the wash basin on a daily basis.

A rainy summer day was the perfect time to wash in really clean water. When it started to rain we would strip down to just a pair of shorts, grab a bar of soap, and run out into the rain. I would always try to be the first one to get under a downspout where there was a good flow of water off the roof. We would all lather up and rinse off in the rain. Once the bathing was over, we would just run-around and play in the rain. By the time the rain had stopped, I am not sure we were as clean as we had been when it started. Quite often Mom would join us and wash her hair. She always told us that rain water was the best water to wash hair. Even in the fall and early spring, she would often catch a bucket of rain water just for that purpose.

While now and then we had the rains for bathing, the weekly bath was a regular weekend routine. When I stayed with Grandpa Myerholtz, he always told me that he started with his face and washed down as far as possible. Then he started on his feet and washed up as far as possible. Then, "To hell with possible." I usually followed his advice.

Tractor rides were always fun, and whenever possible I tried to ride with Pa from the barn to the field. Once he started working the field with whatever equipment he may have hooked to the tractor, I walked back. He did not let me ride with him while he was working because he was afraid that I might fall off and get caught under whatever he was pulling. When he was done working, and I could see him coming in from the field, I would run out to him for a ride back to the barn. It was especially fun to ride on the John Deere tractor. It had steel wheels and the rear drive wheels had triangular shaped lugs on them. As long as we were driving on dirt, the lugs would just sink into the dirt, and the ride was fairly smooth. But, when we had to cross Route 20 on the pavement or drive down the stone driveway, the lugs would not sink in and the vibration they caused on a hard surface would just about shake a lung out of me. I had to hold on with both hands, but that was the best part of the ride.

Days when Pa returned from working in the fields with the team of horses, I would also run out to meet him because this was the time when I could get a ride on a horse. Pa would stop the team, pick me up, and put me on the back of Bob, the big black horse. Bob was so broad across the back, that my legs would almost stick straight out to each side as I held on to the harness hames. I never was on the back of Bill; he was not about to let anyone sit on his back.

When there was work to be done in the field, and it was too muddy to take a tractor and a wagon into the field, the team of horses was used along with a piece of equipment that we called a mud boat. A mud boat was basically a wood platform about six feet by six feet, mounted on a set of wooden skids. It was somewhat like a big sled. The team could pull this mud boat over any kind of ground, grass, mud, snow or whatever. Riding on a mud boat took a bit of skill because I usually stood up, and there was nothing to hang onto except for Pa's legs. With the horses pulling the mud boat, the ride was pretty slow and easy, unless we went over a dead furrow[1], and then I could lose my footing and be rolled off and end up face first into the mud.

But every now and again, Pa would hook the mud boat to the Silver King tractor and this was a whole different kind of ride. When hooked to the tractor, Pa was not on the mud boat so his legs were not available to hold onto. It was necessary for any of us kids riding on the mud boat to sit down and hold onto each other. The ride was a lot faster than with the horses, especially if the ride was in a field where wheat or oats had been harvested. Straw made a very slick surface for the mud boat, and it was almost like being on ice. If Pa had the older kids like me and Louise and some of my cousins on the mud boat, he would sometimes turn the tractor sharply and the mud boat would whip around to the point that we

---

[1] An area of ground with a different surface because of a change in the plowing pattern.

rolled off into the straw. It sounds more dangerous than it was, or at least that's what I remember.

Most of the fenced in areas of the farm had a wooden gate that was used to enter this area. The wooden gate was usually wide enough to allow for the passage of the various pieces of equipment that were a part of the daily farm activity. All of us kids liked to be on hand when it was time to open or close one of these gates. We would stand on the lower wooden rail of the gate near the opening end and hang onto the top wooden rail. As Pa would unlatch the gate and give it a push to open it, we would get a swinging arch ride on the gate as it went from a closed to open position. The ride would be repeated as Pa swung the gate closed.

CHAPTER 7

"DON'T TELL YOUR MOTHER!"

Pa in Woodville

I am not sure when or if I really ever realized that Pa had a drinking problem while we were living in Woodville. Of course, as I got older I knew, but in Woodville I was just a kid, and I don't remember that I thought of his drinking as a problem. However, I do remember going with Pa to the two bars that were on the main street of downtown Woodville. One bar was the Victory Bar, and the other was Dunn's Night Club. The other thing that I remember is that most family members referred to the bars as either *beer gardens* or *beer joints*. Mom usually was upset when she was talking about the bars and would refer to them as a "Darned old beer joint."

Pa often took me with him when he went into town, and many times we would end up at one of the bars. He would usually have a couple of beers and buy me a bottle of pop or soda. I always wanted a Variety Club Lemon-Lime Soda, and Pa would get it for me and say, "Now don't tell your mother that we stopped here." I never did tell, but I did develop a real taste for Lemon-Lime Soda.

Blue Laws were in effect in most states at that time, including Ohio and Michigan. Blue Laws were intended to keep Sundays as a religious day and the sale of liquor and beer was prohibited on Sundays. In fact, most stores were closed on Sundays so buying anything on Sundays was difficult. However, to get around this problem, the beer companies sold what was called 3/2 beer. This was beer that was only 3.2 per cent alcohol which was below the defined legal six per cent alcohol content of most beers. Like most true beer drinkers, Pa said that he did not like the 3.2 beer, but he would drink it on Sunday, because it was the only beer he could buy.

I was told that Mom had tried to get Pa to quit drinking from the time they were married, and that he had, on a number of occasions, promised he would quit. But it seemed that with all of the family get-togethers, and all of the drinking that the rest of the family did, it was hard for Pa to hold up his side of the agreement. I am sure it was especially true when Grandpa and my uncles would tell Pa, "No damned woman is going to tell me if I can drink or not."

CHAPTER 8

THE 1933 CHEVY

Pa had the ability to fix anything that had an engine or was a piece of mechanical equipment. One story he told me demonstrates this talent he had to fix any engine.

He, Mom and us kids were driving home from a visit at Grandma and Grandpa Myerholtz's house, and the Chevy just quit running. Pa got out to check the engine and soon determined that the rotor in the distributor was not rotating. Pa only had a screw driver, a pair of pliers, and an ice pick in the car. He removed the bolt holding the distributor in place, and he pulled the distributor out of the engine block. He found that the gear on the end of the rotor shaft had come off and was still in the engine block. He cut a piece of wire off a nearby fence and was able to use the wire to fish the gear out of the engine. He used the ice pick as a drift pin to reattach the gear to the distributor shaft, and he broke off the rest of the ice pick. He then had Mom turn the engine over while he held on to the No-1 spark plug wire. When he got an electric shock, he knew that the No-1 cylinder had just fired. He put the distributor back in place and set the timing for the No-1 cylinder. As it started to get dark, Mom struck and held lit matches to give Pa a little light. With a little adjustment, the engine was running again.

The other memory I have about Pa and cars was the fact that he found it hard to drive by a car that was broken down on the road. Many a time when we were going somewhere, and we passed a car stopped on the side of the road, Pa would make a U-turn and go back to see if he could help whoever it was that was having a car problem. Whether it was a stalled engine or a flat tire, Pa was always willing to stop and help even if the rest of the family had to sit in the car for awhile.

Usually, I was allowed to get out and help Pa by handing him wrenches. Quite often, the person would offer to pay him something for his help, and Pa would never take any money. However, a few times when I was with him, he would tell the person, "If you would like to give the boy a little something, go ahead." I would usually end up with fifty cents or sometimes a dollar so I did not mind when Pa would stop to see if he could help someone.

The first car that I can remember Pa having was a 1933 Chevy. It was a four-door sedan, and the main thing that I remember about this car was that it almost killed Pa. The Chevy had a problem with the differential, and Pa took the car into the cow barn to fix it. He asked my cousin, Bill, to help him with this repair as the differential was too heavy to handle by himself. Bill was my Aunt Carrie's oldest boy. Everyone called him Pug for whatever reason, and he was about thirteen at the time. Pa hooked a chain to each side of the rear bumper supports and hooked a chain fall hanging from a barn beam to this chain to lift the back end of the car up off the floor. He disconnected the rear springs and differential housing and removed them from under the car.

At this point, the rear end of the car was suspended about three feet off the floor with nothing under the body of the car except Pa. The bumper support on one side of the Chevy suddenly broke off from the frame of the car, causing the chain to let loose, and the car to fall three feet, landing with the gas tank on Pa's chest. Pug came running into the house telling Mom that the car had fallen on Pa. Mom and I went with Pug back to the barn. We used a long piece of wood as a lever, and with the chain fall hooked to another part of the car frame, we were able to lift the car up enough to pull Pa out from under it. I am not sure how much I was able to help. All I can remember is pulling on Pa's pant legs as we were trying to free him. It turned out that Pa had five broken ribs in the area over his heart, and he also had several cuts on his face and nose.

We somehow got Pa into Woodville to Dr. Drossel's office. At that time it was common practice to wrap the chest with tape to help hold the broken ribs in place. Pa had his chest taped for several weeks, and when the doctor took the tape off, the tape took a layer of skin from his chest. Pa was laid up for about a month, but he did eventually finish the repair to the '33 Chevy and we had a car again

Pa did not always have a license plate for the Chevy. I can't remember if we did not have a license because we could not afford one or what; I just remember that this was a problem at times. Sometimes when we drove

into town, Pa would stay off Route 20 in downtown Woodville to avoid being seen by the local police. He said a number of times as we headed out of town, that as long as we reached the village limits before we were spotted, we would be safe because the village police did not have any authority in the county. At least that is what he thought. He sometimes even drove down the alley behind the Red and White Store with the lights out to avoid being seen, and I worried we would end up in jail if we were caught.

Pa told us that at one time he and Esty each had a car, but neither had enough money to buy license plates. They pulled together enough money to buy one set of plates and put one plate on each car. The problem was that they both went to a beer garden downtown and parked beside each other. The Woodville Police Chief was named Gummy Raberg, and he had known Pa and Esty for a number of years and had personally witnessed some of their youthful antics in Woodville. Gummy saw the two cars parked together with the same license plate and told them to at least not park side by side on Main Street.

CHAPTER 9

GRANDMA MYERHOLTZ

Grandma and Grandpa Myerholtz at the Tubbs Farm
Palmyra, Michigan

Grandma and Grandpa were the only people who ever called me Davy, and it was during this time, when I was about five to six years old, that I have my first real memories of them. They were living on a farm on Rogers Highway near Palmyra, Michigan and were tenant farming on a Registered Hampshire hog farm owned by Doctor Tubbs, a medical doctor who lived and practiced medicine in Blissfield. I began spending part of my summers with Grandma and Grandpa on the farm, and sometimes other cousins would also be staying there. When Mom and Pa would go to Palmyra to visit, they would leave me there for a week or two at a time, and quite often Carl and I were there together. Of course, my Uncle Bob and Aunt Lois were still living at home with Grandma and Grandpa.

Grandma was about five-feet tall, she was always overweight, and she had a lazy eye that drooped. She wore glasses on the end of her nose, and most of the time she looked at me over the top of the glasses, primarily with her good eye. Grandma had palsy in her right hand and her thumb and index finger were always in motion. The two fingers looked as if they were rubbing together in a jerky, uneven movement.

Grandma had a lot of problems with her legs and feet. Being overweight and having given birth to eleven children, plus the physical work that she did, left her with bad knees, bunions, and varicose veins. She also had hammer toes, toes that over-lapped each other, on both feet. She walked with a limp, and wore heavy-gauge stockings to give her legs additional support. Most of the time she wore rubber boots on her feet instead of shoes, and she always wore an apron, the full apron type that looped around her neck and tied at the waist.

I am not sure as to Grandma's education, but she did read and write and loved to talk, especially to her grandchildren, and she liked to laugh. She enjoyed sewing, and she did embroidery work, and most of the time, she was working on a patchwork quilt or doing some embroidery work on a pillow case or dresser scarf.

One other thing that I remember about Grandma was she loved to have a canary in the kitchen. The last thing that she did every night was cover the cage with an old apron, and the first thing she did every morning was uncover the cage and talk to the canary. I remember that whenever she would see a gold finch, she would call it a wild canary, and say that she would like to catch a wild canary someday.

At this time, flies were a common occurrence in the house and especially in the kitchen, and like every other kitchen of that time, Grandma had the standard amount of fly paper spools hanging from the ceiling. But Grandma also used to herd her flies out the door. She would open the kitchen screen door, and then go to the opposite corner of the kitchen with a dish towel in each hand and begin swinging the dish towels in a circular motion chasing the flies toward the open door and out of the kitchen. It was something to watch, and I would join in with dish towels of my own. It was also more effective than trying to swat each fly individually.

Grandma did have a fly swatter hanging on the kitchen wall, and her size and bad knees did not slow her down when she was determined to swat a bothersome fly.

Grandma had a large, heavy, cast-iron woodstove that was black with chrome trim in her kitchen. The stove had two water reservoirs located on each end that were filled with water in the morning so that hot water was available at any time of the day. There were four lift-off burner lids that could be taken off with a lifter so a pan could be set directly over the open flame of the stove.

Two things always sat on the stove no matter the time of day or night. One was the coffee pot. Grandma had a black and white porcelain coffee pot that she used to make coffee. She put the coffee grounds directly into the pot and added the water. She would usually throw in an egg shell to cut down the acid taste and place the pot on the stove. The pot was taken off the stove only to pour coffee into a cup. Then it was returned to the stove where the coffee would continue to brew until someone wanted more coffee. When the pot was empty, Grandma would just add more grounds and water, and the occasional egg shell. This process was repeated daily until the bottom fell out of the coffee pot, and Grandma would get a new pot and start over. I can recall my Uncle Esty used to say as he left Grandma's that he needed to take a cup of coffee with him so he could patch the leak in his roof when he got home.

Mom and Pa would not let me drink coffee at home, but Grandma would let me drink it when I stayed there, and of course, I had to have a cup of coffee for breakfast wherever I could just because it made me feel so grownup. However, my young taste buds and stomach were no match for Grandma's coffee. I could not put enough cream and sugar in that coffee to make it drinkable for me. I love the smell of coffee in the morning, but to this day, I cannot force a cup of coffee down my throat.

The other item that always sat on the stove was the little brown crock that held the bacon grease. In those days it was a common practice to catch and save bacon grease to have grease handy for whatever was cooking. The problem was that Grandma saved the grease from everything that she cooked so over time, the crock would become full of various layers of grease and tiny pieces of cooked meat. When she would take a spoonful of grease out of the crock, it would almost look like she was dipping a scoop of chocolate swirl ice cream. I have to admit that at times the grease crock did not look all that appetizing, but I always liked the way that her meals tasted. I don't know for sure, but I think that the grease may have been the secret to Grandma's cooking.

Grandma's kitchen was always full of aromas. She baked most of her own bread, she made pies quite often, she canned vegetables from her garden, and, of course, no meal was complete without some kind of cooked meat, usually fried in an iron skillet with bacon grease. Breakfast usually consisted of fried eggs, pancakes, and either bacon or pork chops, or sometimes both. Grandma made fried mush which is something that I came to really like. She would cook up a batch of cornmeal mush the night before and let it set in a loaf pan overnight to solidify. The next morning she would slice the mush, like she was slicing bread, and fry the mush in bacon grease. She would then butter the fried mush and pour syrup over it. The syrup that Grandma used was made that day by boiling sugar and water with a little maple flavoring until all of the sugar was dissolved and the mixture started to thicken. It was delicious.

Sometimes in the winter, Grandma would make oatmeal for breakfast. The problem with Grandma's oatmeal was that it was very sticky, to the point that I practically had to pry it off the serving spoon to get it into my bowl. Adding milk seemed to make it almost slimy, so I usually passed on the oatmeal. Pa used to kid Grandma that he was going to use her oatmeal to hang wall paper. One other food that Grandma cooked for breakfast was something that she called bap. I am not sure where the name came from, and I am not sure what it was supposed to be, but I think that it was a form of gravy because it was served over toast or bread. When Grandma made bap, she would brown flour in (you guessed it) bacon grease, and then add milk and cook it until it thickened.

Grandma's kitchen was always a source for snacks during the day. She usually kept a plate of longhorn cheese on the table with a glass cover to keep the flies away, and during the hot days of summer, the cheese would heat up to the point that the oil would start to collect on the plate. But the cheese seemed to taste better when it was warm and a little moist. Grandma usually baked cookies every couple of days, so there was always a plate of cookies waiting on the table for whoever was passing by. I am sure that Grandma baked other cookies, but the ones that I remember were her sugar cookies. These cookies were about the size of a saucer and were about a half an inch thick. I think that Grandma used an old coffee can to cut out these cookies. By the time I finished eating one of them, I needed a glass of milk to wash it down.

The other snack on the table was a dish that contained what Grandma called candy, but I was never convinced that her horehound was candy. It tasted like bad cough syrup to me but she liked it. She also liked licorice but this was the kind of licorice that was vary tar-like in consistency, and again it tasted like bad cough syrup to me. Every once in a while, she would have a dish of wintergreen mints on the table, the big flat pink ones that I came to love.

Grandma had a large garden full of just about anything that you could grow. She was a little superstitious about some things, and one of them was when to plant the peas. Peas were planted on Good Friday, period. It didn't matter if Good Friday was in late March or early April, you planted peas on Good Friday.

During the day, I would sometimes stop in the garden to eat a few fresh-picked green beans, or a radish or two, or a couple of carrots, or a tomato. I never worried about washing off the vegetables; I would just knock off the loose dirt, rub the radish or carrot on my pant leg for a second, and then eat it. One vegetable that I really grew to like was small onions. I would pull a couple of small onions out of the ground, knock the dirt off, and take the onions into the kitchen. I would remove one of the stove lids and drop the onions into the hot coals in the stove fire, and I would leave the stems of the onion sticking out of the opening to be able to pull the onions back out of the fire. It only took a couple of minutes to get the onions steaming in their own skins. When I could see a little steam coming out of the onion, I knew that the onions were ready to eat. They tasted great.

One vegetable that was always in Grandma's garden was potatoes, and where there are potato plants, there are potato bugs. When I stayed at the farm, my job was to take a coffee can half-full of kerosene, walk down the rows of potato plants, picking off any potato bugs that I saw, and drop them in the can of kerosene.

Grandma also had quite a collection of house plants that she cared for daily. She had tall green and white snake plants, a vine type plant that she called a Wandering Jew, sweet potato vine which she grew by putting a sweet potato in a fish bowl filled with water, and geraniums in pots all over the house, inside and out. She would take the outside geranium plants out of the ground and hang them upside down on a clothes line in the cellar for the winter and replant them in the spring. She also had one of the largest Christmas cactus plants that I have ever seen. She grew it in a concrete urn, and it sat on the porch from spring to fall and in the house during the winter months. It took two men and a boy to move it. I believe that cactus was older than any of her children.

Grandma made her own cottage cheese so it was not unusual to walk up on the back porch and see a cheese cloth bag of fresh milk curd hanging from the porch roof rafters as the cottage cheese cured out. This dripping bag always attracted the cats that lived in the barns and they would gather under the bag and lick up the milk dripping onto the porch floor.

There was another cheese that Grandma used to make. She did not make it all that often as I recall. In fact, I think that I only saw her make it one time, but that one time was enough. This is another story that requires a little background information.

Grandma and Grandpa would occasionally butcher a hog, and I witnessed this one time. I recall a large kettle of boiling water over an outdoor fire, plenty of blood, plenty of squeals, and plenty of smells, none of them pleasant. As Grandpa used to say, when they butchered a hog, they used everything but the squeal to prepare the standard hams, bacon, chops, side meat, and then everything else went into the sausage. Even the skin was deep fried in bacon grease and made into what was called 'cracklings,' a kind of potato chip made out of pig skin. The only thing left was the head and the feet.

That brings us back to the cheese. The head was taken into the house and placed into a large pot of boiling water, along with any of the pig's internals that were available. This concoction was then cooked until all of the meat, skin, brains, and whatever else may have been in the pig's head were cooked off the bone. The skull, teeth and any other boney items were removed, and Grandma added various spices and herbs and continued cooking until most of the liquid had been boiled away.

Now there are certain things in a pig's head, that when cooked, make the resulting mixture become very viscous, to the point that it is jelly-like, and given a little time, these items will solidify and take on the consistency of cheese. What Grandma made was called head cheese, and it had the strangest combination of different colors and textures, all suspended in what looked like a shiny, clear, jelly-like substance. The intent was to slice this loaf of jellied pig's head into lunch meat-type slices and eat it on bread like a sandwich. Mustard was optional and preferred. I can only guess what this may have tasted like, as I never was able to bring myself to the point of actually putting even one little taste in my mouth.

The pig's feet were a different story. They were also boiled to totally cook them, but then they were canned in a pickling liquid, and once sufficiently pickled, they were quite good and were one of Grandpa's favorite foods. I do have to admit, I felt a little funny about eating my way around the pig's toes the first time I tried one.

Grandma was usually the one to feed the chickens and gather the eggs, and when I was there, I always helped with these chores. Grandma kept a slop bucket in the kitchen, and any leftover food, garbage, and whatever was no longer useable in the kitchen went into the slop bucket. When the bucket was full, Grandma would take it out to the hog pen and pour the contents of the bucket into the hog trough, and then she would call the hogs. Grandma would let go a loud, "Sue-wee," and by the time she was on her third, "Sue-wee," the trough would be surrounded by hogs eagerly eating the feast that Grandma had poured from the slop bucket.

One time when I came to visit the farm, I walked into the kitchen, and I let go with a loud, "Sue-wee." Grandma laughed and returned an equally loud, "Sue-wee." From that time on, whenever I entered Grandma's house, wherever she was living until the day that she died, I would call out "Sue-wee," and she would always answer, "Sue-wee."

CHAPTER 10

GRANDPA MYERHOLTZ

Woodville Brown Baseball Team Players
Grandpa Myerholtz is on the Right

Grandpa was a small man in height and weight. He stood about five-feet, six inches tall, and he probably never weighed more than a 125 pounds, unless he had his pockets full of rocks. He always seemed to have a two or three day growth of whiskers on his chin. Grandpa was missing more teeth than he had, so when he smiled I would only see a couple of teeth. His face was tanned all over except for the area of his forehead that was covered by the baseball cap that he always wore. The back of his neck was also deeply tanned and heavily creased like a piece of old leather. Grandpa worked outside as a tenant farmer, but for awhile early in his life, he worked at the Woodville Lime Plant. During this time, his main job was setting and detonating dynamite charges for the blasting that was a part of the quarry operation.

Grandpa usually had a cigarette in his mouth or in his hand, and he usually had a chaw of tobacco in his cheek. He liked to roll his own cigarettes out of Bull Durham tobacco, but every now and then, he would buy a pack of Camels. Grandpa was able to keep the ash in place on the end of his cigarette longer than anyone I had ever seen before. He held the cigarette between his fingers, and when he talked, he moved his hands constantly. All of us kids would watch his cigarette as he waved his hands and talked to see if the ash would stay in place. We were especially watchful when he was sitting at the dinner table to see if the ash would stay in place or fall into the food on the table. He chewed Red Man Chewing Tobacco, and there were empty coffee cans sitting around the house which Grandpa used as spittoons. Quite often there was tobacco juice on his whiskers where he had not quite dispelled all of the juice cleanly. I can remember thinking at one point that Grandpa looked a lot like the B. O. Plenty character in the *Dick Tracy* Comics.

Grandpa liked his beer. He usually drank two or three bottles a day during the week and a case of beer over the weekends. Grandpa did not seem to swear that much, except when he was drinking, and at that time his language became very colorful. We could tell when Grandpa had had too much to drink because he would either want to dance with Grandma or argue with someone. When he wanted to dance, he would begin to slide his feet around the floor in a slow motion waltz movement with his right hand extended up and out away from his body. At this point Grandma would usually tell him, "Sit down you old fool." When he wanted to argue, he would usually make a firm statement about something or other, and then demand of no one in particular, "Am I right? Am I right?" And then he would jab the air with his right index finger and declare, "You're god damned right, I'm right!"

I was told that when Grandpa was drinking, he sometimes would get into a poor-me attitude and occasionally threaten to kill himself. One time when Mom and Pa came to visit Grandma and Grandpa in Woodville, Grandpa got into one of his drinking moods and got upset to the point that he told everyone that he was going to walk down the road to a large old tree and hang himself. He got a rope out of the barn and started walking down the road. Grandma convinced Pa that he should go and get Grandpa. Mom and Pa drove down the road and found Grandpa sitting on the ground, leaning against the hanging tree with the rope in his lap. Pa rolled down the window and asked Grandpa if he was alright, and Grandpa replied that he was just getting ready to walk back to the house for supper. Mom and Pa said their good-byes as Grandpa got up and started back to the house, carrying the rope as he ambled along.

I witnessed his poor-me attitude on more than one occasion when Grandpa was drinking. He would talk about his death and tell anyone who was listening, "When I die, just put me in an old burlap bag and leave me by the side of the road." I was never quite sure what was supposed to happen when he was left at the side of the road in a burlap bag.

I don't remember anytime that Grandpa owned his own car, and I don't think that he ever had a driver's license. It wasn't that he did not know how to drive a car or a truck. It was just that he never owned one, and he saw no reason to have a license. Whenever we visited the farm, Mom and Pa would take either Grandma or Grandpa or both to the store to shop. They mostly shopped in Blissfield. Grandma would usually ask, "Can you take us to the store in your machine?" She never called a car a car, it was always a machine. If they really needed something and no one was around to take them, Grandpa would fire up the tractor and drive it into Palmyra.

Grandpa loved baseball, and he especially loved the Detroit Tigers. I remember that Hal Newhouser, Virgil Trucks, George Kell, and Hoot Evers were some of his favorite players at that time. I also remember that Pa and Grandpa would always have friendly debates about which was the better team, Pa's favorite team, the Cleveland Indians or Grandpa's favorite, the Detroit Tigers.

One of the reasons that Grandpa liked the game of baseball so much was the fact that he had played it as a young man. I was told that the Village of Woodville had a semi-pro baseball team called the *Woodville Browns*, and I have an old post card of three players from the Woodville Browns and Grandpa is one of them. Grandpa played for this team at some point, but when and how long he played I have not been able to determine. All I know is that Grandpa would talk about his playing days, and he would show us his crooked, stiff, index finger on his right hand

and explain how he had broken that finger catching knuckle ball pitches from Merle Reyome while he was playing for the Browns.

Baseball was not the only sport that Grandpa played as a young man. I was told that he liked to ice skate, and he particularly liked to jump barrels on ice skates. At one point he took part in a barrel jumping contest on the Portage River which runs through Woodville, and he won the contest. I am not sure how many barrels he jumped to win, because I have heard that it was five barrels, and I also heard that it was seven barrels. The amazing thing was, he did his barrel jumping with the old-fashioned ice skates that were strapped to his shoes and did not provide any support for his ankles.

Grandma's brother, Oscar Layman, told me a story about Grandpa that occurred when he was a young man and would come to visit the Layman family. Grandpa would often take a seat in the kitchen next to the cook stove. He would open the oven door and put his feet up on the door and then rock back and forth on the back legs of the chair. As Grandpa talked, he would spit his tobacco juice into the open oven and watch it sizzle. Oscar was in his nineties when he told me this story, and from the way he told the story, I don't think Grandma's family was too impressed.

I have a number of memories of Grandpa and events that happened on the Tubbs Farm, some of which I took part in, and others that I became aware of from talking with family members who were there at the time.

On one of my stays at the farm, the milk cow was about to give birth. I was out in the barn with Grandpa when the cow decided it was time to deliver. Grandpa could sense that something was wrong, so he got the cow into a stall and kept her in one place by tying her halter to the feeder in the stall. He then got behind the cow and tried to assist in the birth of the calf. Now I had seen kittens being born under the cook stove at one time, and quite often I had seen pigs being born, but I was not prepared for what I was about to see with the birth of a calf. Grandpa told me that the calf was coming feet first and that unless he could reposition the calf, the cow and the calf could both die. He took off his flannel shirt and reached his bare arm and hand into the birth canal of the cow to a point that his whole arm from hand to shoulder was inside the cow. He then tried to reposition the calf to move the head into proper position for birthing. I don't know how long he worked at this, but at one point he became quite discouraged and began to swear.

He removed his arm from the cow, and I could see that he was covered in blood and other matter. He then asked Uncle Bob to go get a short piece of chain that was hanging in the tractor shed. When Bob returned with it, Grandpa took the end of the chain, which had a hook, and began placing the chain inside the cow. He positioned the calf to a point that he had both hind legs together with the chain around these two legs. He then began pulling the chain from the cow and was able to pull the calf out with it. The calf was dead, and Grandpa was covered with blood and sweat, but the cow was saved. I think I was seven when this happened.

I also was at the farm a number of times when pigs were born. Since the Tubbs farm was a pig farm, it was not unusual to breed a large number of sows around the same time of year. So once the birthing started, it continued for a period of time. The main problem with birthing pigs was that accurate records of breeding and projected dates of giving birth were not something that Grandpa kept. Under normal conditions Grandpa was able to watch a particular sow and guess fairly closely about when she would give birth, and then he separated her from the rest of the pigs and placed her in a farrow pen, a pen that held a sow while she gave birth. The reason for separating the sow was that most pigs eat anything, including afterbirth and newly born piglets, and to keep other pigs away from a new litter of piglets, the sow is isolated. On more than one occasion, I can remember Grandpa jumping into the main pig pen and pushing other pigs away from a sow that was giving birth in an effort to save the piglets. When this happened, anyone handy, including me, jumped in to help carry the newly born piglets into the farrow pen while Grandpa stood guard over the sow.

Grandpa had an Allis Chalmers tractor on the farm. It was orange, as all Allis Chalmers tractors were at that time, and he kept it in a shed to the right of the rear of the house when it was not in use in the field. It was something that all of us kids liked to play on and around when we were there on weekends. On one weekend, a number of us were at the farm and, of course, we all played on the tractor.

Now I have mentioned that Grandpa liked his beer on weekends, so sometimes on Monday mornings, Grandpa was not at his best. On this particular Monday morning, it had rained most of the night before, and the area in front of the tractor shed was quite muddy. I don't know if one of us had put the tractor in gear the day before, or if Grandpa even checked the gear shift to see if the tractor was in neutral. Grandpa set the ignition and the throttle on the tractor, and then walked around to the front, engaged the hand crank, and turned over the engine in an attempt to start the tractor. I cannot remember if this tractor ever started on the first crank or not, but this morning it did, and the tractor was in gear.

As the engine came to life, it lunged forward, knocking Grandpa into the shed door which was still closed. As the tractor broke through the door, Grandpa was knocked to the ground, directly in front of the rear wheel. The large rear rubber tire rolled directly over Grandpa's face, forcing his head into the mud under the shed eave, as the tractor chugged out of the shed and into the farmyard.

Grandpa survived having his head run over by a tractor, thanks to a very large mud puddle. He ended up with a couple of broken ribs and bruises and scrape marks on his face from the rubber lugs on the tires. Uncle Bob was at our house in Woodville at the time that we got word from Grandma about the accident, and it was the next morning before Uncle Bob and Pa drove up to the farm to find Grandpa working in the field. I remember thinking that Grandpa and I both must have very hard heads. I survived a kick in the head by a horse, and he survived having his head run over by a tractor.

That tractor got Carl and me into trouble once. We were at the farm together and were out in the field across the road from the house where Grandpa was working with the tractor. I can't remember what we were doing exactly, but at one point Grandpa had to get something out of the barn, and he left the tractor running. There was a wooden gate and fence at the road to separate the field from Rogers Highway. Before I knew what was happening, Carl was up in the driver's seat of the tractor, and he had put the tractor in gear. It took off with Carl doing more to just hang on than steer. Carl drove the tractor through the wooden gate and onto Rogers Highway. He managed to do a U-turn in front of the house, going back through the broken gate, and finally stopping the tractor in the same general area that the tractor had been when he first climbed on it.

We both ran up and sat down on the front porch and tried our best to act like we had no idea what happened to the gate. Since the tractor was facing the opposite direction from what it was when he left, and the wooden gate was broken, it did not take Grandpa too long to figure out what we had done. As I said, we got into a little trouble on that one.

Chapter 11

THE TUBBS FARM

Harmon Myerholtz Family
Abt. 1946

Upper Left: Grandma, Pa, Uncle Esty, Uncle Bob, Grandpa
Lower Left: Aunt Gusty, Aunt Lois, Aunt Annie, Aunt Carrie
Not pictured: Uncle Harmie who was in Japan at this time

For as long as I can remember, I suffered from toothaches, and I often had a toothache when I visited my grandparents at the Tubbs Farm. Growing up at that time did not include much dental hygiene on my part, so I usually had at least one bad tooth and a lot of pain. In those days a trip to the dentist was something that other kids did. When I had a toothache I had just a couple of options to relieve the pain, and they relied mostly on heat to eliminate the ache. Option one was to fill a water bottle with hot water and hold it to the side of my face where the bad tooth was and wait for the heat to relax the nerve to the point that the hurting stopped.

The problem with this option was that the water cooled down quickly, and I had to constantly re-heat it. The other option was to pour salt into a pan, heat up the salt, and then pour the hot salt into an old sock. I would hold the sock full of hot salt to the side of my face, and hopefully this would have the same effect as the hot water bottle. While the salt stayed hot longer, it was not as comfortable against the side of my face as was the hot water bottle.

When I was at Grandma's house she had other options that she referred to as remedies. One was to rinse my mouth out with warm saltwater. The problem was, if I did this for a long period of time, I ended up swallowing a lot of saltwater. After awhile, I was more uncomfortable with a stomach ache than I was with the toothache. The next option was to pack the area around the aching tooth with chewing tobacco. The theory was that the tobacco would deaden the feeling in the gum and ease the pain of the toothache. The problem with this remedy was that a six or seven-year-old boy does not do well with a cheek full of chewing tobacco slowly oozing down the back of his throat. Very soon I learned to say the toothache was gone, just so I could spit out the tobacco and the mouthful of tobacco juice. One result was, the larger the wad of tobacco and the more tobacco juice I produced, the better the salt water remedy started to sound. The last option was only tried once which was enough for me. With this option, the chewing tobacco was first soaked with whiskey and then placed in my mouth and around the tooth. The whiskey was supposed to speed up the ability of the tobacco to deaden the pain of the toothache. I began to wonder if these toothache cures were ones that Grandpa preferred when he had a toothache. Needless to say, there were a number of times that I opted for a sock full of hot salt.

In addition to the couple of weeks that I spent every summer at Grandpa's farm, there were many other trips to the farm. It seemed that whenever our family traveled somewhere, it was to Grandma and Grandpa's house. We usually visited on Sunday for dinner, but sometimes we would drive over on a Saturday evening and spend the night and stay for the Sunday dinner before driving home. I remember on most of our Saturday night trips, Pa would repeat the same comment as we drove up to the house in the dark, and one time I beat him to the punch and said, "The house is lit-up like a whorehouse on Saturday night." Mom was not pleased. She yelled my name, and said to Pa, "Listen to that Myron. That's right from you." That was when I began to realize that parents could say things that kids were not allowed to repeat.

Quite often other aunts, uncles, and cousins showed up on Sunday and occasionally on Saturday night. At this time, my uncle Esty was married to Mom's sister, Kate, and they had three daughters, Cathy, Marie, and Barbara. Also, Pa's older sister, Carrie, was married to Frank Reyome, and they had had five boys and two girls. Bill, was the oldest, and he was followed by Dick, Ted, Don, Jerry, Ocie May, and Sharon. Aunt Gusty and Uncle Melvin and their four kids were also likely to show up on any Sunday as they were living close by in Blissfield.

Dinners usually consisted of fried chicken with mashed potatoes and gravy, corn, beans and whatever else was growing in the garden. Grandma also did a lot of canning, so pickled beets and a variety of jams and jellies and pickles were on the table. Grandma made her own egg noodles, and usually there was chicken noodle soup with all of the chicken innards that I mentioned earlier. Grandma always had fresh pie for dessert, usually apple, pumpkin and mincemeat. Grandma made her own mincemeat, and I developed a real taste for it. Pa did not like mincemeat pie and referred to it as 'rat' pie, but that didn't keep me from eating it. She added cinnamon to the top of the pumpkin pie after baking, and I would have to blow off the cinnamon before I could eat the pie. For me, the eggs pickled with the beets were the best part of the meal.

Beer was always a part of these get-togethers. Grandpa loved his beer, as did all of his sons and sons-in-law, and my Aunt Gusty could hold her own when it came to drinking beer. Pa would usually stop and pickup a case of beer, twenty-four bottles, when we drove through Blissfield on our way to Grandma's house. Grandpa's favorite beer was Old Dutch, The Good Beer, and Pa's favorite was Buckeye, so he would usually buy one or the other. I am not sure if Pa bought these beers because they were his favorites or because they were the cheapest. If other aunts and uncles came, they usually also brought beer. For the most part, drinking beer was a normal part of a fun family gathering. However, every now and then, tempers did get a little high, and sometimes an argument broke out. Usually the argument was between Esty and someone or Grandpa and someone. The swearing would increase as the voices became louder, until someone would eventually threaten to kick someone's ass. At this point calmer heads (the women folk) would intervene, and things would slowly get back to normal. I never saw an actual fight at one of these gatherings, even though I can remember thinking that there was going to be one any minute.

With all of the grandchildren that were a part of these gatherings, it was not unusual for one of them to try to sneak a sip of beer from one of the many beer bottles that were sitting around. This occurred more with the boys and was usually the result of someone saying, "I dare you to sneak a drink of the beer," and sometimes a couple of the boys would try to get one of the girls to taste it. The first problem with tasting beer was it needed to be done quickly in order not to get caught. The second problem was that most everyone drinking the beer also smoked. Quite often when someone finished the beer, he would throw his cigarette butts into the beer bottle. If we did not take a second to look into the beer bottle that we grabbed, we could get a very unpleasant surprise when a wet cigarette butt ended up in our mouth.

There was never any hard liquor at these gatherings except when some of Grandma's Apply Jack was available. Pa said that Grandma started with a gallon of apple cider and added such things as raisins, brown sugar, yeast and licorice. Grandma would put the jug in the cellar and let it work and harden for a period of time. If the jug did not explode, it was ready to drink. I never personally tasted this home brew, but I was told that it had a real kick.

Whenever we went to Grandma and Grandpa Myerholtz's house, Pa would take along a shoe box that contained a pair of barber scissors, a barber's comb, and a pair of hand clippers. At some point during the visit, Pa would give a haircut to any of the men or boys that wanted one. Pa would usually cut Grandpa's hair and sometimes, depending who was there, he would cut three or four heads of hair during the visit. Pa always cut my hair for as long as I can remember, and every now and then, one of my uncles, especially Esty and Harmie, would stop at our house and ask if Pa had time to cut their hair. I think that for Pa, cutting hair was a way of saving the family a little money, and it was something that he enjoyed doing. He again would tell me, "You learn by watching and then doing," and that is how he learned to cut hair.

Before and after dinner, when other aunts, uncles, and cousins were present, there were tractor-wagon rides, and games of tag and hide and seek for anyone who wanted to play. There often was a softball game that everyone played, youngest to oldest. At that time, my Aunt Lois and Uncle Bob were taking Hawaiian guitar lessons, and they would usually play whatever they were practicing, and everyone would listen. Sometimes we would tune in the *Grand Old Opry* on the radio, and we would all square dance in the living room, adults and children alike. Quite often, Uncle Bob did the calling. When we stayed the night, us kids mostly made beds on the floor in the living floor using blankets and feather ticks.

The trips home were long and always started as it was getting dark. The drive home in the '33 Chevy would take about two hours. There was no radio in the Chevy, and four or five kids in the back seat soon became a repetition of, "Quit leaning on me," or "I need more room," or "When are we going to get there?" Pa would get irritated and threaten us with bodily harm when we got home if we didn't stop. At that point, Mom would start to sing to entertain us. She had a great voice and knew quite a number of songs that we all soon learned, and at times we would sing along. Songs like, "Put My Little Shoes Away," "Two Little Orphans," "Careless Love," "Cowboy Jack," "Red River Valley," and "Amazing Grace," were ones that she always sang. She told us that she had learned the words to many of these from listening to Grandma Myerholtz sing the same songs. After awhile, I would start to get sleepy, and the movement of the car would start to fall into the same rhythm as Mom's voice, and I would drift off to sleep. The next thing that I would be aware of was Pa carrying me into the house and putting me into my bed.

CHAPTER 12

UNCLE BOB

My Uncle Bob is only five years older than me, and he was at the farm whenever I was there. I spent most of my time with Carl and him and other male cousins doing what young boys do when they are together. I mentioned that Grandpa smoked Bull Durham, and on one occasion, Bob, Carl, and I decided that we should try out this smoking thing. Bob had managed to sneak out a bag of the Bull Durham tobacco, but he did not get any of the paper that was needed to roll a cigarette. Usually the only paper to be found in the outhouse on the farm was an old Sears and Roebuck Catalog, but on this particular search for paper, we found a small roll of honest to goodness toilet paper. Thinking that toilet paper and cigarette paper were basically the same thing, we rolled, as best we could, a cigarette for each of us. We learned quickly that unlike cigarette paper, toilet paper bursts into flame when it comes into contact with a lit match. I think that we all lost a few eyebrow hairs that day. Another time, we tried to make cigarettes out of dried corn silk and found that dried corn silk also produces an open flame under the right conditions. I can't recall that we were ever successful in our smoking attempts.

Uncle Bob is the one who introduced me to the joys of riding a pig. Again, Bob, Carl and I were at the farm together and looking for something to do when Bob suggested that we ride a pig. Bob got up on the wooden fence near the corner of the pig pen, and Carl and I singled out a pig and herded her over to the corner where Bob was. When we got the pig near enough, Bob dropped down from the fence onto the pig's back, grabbing hold of each of the pig's ears and wrapping his legs around the pig's belly. The pig did not see the fun in this, and she was off and running. It was really funny to watch the pig running around the pen with my Uncle Bob holding on for dear life. At one point Bob basically relaxed his legs and stood up, letting the pig run out from under him.

Then it was time for Carl and me to try our luck. The first thing that we both learned was that our legs were considerably shorter than Bob's so we had a problem with holding on, and even more problems with standing up and letting the pig run out from under us. But we both managed to take a short ride and then get off, which was more or less just sliding down the pig's back and landing on our feet behind the pig.

Bob wanted to try it again, so Carl and I herded another pig over to him. Only this time, whether by chance or by choice, Bob ended up facing the rear of the pig, and he grabbed hold of the pig's tail. Carl and I could not stop laughing as we watched the pig running around the pen with Bob holding tightly to its tail. Since all of this took place in the main pig pen, there were a number of small triangular-shaped hog houses in the pen that were just large enough to give shelter for one or two pigs. For some reason this particular pig made the decision to seek shelter and ran head first into the opening on one of the hog houses. As the pig entered the hog house on a dead run, the front of the house caught my Uncle Bob in the middle of the back, pushing him off the pig, face first into the mud of the pig pen. The whole sight caused Carl and me to laugh even harder. I was content to let Bob have bragging rights about riding a pig backwards. Somehow I did not think that ending up face first in the pig pen was worth the effort of keeping up.

One more adventure I had with Uncle Bob on several occasions involved an abandoned farm house on the property next to the Tubbs farm. This house was haunted, at least that is what my Uncle Bob tried to tell all of us kids. He used to take us over to the house after dark and walk us through it, lighting our way with a kerosene lantern while telling us scary tales about the ghosts he had seen there. The older boys and I went along and tried to act frightened mainly to make sure that the younger kids, especially the girls, were really scared. I have to say that a few times I was probably more frightened than I was even pretending.

CHAPTER 13
OUTHOUSES

The first time I can remember using an indoor bathroom was when we visited Grandma and Grandpa Dickerson at their apartment in Detroit. I have been told that we had indoor plumbing in the houses when we lived in Toledo when I was very young. And then later, there were indoor bathrooms in school. However, for most of my growing up years, we had an outhouse.

Both the farm in Woodville and Grandma and Grandpa Myerholtz's farm had outhouses, as did the homes of my aunts and uncles. These outhouses were basically the same. They were usually two-holers, but sometimes they were three-holers. Each one had the little crescent moon-shaped air vent above the door which did not do all that much to get rid of the odor. Some outhouses had lids for the holes and others did not, and some had real toilet paper with a wire roll hanger, and some just had whatever paper was available, including old Sears catalogs. There was a rod or a stick of some sort in the outhouse which was used to knock down any spider webs that had been spun in the holes overnight. A bag of lime with an empty coffee can was kept in the outhouse so that occasionally someone would dump a little lime into the pit to help cut down on the smell.

I can't remember when I first started having these thoughts, but at some point I remember being in the outhouse and wondering to myself, why is there more than one hole in an outhouse? I had never seen two people using the outhouse at the same time. Who would I really want to have sitting beside me here? Thankfully, these are questions that I no longer need to ponder thanks to the wonders of indoor plumbing.

The other thing about being a young boy on a farm was that in some cases the world was my outhouse. When I was with other young boys, my uncles, my dad, or my grandpa, playing and working on the farm, it was not necessary to go clear back to the outhouse, and the back of the barn, a nearby tree, or just some tall weeds or grass provided the perfect place with a minimum of effort and wasted time.

I remember that Grandpa often would go out on the back porch late in the evening of a summer day to have one last cigarette before going to bed. Sometimes I would go out on the porch and see him standing by the rail looking out at the field and the stars as he smoked, relaxing from a hard day of work. One time, just before he went inside for the night, he turned to me as he un-buttoned his fly and said, "Sometimes it just feels good to piss off of the porch."

CHAPTER 14

SCHOOL DAYS AND THE RAMIREZ BOYS

1946

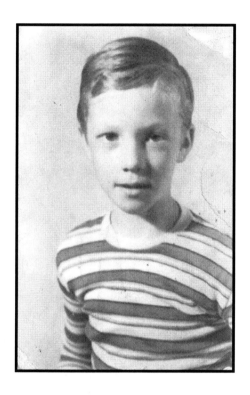

My First Grade Picture

The summer of 1946 was the first time that I remember the Fourth of July, and in Woodville, the Fourth of July was a real event. The town blocked off Route 20, Main Street, for a carnival on the main drag, and I can remember riding on the Ferris Wheel and seeing the tops of all of the buildings in downtown Woodville. One carnival attraction that Pa could not pass was *Ring the Bell*. He loved to swing the big hammer and try to ring the bell at the top of the scale. He told me that the whole secret to ringing the bell was not to hit the lever squarely in the middle, but to hit it on the front edge for more leverage. He was good at ringing the bell. All carnivals had a guy who would guess a person's weight or age. If his guess was more than five pounds or two years off, that person won a prize. Now Pa always looked younger than his real age, so he would have Mom and us kids wait for him a little ways off from the booth while he went over and had the guy guess his age. Pa almost always won a prize because the carnival workers guessed his age at least five years younger than he really was.

At that time, Woodville had one of the better fireworks displays of any small town in Northwest Ohio. We would go down to the City Park on the banks of the Portage River and sit on our blankets and watch the fireworks. We would count the number of sky rockets, and there was always over a hundred.

In September I started school in Woodville. We were living about a mile out of town so we had to ride the school bus each day. Our bus driver was Gummy Raberg, the Police Chief. Louise had started the year before, and her teacher, Mrs. Bowersox, had also been one of Pa's teachers when he was in school in Woodville.

I mentioned earlier that Pa had quit school in the ninth grade. The story he told is that one day during recess, a boy in his class fell and ran his arm through a school window, breaking the glass and cutting his arm pretty badly. Pa said that the teacher told all of the kids to go back into the school except the only black girl in the class. She told her to get a bucket of water and clean up the blood on the concrete. Pa asked the teacher, "Why are you making her clean up the blood? Is it because she is black?" The teacher told Pa to go to the principal's office and threatened to have him expelled for interfering with her authority. Pa said that he just left the school and never went back.

My first grade teacher was named Mrs. Beaker. I don't remember that much about the first grade except that I met a boy named Kenny who lived on Route 20, just outside of the village limits. I used to get off the bus at his house to play after school and then walk the half-mile home. I also remember that first grade was the first time I realized I liked a girl. Her name was Veronica, and I had never heard of the name Veronica so both the name and the emotions were something new to me. Unfortunately, Veronica did not share my feelings.

We had a tuberculosis scare in first grade, and everyone took a TB test. Students wore a tape patch on their upper arms for about a week, and then the patch was removed to determine if anyone was positive. For whatever reason, when they tested my patch, they told my parents that the result was positive for TB. Mom and Pa had to take me to a Fremont clinic where I was given a chest X-ray to determine if the test had been accurate. I remember that Mom was really worried all the way to the clinic, but fortunately the X-ray was negative.

It was in the first grade that I got to know the Ramirez boys. We all rode the bus together and even though the two Ramirez boys were older than me, we sat together on the bus. They looked out for me on the playground during recess, and one time when an older boy was picking on me, the Ramirez boys came to my rescue. As my friendship with the Ramirez boys grew, so did the time that I spent with them. I began to pick up some words in Spanish and learned to like tamales, a treat to the Ramirez family. Whenever a major holiday occurred, Christmas, Easter and such, large quantities of tamales were handmade by the family, and usually some of them ended up at our house. Mrs. Ramirez also made tortillas and fried them directly on the top of the kitchen stove. I discovered that a tortilla fresh off the stove top with a little butter was great eating. I learned that I had a low tolerance for hot, spicy Mexican food. Mrs. Ramirez had a little mortise and pestle that was made from a kind of black stone, and she would hand-grind peppers in it. It occurred to me that it was good that it was made of stone because if it were wooden, it would probably catch fire from the heat of the peppers.

Another thing I started doing with the Ramirez boys was working in the fields during the tomato and sugar beet seasons. One of the first things that I learned how to do was to block beets. Beets are planted in rows by a seed drill, but not all of the seeds are planted uniformly. Once the beet plant started to grow, it was necessary to have workers go down each row and move plants that were too close together and pull out excess beet plants. This was necessary to ensure that the growing beet had enough room to develop, and the process was called blocking. In the fall, harvesting the beets was done by hand. Workers would pull the beets out of the ground with one hand, chop off the tops with a machete type knife, and toss the beets onto a truck. When it was too muddy to get a truck into the field, it was necessary to haul the beets out with a team of horses. When the horses were needed, I sometimes got to drive the team.

This was the first year that I can remember picking tomatoes. One thing I learned about picking tomatoes was when tomatoes get over ripe, they are like a water balloon. The skin of the tomato is strong enough to hold the juice inside, and if I could slide my open hand under the tomato for support, and carefully break the stem off the plant, I could then toss the tomato at an unsuspecting friend when he was not looking. Even if I missed the person I was throwing at, there was a big splash of red juice when the tomato hit the ground. I also learned that everyone else already knew how to do this, so quite often I was on the receiving end of these red juice bombs.

The first time that I ever fired a gun was with the Ramirez boys. Raymond had a single shot rifle. He had sawed off the wooden stock just behind the trigger guard to form a revolver-like handle. He then sawed-off the barrel so it was about twelve inches long. It looked a little like an old pirate's pistol, and he used it to hunt rabbits and other small animals. We were out playing in the woods one day and Raymond had the gun in a bag over his shoulder. He saw a red-headed woodpecker in the tree and took out the gun and shot at the woodpecker. He did not hit it, and then asked me if I wanted to shoot the gun. Of course I had to say, "Yes." I think I shot at a tree and missed, but it was the first time I fired a gun.

A few weeks later, Pa had his rifle out to shoot at a rabbit or something, and I told him that I had shot Raymond's gun. Pa was not pleased that I had done this, but took the opportunity to teach me about shooting a rifle. He sat up a bale of hay in front of a mound of dirt behind the barn. He then placed a couple of tin cans on the bale and sat me down behind a second bale of hay. He laid the rifle across the bale and gave me instructions on how to hold the rifle and sight the target. I missed the first shot but hit one of the cans with the second shot. I thought that I going to be the next Roy Rogers.

Pa was an excellent shot with a rifle. I can remember him taking the rifle with him on the tractor as he worked in the fields in the fall and coming home with a couple of rabbits and occasionally a pheasant. Shooting rabbits and pheasants from a tractor with a rifle is not an easy thing to do.

At that time in Woodville there was a small community made up of Mexican families just west of the Woodville Lime Plant. The Ramirez family had bought a property lot in this area, and they were in the process of building a house there. Also at that time in Woodville, there was a movie theater called the Limelight. There were enough Mexican families in the area that once every week or so, there would be a movie in Spanish. I remember seeing a number of western movies in Spanish with the Ramirez boys. I could still follow the plot of the movie, and I knew who the hero and the bad guys were. I just did not know when to laugh at the funny parts.

It was the Ramirez boys who introduced me to chewing tar. For some reason, they liked to chew tar like it was chewing gum. Often in the summer, area roads would be resurfaced with hot tar. Whenever a road was resurfaced, they would ride their bicycles over to the road and scoop up some fresh tar into an empty can and bring it back to their house. They rolled out the tar into a tootsie roll shape and let it harden. They then bit off a little bit of the tar roll and chewed it like it was gum. I tried this on a number of occasions and decided that except for the chewing motion, chewing tar did not have a lot to offer.

When I started school, Pa thought it was time I learned how to milk a cow. Pa showed me how to grip the udder with my thumb pointed down and the rest of my fingers wrapped around the udder, holding it tightly against the knuckle of my thumb. Then, with a downward pulling motion and a squeeze, the thumb knuckle stripped the milk from the udder. We always seemed to have at least one barn cat which would come around whenever we were milking the cow. When this happened, Pa would aim the udder in the direction of the cat and squirt a stream of milk into his open mouth. The first few times that I tried this, I squirted more milk on the cat than I did in his mouth, but after a few tries, I could control the direction of the stream of milk.

There were two important things I learned to watch out for when milking a cow. I usually sat on a milking stool with both of my feet under her belly, and the first lesson was that a cow does not like to stand still, even when she is restrained in a milking stall. She would often shift her weight from foot to foot, and when she did this, if I did not pay attention to where my feet were, she was likely to step on my foot. It was not pleasant to have my foot stepped on by a 1,000 pound cow.

The other lesson I learned was where there are cows, there are also flies. When a fly lands on a cow and bites, the only thing a cow can do is swat at the fly with her tail. Since I was sitting near the back end of the cow when she suddenly swung her tail at a fly, often my head got in the way. Getting slapped upside of the head by a cow's tail is not fun, especially if she had been a little careless the last time she made a cow pie.

For whatever reason I don't have a memory of Christmas before the one in 1946. That year, we did not have a tree or anything until one night when Mom and Pa came home from downtown Woodville. They told all of us to go into the bedroom and close the door. We waited in the room for what seemed like a long time and when finally they called us out, we found the a room filled with a Christmas tree, gifts, and everything. My gift, a brand new wooden Radio Flyer wagon with red trim, was sitting under the tree. It was a Christmas to remember!

Pa loved to have oranges and tangerines at Christmas, and that Christmas we had both. I don't know if it was the war and rationings that caused us to not have oranges and tangerines up to this time, or if it was just the cost of the fresh fruit, but I know that Pa was really excited about having both. That Christmas I learned Pa also loved chocolate covered cherries. Mom gave him a box of them, and he shared one with each of us kids. It was the first time that I remember eating a chocolate covered cherry, and I could see why Pa liked them so much.

My memories of winters in Woodville include heavy snowfalls that were at least knee deep. While my knees were closer to the ground, I did hear Grandpa use the expression, "The snow is knee deep to a tall dog." We spent a lot of time playing in the snow, and there never seemed to be enough gloves for everyone. We often wore old stockings on our hands, and they worked just fine.

Mom used to make snow ice cream whenever we had a fresh snow. She would go out and scoop up a big bowl of fresh snow from a deep drift. She would add a little milk, a little vanilla, and a little sugar. She would stir this all up and serve us a bowl of delicious ice cream. I think that this was the time when I first remember Pa warning us kids, "Don't eat the yellow snow."

I learned a very painful lesson that winter. I had a rather large old tricycle that I rode around the driveway and sidewalks, and I had Pa's old 1945 license plate wired to the back. I was out riding the bike on a cold winter day, and for whatever reason, I put my lips down on the handle bar of the bike. Instantly my lips were frozen to the handle bar. I tried to pull away but could not. I tried to call out for help, but again, when my lips were frozen to a metal object it was not easy to say anything. I finally was able to pull my head back from the handle bar, but I left a good portion of the skin from my lips attached to the handle bar. They were bleeding as I came into the kitchen, and Mom put a wet wash rag in my mouth, and soon the bleeding stopped. Pa was not too sympathetic about the whole thing and told me I should have known better.

CHAPTER 15

A MOVE TO MICHIGAN

1947

Our Family in Ogden Center, Michigan
(Girls and Mom in Feedbag Dresses)

Upper Left: Pa, Raymond, Mom
Lower Left: Me, Louise, Caroline, Janet

I think that the summer of 1947 was the first time that Pa took me along on one of his overnight fishing trips. Pa liked to fish and during the summer, he would sometimes drive up past Oak Harbor on a Saturday evening and fish all night in the Portage River, returning home on Sunday. I can't remember who else went with us, except that it was two other men that Pa knew. I had a cane pole that was at least twelve feet long, and we stuck the end of the pole against the rear fender of the car, resting it on the running board. We then laid the tip of the pole over the headlight on the front fender. I thought for sure that the pole would fall off the car, but it never did. That first time, I got sleepy soon after dark and slept more than I fished. But the more I went along on the overnighters, the more I got used to staying awake longer, although I don't think I ever got to the point where I could stay awake all night.

Pa always went to the same place on these fishing trips. There was a boat dock called Mechens Grove with a bait shop and a boat rental on the Portage River near La Carne, a small town on Route 105 just past Oak Harbor. Pa usually did bank fishing when he fished all night. He gathered some wood and started a fire, and we roasted hot dogs on a stick for supper. Pa brought a kerosene lantern for light, and he sometimes cut dried cattails, soaked them in kerosene, stuck them in the ground, and lit them for additional light.

We caught mostly bull heads and cat fish. Both of these fish have sharp barbs in the fins near their heads which would give me a nasty sting if I was not careful when I was removing the hook. Pa taught me how to hold these fish so that they could not sting. He also taught me how to skin these fish as both are good eating. We usually threw back the sheep head, and we did catch plenty of carp. The best thing about catching a carp is that it puts up a great fight once it is hooked. Pa usually took the carp home along with all of the bull heads and cat fish. Mom would fry up the bull heads and cat fish after she rolled them in flour or Saltine cracker crumbs. Although the carp were very boney and never tasted that good to me, Mom would cook them up and Pa ate them. Grandpa used to say, "The only way to cook a carp is to stuff it full of horse shit and then nail the carp to a wooden board and bake it in an oven. When the fish is fully cooked, throw away the carp and eat the horse shit and the board." I don't recall that Mom ever followed his recipe. Another of Grandpa's colorful recipes was for cooking a skunk. He said that all you had to do was "Boil the piss out of the skunk."

I started the second grade in 1947, and shortly after school began that year, my brother, Raymond, was born. I had gone to the Limelight Movie Theater with the Ramirez boys on their bikes, with me riding on the handle bars of Raymond's bike. When we returned, all of my sisters and Pa were sitting on the back porch. Pa explained that Dr. Drossel was in the house, and that Mom was having a baby. In a short time, my brother Raymond was born. One of the family stories that everyone enjoys to this day is that Ray would never have been born if it weren't for my sister Caroline. She had played in Mom's bedroom and somehow found her diaphragm. Caroline was only three years old, and she did what most three year old would do, she put it in her mouth. When Mom found Caroline with the diaphragm in her mouth, she did not detect the small hole that Caroline had put in it.

A couple of weeks later, my Aunt Kate and Uncle Esty moved upstairs for a few weeks. I can't remember why they moved in, or why they moved out, I just remember one incident that happened while they were there. I was getting ready for school one morning, and Ray was crying quite a bit, and Mom was trying to get him to settle down. He kept crying and would take long breaths of air between the fits of crying. At one point the crying suddenly stopped, and Mom yelled out, "I think Ray swallowed his tongue." My Uncle Esty was upstairs shaving when he heard Mom yell, and he came running down the stairs with soap on his face and hands. Mom was holding Ray, and Esty reached a soapy finger into Ray's mouth and pulled his tongue forward. Ray immediately started to cry again, and we were all quite relieved, especially Mom.

Esty was Pa's older brother. He was taller than Pa, and looked more like the Layman side of the family. He too, like Pa, had been farmed out as a child, but I don't think that he stayed in school as long as Pa did. Esty's left leg was bowed due to an accident that happened shortly after he married Aunt Kate. He had taken a job driving a semi-truck, and on one of his trips, the trailer had a flat tire. He was lying on the edge of the road, putting the jack under the trailer axle. A passing car ran over his left leg, breaking the bone between his knee and his ankle. He was put into a cast, but he grew tired of wearing it and not being able to go to work. One night after he had been drinking, he cut the cast off and laced up a knee high boot on that leg and told Aunt Kate he was going back to driving truck. He ended up with a permanent bow in the bone of his leg and walked with a slight limp because the one leg was shorter than the other. This leg problem kept him out of the war.

Esty had a short fuse and a temper that was magnified by the amount of beer that he drank. He was the first one to get angry when he was drinking with other family members. Also, Esty could string together the longest and most varied combinations of swear words that I have ever heard, then or now. Grandpa and Pa both knew their way around cuss words, but Esty stood head and shoulders above either of them when it came to stringing swear words together. The other thing about Esty and his temper was if he got angry while he was working on something, whatever was in his hand got tossed as far as he could throw it. Working on a car with Esty was no fun because you were either ducking the wrench that he was throwing, or you were looking for the wrench that he had just tossed. I once saw him become so angry that he picked up a hammer and broke out both headlights on the car. I also saw him stab a screw driver through the windshield of another car, and both cars belonged to him.

Esty was introduced to my mom's older sister, Kate, by Pa, who brought Esty along for his second date with Mom. That was their first double-date, and at one point early on, they all agreed to switch dates for one night, with Mom going to a movie with Esty, and Pa going to a different movie with Kate. According to Mom, this only happened one time, but my Aunt Kate used to tell people that she had met and dated Pa first. This made my Mom quite upset then and still does today when she talks about it.

My Aunt Kate and Mom were quite different. Mom did not smoke, and I think that she would die of thirst before she would drink a beer. Mom hardly ever said a cuss word, preferring to use, "Gosh darn, dang, and heck." However, my Aunt Kate did like a beer now and then, she did smoke, and she was known to throw a cuss word or two back at my Uncle Esty when they were arguing. And they did argue. My Aunt Kate just seemed to be more worldly than my mother. Kate and Esty married about six months after Mom and Pa, and their first child, Cathy, was born about six months after my sister, Louise, and about seven months before me.

As the winter of 1947 approached, Pa made a decision to quit farming and take a fulltime job driving a truck again, so we had to move out of the Sander's farmhouse. The Ramirez family had finished building their new house near the lime plant and their three-room beet shanty house was empty. Pa made arrangements to rent the house, and we moved into it. There was one room that served as the kitchen and dining room, and two small rooms that served as bedrooms. Mom, Pa, and Ray slept in one bedroom, and Louise, Janet, Caroline, and I slept in the other. There was an outhouse and an outside well. We had a very small wood cooking stove, and a small coal stove heated the house.

What I remember most about this house was that it was always cold and dark. We moved into the house about November and moved out of it the following February, but it seemed like we were there much longer. It was winter and often snowed at night. When we awoke in the morning, there would be a thin layer of snow on the kitchen floor in front of the outside door. Also, if we left any water in a glass overnight, it would be frozen in the morning. The house did not have electricity, so the lighting was by kerosene lamps. Pa was gone often, driving long-distance hauls, so Mom and us kids were there alone a great deal of the time. In fact, Pa was gone so much, Mom finally told him that he would need to get a different job because she could not live in that house with five kids on her own.

I guess Pa took her seriously because he soon found a job in Blissfield, Michigan. My Uncle Esty was working at the Peale Alfalfa Mill in Raga, Michigan, and heard that Peale was looking for someone to run his Blissfield plant. Esty suggested Pa for the job. Peale hired Pa to run the third shift from 11:00 PM to 7:00 AM, and we moved out of the beet shanty and in with Grandma and Grandpa Myerholtz on the Tubbs farm.

We lived with Grandma and Grandpa for about two weeks while we were looking for a house to rent. At this same time, Kate and Esty were also living with Grandma and Grandpa, so we had a houseful. I remember going to school briefly at the school near Grandma's house. It was a one-room schoolhouse with grades one through nine, and on cold mornings, we all pulled our chairs around the stove in the center of the room to keep warm. I got on the bus in front of Grandma's house, along with my Uncle Bob, my cousins, Cathy, Marie, and Barb, and my sisters, Louise and Janet. We were seven of the twenty kids at that school. The only other thing I remember is one day the teacher gave a number of us younger kids pictures to color while she taught the older kids. The picture that I had was of a child sleeping in a bed with a teddy bear. The bed had a quilt on it, and I colored the squares of the quilt red and pink. I remember that she held up my picture to the class and used it as an example. She said, "Never use red and pink in the same picture because red and pink do not go together." She told me that I should know better than to use red and pink together, and I guess she must have been right. After all, I was in the second grade.

Mr. Peale, Pa's boss, offered to rent him a house just outside a small town called Ogden Center, Michigan, which was about eight miles from Blissfield. It was located on Crocket Highway, south of the intersection with Weston Road, and there was an open ditch between the house and the road. I remember the ditch specifically because in the spring of 1948, I had been given my first bicycle. It was a used bike that Pa had picked up somewhere, and he taught me how to ride it in the driveway. Pa held the bike by the seat as I tried to get my balance and pedal at the same time.

I guess he thought that I had finally gotten the hang of it because he let go of the bike. I pedaled it in a weaving fashion down the drive, across the front yard, and directly into the ditch which was half full of water. I was not hurt, but I was totally drenched, as I struggled up the ditch bank dragging my bike up out of the water.

At this time, Dutch and Melvin were living in Blissfield, Grandma and Grandpa were living on the Tubbs Farm, and Esty and Kate were living in Ottawa Lake, so we were all quite close, and often we would all be at Grandma and Grandpa's house on Sundays. It was on one of these Sunday visits that I came home with a dog. This dog showed up at Grandpa's house at some point and stayed around there for a couple of weeks. Grandpa had a small brown dog named, Shep, so he did not need another dog. Esty had tried to chase this stray dog away a couple of times by hitting it with a stick or throwing rocks at it, but the dog kept coming back. The day we were there, the dog showed up again, and immediately Esty started chasing him around the house, trying to get him to leave. Grandpa said, "I wish someone would just take that dog, so he would quit showing up here." I asked Pa if we could take him, and to my surprise he said, "Yes." We took the dog back to our house, and I named him Mike. He was medium-sized, tawny-colored, and he had longish hair like a Collie but without the long nose of a Collie. He was my dog, and I was responsible for feeding him and cleaning up the dog messes that were in the front yard. Mike was good with all of us kids and was fun to play with in the yard. But whenever Esty was at our house, Mike growled at him, and tried to find a place to hide.

I do not have as many vivid memories of this house as I had for the Woodville house. Maybe it's because we only lived here about a year, or maybe it's because the house was the only part of the farm that we had access to. Mr. Peale rented the barns, out buildings, and land to another person who was running the farm, and we were not allowed in the buildings and were supposed to stay out of the fields.

I do have a few memories of the inside of this house. One of the interior walls of my bedroom had two glass windows that were the backside of a china cabinet that opened to the dining room. This china cabinet had glass doors on the dining room side, and glass shelves inside of the cabinet area. One day I was sent to my room for something I had done, and I was not happy about being there. As I lay on my bed, I began kicking the wall where these windows were located, and with each kick, the items that sat on the glass shelves in the china cabinet rattled. I remember that Mom told me a couple of times to, "Quit kicking the wall," but evidently I did not follow her suggestion because suddenly Pa was in the room, belt in hand, and he was not happy. I am sure that I did not kick the wall again after that.

Another memory of this house is that I started washing dishes here. Mom decided that because she needed to take care of Janet, Caroline and Raymond, and get them ready for bed each night, it was time to have Louise and me do the dishes after supper. We took turns washing and drying the dishes every other night. I didn't mind doing the dishes, but I wondered if any of the other boys in school thought that I had dish pan hands. I even asked Mom, "Can you really tell if someone has been doing dishes by looking at their hands?"

When we moved into this house, I immediately started school at another one-room schoolhouse. The school was located on the northeast corner of the intersection of Crockett Highway and Weston Road, and the school building is still standing. The best part about this school was that it was just about 200 yards down the road from our house. Louise, Janet and I were three of about twenty kids that made up the classes from first through ninth grade, and our teacher's name was Miss Vick. The two ninth grade boys came to school early and started a fire in the coal stove to heat the building for us. Miss Vick would start each day with the *Pledge of Allegiance*, and then she would give each class of two or three students instructions and an assignment to work on while she went from class to class. When she finished the ninth grade, she would go back to the first grade and check the students' work and continue checking each class. If we got our work done, we were supposed to read until Miss Vick got back to us.

The school had an outhouse, and if we needed to use the facility, we were to raise our hand with the traditional one finger, two finger signals. Miss Vick would give us a nod of her head to indicate that we could quietly exit out the back door to the outhouse. Some days, especially in the spring when the weather was nice and the schoolwork was boring, almost everyone would have a hand up just for an excuse to go outside. Miss Vick would become a little more selective with her head nods, and at times, would simply tell us to wait for recess.

The school also had an outside well for water. It was the responsibility of the younger boys, including me, to take turns filling the water bucket in the morning before school and placing the filled bucket on the bench at the front of the room. There was a dipper hanging on a hook by the bucket, a towel to wipe the dipper after using it, and a small washbasin and another towel to wash our hands after we made a trip to the outhouse.

There was one other boy in the second grade with me. His name was Don, and one day during recess, Don and I got into a wrestling match on the playground. Miss Vick made us go into the schoolhouse, and she told us to wrestle on the floor in front of the rest of the kids. I am still not sure what she was trying to prove by making us wrestle because after about five minutes, she just told us to stop and take our seats. If there was a lesson in this, I missed it.

Chapter 16

GRANDMA AND GRANDPA DICKERSON

Helen Louise and Charles Raymond Dickerson

At this time Grandma and Grandpa Dickerson were living in Detroit. I can't remember going to Detroit before this, but I am sure that we had traveled there at some point. It seemed that Pa made most of the decisions about where we went and who we went to see, so usually we went to one of Pa's relatives. But every now and then, Mom would put her foot down and insist that we go to see Grandma and Grandpa Dickerson. However, we just did not go that often, and I think that Pa would use the excuse that the tires on the car could not be trusted to safely drive that far.

Most of the tires on the car were quite worn, and Pa had to install what was called a boot inside of the tire to give added thickness to the worn spots. The boots caused the tires to be out of balance, and we could feel the shaking of the car each time the tire with a boot rotated. When all of the tires on the car had a boot, the car shook all the time.

Pa sold the '33 Chevy and bought a 1939 Plymouth that needed some engine repair. I remember holding the lead cord light and handing Pa tools as he worked on the engine. I was seven years old, and this was the start of many a night helping Pa work on not only his car, but many other cars that he fixed for other people. The Plymouth was always difficult to start whenever it rained. The ignition seemed to have a problem with moisture shorting out the distributor. I can remember Pa saying, "If someone would spit on the driveway next to the Plymouth, it wouldn't start."

Now that we were living in Michigan, Detroit was closer than when we were living in Woodville so we visited more often. In addition, Pa had the '39 Plymouth instead of the '33 Chevy, so he was more confident about being able to drive to Detroit and back without having to worry about engine breakdowns or multiple flat tires. Driving to Detroit, we kept an eye out for a factory that made cook stoves where a very large iron cook stove was all lit up in front of the factory. When we saw the stove, we knew that we were almost to Grandma's house.

My early memories of both Grandma and Grandpa Dickerson are sketchy. I can't remember too many specifics, and I think that this is because I didn't see them that much. Grandma always lived in an apartment in the city, and there were no yards to play in and not much room in the apartment. I usually took a seat and stayed there for the entire length of the visit. This was partly because Grandma Dickerson seemed to have nicer furnishings in her house, and we were not supposed to touch anything.

My Uncle Richard always lived with Grandma. As I mentioned, Richard was mentally challenged, and he had his own room where he would go and shut the door the minute that we arrived. He would tell us not to get into any of his stuff. Grandma mostly talked with Mom and seemed to have very little to say to us kids. She was a large woman, slightly taller than Grandpa, and she outweighed him by at least fifty pounds. In all of my memories of Grandma Dickerson, she always had white hair.

Grandpa Dickerson was short, about 5'6" tall and quite thin. He had lost most of his hair and was bald except for a small band of hair directly above his ears. He had lost all of his teeth, and he did not always wear his false teeth. Sometimes after a few drinks and with his teeth out, Grandpa would put on a sailor's hat and entertain us all with his imitation of the cartoon character, Popeye.

Grandpa liked to drink, and if he were not at home when we arrived, it was generally because he had gone out for something to drink and not come home. Grandma would ask Pa to go out and look for him, and sometimes Pa would return with him but mostly not. Pa used to tell us that during prohibition, Grandpa would take whatever he could find that contained alcohol and mix that with water and drink it. Pa claimed that Grandpa drank hair tonic and water because the hair tonic was about forty percent alcohol, and Wild Root Hair Tonic was his drink of choice. Mom told me that during prohibition Grandpa Dickerson made his own beer in the basement of the house where they lived, and at times one of the bottles of beer would explode and send glass flying all over the basement floor.

Throughout my childhood, my dad, and both of my grandpas and most of my uncles struggled with drinking. But Grandpa Dickerson was the only one that seemed to be an alcoholic. Grandpa Myerholtz and Pa usually drank beer and would occasionally have a drink of the hard stuff at weddings and special occasions. I was never aware that drinking kept Pa or Grandpa Myerholtz from working at their jobs. Grandpa Dickerson on the other hand, would drink beer, but preferred the hard stuff. On a number of occasions, he would leave the house and be gone for days at a time, as Mom put it, "out on a drunken jag." Grandpa Dickerson worked at the Libby Owens Ford Company as a glass cutter, and he would sometimes get fired from his job because of the drinking. He would leave home for work, but instead of going to work, he would go on a drunken jag and not show up for a few days or more. Once he did come home and sober up, he would go see his boss and promise not to miss work again. His boss would eventually take him back because when Grandpa was sober, he was a very skilled glass cutter.

The one thing that I do remember about Grandpa Dickerson is that he could, and often did, recite the entire words to the poem, "Abdul Abubul Amir." I can't remember the first time that I heard him do this, but I did hear it a number of times. Grandpa Dickerson also was quite fond of limericks and would sometimes recite one. I knew that they rhymed, but I did not understand the off-color lines until I got a little older.

The other thing that I remember about our visits to Grandma and Grandpa Dickerson's in Detroit is that although both my Aunt Juanita and Aunt Shirley were still living at home, I cannot remember them being in the house when we were there. My Aunt Juanita is about seven years older than me, and my Aunt Shirley is about five years older than me, so they would have been in their teens at this point. I do not know why I have no memory of them during this time, except that my Aunt Juanita told me later that they didn't like being there with all the "noisy, crying kids."

One time when we were coming home from visiting Grandma and Grandpa Dickerson, another driver passed Pa and got too close to our car and ended up side-wiping us as he passed. I remember that Pa swore and took off after the other car, chasing it through the city streets. Mom finally got Pa to slow down and continue our drive home, but not until all of us kids were scared to death by the wild ride we had just been taken on through the dark streets. I don't even think that Mom's singing had a big effect on us that particular ride home.

Another set of grandparents that I first remember visiting at this time was my Great Grandma Laura Polly and her husband, Joe. Grandma Polly was the mother of my Grandpa Dickerson. Grandma Polly was a Mize from southern Kentucky, and she met and married Robert Richard (Bobby Dick) Dickerson in Science Hill, Kentucky. They had four children: Irene, Freda, Clarice, and my Grandpa Charles. They were living in Indiana when Grandma left Bobby Dick because of his drinking and carousing. She moved to Detroit where she got a job, saved her money, and then went back to Indiana to get her kids. She later met and married Joe Polly.

The story about Joe is that during prohibition he was working in a speakeasy as a bouncer somewhere in Indiana, and one night a fight broke out and a man was killed. Joe spent time in prison because of his involvement in the fight. Joe was a tall, stocky, white-haired man who liked to hunt, and who operated a saw sharpening business in his garage. Grandpa Joe Polly did not have a high tolerance for kids. The first time that I was in his saw shop, he kept telling me not to touch things, and warned me that "If you aren't careful, you are going to lose a finger." He had an Irish Setter dog, Pat, that he used to hunt pheasants, and he hunted up to the time that he lost a leg. I don't remember exactly when it happened, but it was after I knew him. He was climbing a ladder and slipped and fell, skinning the shin of his leg on the ladder rungs. He developed gangrene in the leg, and it had to be amputated just above the knee.

Great Grandma and Grandpa Polly lived in a house on Robb Highway in Palmyra, Michigan so they were quite close to us. We could stop and see them when we went to Grandma and Grandpa Myerholtz's house. At this time, my Great-Great Grandmother Mize was living with Great Grandma Polly, and I remember seeing her in her bedroom off the living room, but I do not remember anything else about her. My Great Aunt Freda and her husband Ed were living in a small house behind Grandma Polly's house. I never got to know Freda and Ed very much, but they were always at Grandma's house whenever we visited. Freda had a small dog, and whenever Freda would have a beer, which was often, she would pour a little of the beer into the dog's water dish, and the dog would quickly lap up the beer. This would continue until the dog began to stagger and fall down as he crossed the room. Freda would then quit giving him beer, and he would go over and lie down in the corner of the room and sleep it off.

When I was older, I was told the following story about my great aunts, Freda and her sister, Clarice. I can't remember ever meeting Clarice, as she died early in life of an alcohol-related illness. One time when Mom and Dad were dating, Freda and Clarice needed a ride to work, and they asked Pa if he could give them a ride to downtown Toledo. At the time, Mom always thought that they worked as telephone operators. Pa agreed to give them a ride, but after they had left the house, Freda and Clarice told him to take them to a different location. It turned out that they had Pa take them to a rather large residence that was well-known as a house of prostitution. Mom was surprised and a little shocked when Pa told her the truth about her aunts' profession. It also turned out that both Freda and Clarice had friends and possibly boyfriends that were associated with the Licavolli Gang in Toledo. A number of Dickerson family members claimed that often the men that Freda and Clarice kept company with were seen carrying a gun in a shoulder holster.

CHAPTER 17

DODGING A BULLET OR TWO

1948

Me, Janet, Louise, Caroline on the Tubbs Farm

Late in the spring of 1948, our family was involved in a car accident on one of the Michigan Highways. I can't remember the exact reason why we were driving on one of the few blacktop roads near Grandpa's farm during an ice storm, but we were, and we had a car full of passengers. Mom and Pa were in the front seat of the Plymouth along with Ray and Caroline. Grandma, Grandpa, Bob, and Lois were in the back seat with Louise, Janet, and me sitting on laps or the floor. Pa always told me that the secret of driving on ice was to drive with the two passenger side tires on the berm since the stones were usually loose and not frozen.

We were driving along very slowly, and I am not sure if Pa got too close to the grass along the road or if he ran out of berm, but almost in slow motion the car began to slide down the ditch bank, and eventually the Plymouth lay on its side at the bottom of the ditch. Pa managed to open the driver's side door and crawl out of the car, and then he helped Mom, Ray, and Caroline out through the same door. He opened the rear door and lifted me, Louise, and Janet out, followed by Bob, Lois, and Grandpa. Grandma was lying on her side in the bottom of the car, and I remember that Pa kept telling Grandma that she should not step on the window of the car door when she tried to stand up because she might break the glass and cut herself. Somehow Grandma was able to stand up, and with all of us helping, we were able to get her out of the car. The thing that surprised us all was that when Grandma did manage to standup, she was standing with both feet on the door window and the glass did not break.

Pa walked down the road to the nearest farmhouse and returned with the farmer and a tractor. The farmer was able to hook a chain to the front bumper of the car and pull the Plymouth up out of the ditch. Because of the ice, the car just slid up the ditch bank and slowly rolled back onto its wheels on the road. There was little noticeable damage to the side of the car, so we all climbed back in and continued driving to wherever it was that we were going.

For as long as I can remember, Pa had been a baseball fan, and as I mentioned, the Cleveland Indians was his favorite team. 1948 was the first year that I listened to baseball games on the radio with Pa. Whenever he was working on a car, which was often, or on any other project in the barn, he would have a radio on, and if the Indians were playing, we would listen to the ballgame. Radio in those days was far different from what it is now. For one thing, all stations were AM stations and reception on most stations was usually poor. We would be listening to the game and just when something exciting was happening, the sound would start to fade and the static would get so loud that we couldn't hear what was happening in the game.

Pa would try to adjust the station knob. When that didn't work, he would start to cuss, and soon he would slam his hand down on the top of the radio and follow up with a whole string of swear words. I cannot remember any radio we had that did not have a broken top or at least a cracked top or casing. In 1948, the Cleveland Indians won the American League Pennant and then beat the Boston Braves in the World Series. Larry Doby, the first Negro baseball player for the Indians, soon became my favorite player, and I was hooked on listening to Jimmy Dudley as he did the play-by-play of the Indians games on the radio.

This was really my first exposure to the African American race. There was one boy who was black in my first grade class, but I never got to know him. I did know and have a relationship with the Ramirez family, but they were Mexican, not Black. I had heard comments and talk from the adults in my family about negroes, and in general most of this talk was not complimentary. I had heard Grandpa use the expression, "There's a nigger in the wood pile," on a number of occasions, and I had heard large stones found in the fields referred to as nigger heads. I had also heard Pa tell a number of jokes that included the term, *nigger*. Grandma Myerholtz had some strong feelings about other groups of people. I can recall that she did not trust gypsies. She always told us kids whenever a carnival or circus was in the area that we had to watch out for gypsies that traveled with these groups because they would kidnap kids whenever they could. She also did not trust Jewish people and made references to "Jews cheating people out of their money."

All of these comments were general and not about specific individuals. For the most part, both Mom and Pa were accepting of people of all races and religions. I remember that Mom would tell us that, "Black people are no different than we are, and that it is only by the grace of God that we are not black ourselves." While her statement did make me wonder about why God made some people black and some people white, I knew she felt she was not prejudiced. She believed all people are equal in God's eyes, and she was trying to teach us to be accepting of everyone.

In the summer of 1948, us kids all dodged a bullet so to speak. We were asked by the man who was farming the property to do a cleanup of the brush and trash in the barnyard areas of the property. Evidently, he did not want to do it or was too busy to do this himself, and he was willing to pay Pa to do it. After Uncle Bob and Aunt Lois and all of us kids had gathered the dead branches, waste wood, and other burnable items into a rather large pile in the middle of the barnyard, we stood around watching the pile burn. All at once there was a loud bang that sounded like a gun shot, and Lois let out a short scream.

Apparently, in our cleanup efforts, which included sweeping out some of the building floors, a 22 rifle bullet had been swept up and ended up in the fire. The heat of the fire caused the bullet to explode, and the head of the bullet had struck Lois in the leg. She was wearing shorts at the time, and a thin line of blood, almost like a knife cut, could be seen running across her thigh where the bullet had grazed her leg. We all felt very lucky that the bullet had not hurt anyone more seriously, especially the kids, because the height of the bullet where it struck Lois, could have struck one of us in the chest.

That summer was my first remembrance of meeting two of my uncles. Although I had heard of them before, it was the first time I was with them. Mom's brother, Charles or Corkey, came to visit us one day, and he was riding a motor cycle. What I remember about the visit is that I was fascinated by the motor cycle he was riding and the leather jacket that he was wearing. There was a story about Corkey that Mom told me when I was older. One night, when we were living in Toledo, Uncle Corkey decided he would borrow Pa's car for the night. The only problem was, he forgot to ask Pa. It turned out that Corkey had an accident with the car and as a result Mom and Pa had to lie to the police. They had to say that they had loaned the car to Corkey so he would not be charged with stealing the car.

This was the year that Pa's younger brother, Harmie, came home from the occupation of Japan. I was told that when Harmie was discharged from the Marines, he came to Toledo by bus. He was at the Toledo bus station, trying to get a bus ticket home to Adrian, Michigan, the closest bus stop to the Tubbs farm. At this point, a woman introduced herself and offered to drive Harmie to Grandpa and Grandma's house. It turned out that the woman had a small motor scooter, not a car, but Harmie accepted her offer. The woman was Dorothy Buck, and she eventually became Harmie's wife.

That summer was the first time I stayed for a week or so with my Aunt Carrie and Uncle Frank Reyome at their home in Bowling Green, Ohio. My Aunt Carrie was Pa's oldest sister and had married Frank Reyome when she was eighteen. Carrie looked like a younger version of Grandma. Frank had wavy black hair and a pencil thin mustache. His complexion was quite dark and he told people that one of his grandmothers was a full-blooded Cherokee Indian. Evidently Frank liked to call his children by nicknames, because Bill was Pug, Don was Duck, Ocie May was Kitty, Sharon was Cookie, and the baby, Jack, was called Butch. Frank himself was Pap to most of his friends.

At that time, Frank and his brother, Ivan, ran a gas station on East Wooster Street next to the New York Central Railroad Station. The gas station was called *Puss and Paps* because Ivan's nickname was Puss. I wondered why anyone would have a nickname like Puss, and when I got a little older, I asked Pa how he got his nickname. Pa told me that Ivan earned the nickname because he was very popular with the women.

Pug, who was the oldest Myerholtz cousin and eight years older than me, worked at the Wagon Wheel Restaurant on South Main Street next to the A&P Store. The restaurant specialized in homemade pies, and we would go there to a have piece of pie. I remember how funny I thought Pug looked wearing a white apron and a little white paper cap over his red hair and freckles.

The Reyome house in Bowling Green was located on the east side of Lime Street, across from the Daybrook plant. On the back side of the house was a storage room with a low roof that housed the well pump and the washing machine. This low roof attached to the house just below the window of one of the upstairs bedrooms. During my stay there, I learned that the boys had a routine that they followed most nights. When Aunt Carrie told us all that it was time to go to bed, we would go upstairs and lie around for a little while and wait for a period of time for things to get quiet downstairs. Then we would crawl out the window onto the roof, and with a short jump, we were on the ground in the backyard. We would spend some additional time playing in the neighborhood before climbing back up on the roof and into the house through the window. I was sure that either my Aunt Carrie or Uncle Frank must have known what was going on. But if they did, they never said anything or tried to stop it.

Another adventure with the Reyome boys was playing in the underground hiding places they had built in the storage yard of the Daybrook plant. Daybrook manufactured truck bodies which were stored in a large lot across the street from the Lime Street house. My cousins had somehow managed to dig some fairly deep holes in this lot between the truck bodies. They had placed wooden boards over these holes and then covered the boards with dirt, leaving a small opening to get into the hole. These were great places to hide and play, except right after a hard rain when the hole would fill with water. I couldn't help but wonder what would happen if the walls caved in while I was in the hole.

My Aunt Carrie was a member of the First Pentecostal Church which was located on the corner of Elm Street and Second Street. During my stay there, I went to the church service on Sunday with Carrie and most of my younger cousins. Frank did not go and neither did the older boys. At one point in the service, the Preacher began to twitch and shake around quite a bit and began walking down the main aisle of the church. As he did this, other people in the pews began to twitch and shake and also began moving into the aisle. Before too long, most of the adult women and a few of the men were in the aisle, not only twitching and shaking, but also lying on the floor and rolling and moaning. This group included my Aunt Carrie.

I did not know what was going on or what I was supposed to do. I started to ask my cousin, Jerry, what was happening, but saw that both he and Don had their hands over their mouths, trying hard to hold back their laughter. This display of religious zeal continued for a short while, until the Preacher somehow found his way over and around the other people and back to the front of the church. Everyone returned to his seat and the service continued. Up to this point, I could only remember being in a church once, and that was for a funeral, so I was not sure what to think about what I had witnessed. When I told Mom, she assured me that what I had seen was not how most churches conducted their services. Pa simply referred to the church as, "A bunch of Holy Rollers."

I have mentioned that I had a lot of problems with toothaches, and I was not the only one in the family with this problem. Both Mom and Pa had problems with their teeth to the point that Pa already had a full set of false teeth, and Mom was missing a number of her teeth. No one in the family had been to a dentist, except to have an occasional tooth pulled, and none of us had a toothbrush. Mom had so many toothaches that she finally went to a local dentist and had her remaining teeth pulled. He charged her a dollar a tooth to pull her remaining nineteen teeth. Mom turned twenty-five years old without a single tooth in her mouth.

I attended my first county fair in the summer of 1948. It was the Lenawee County Fair in Adrian, Michigan, and I was going to see a new car with Pa and his friend Maynard Kinsey. Pa met Maynard when he was dating Mom, and they remained friends over the years. Mom and Pa often went to visit Maynard and his wife, Helen, at their home near Ottawa Lake, Michigan.

On this occasion, Maynard was driving his Willies auto, and we were with him, going down one of the dirt-road highways on our way to Adrian. Most of the bridges over small creeks and rivers were constructed with a steel framework that looked like a railroad trestle bridge. We were in the middle of crossing one of these bridges when the hood latch of the Willies let loose and the hood flew up, completely covering the windshield, making it impossible to see anything in front of us. Somehow Maynard managed to get the car stopped without hitting the bridge. He got out, closed the hood, and tied it shut with a piece of rope. We continued on to the fair where the big attraction was a new 1948 Tucker Tornado. Pa always said that the Tucker was the best car that was never made.

Most of the side roads in Michigan were either stone or dirt roads, including the Crockett Highway that ran by our house. Pa could never understand how a dirt road could be called a highway, and he said that the state of Michigan was the only state he had been in that didn't know the difference between a dirt road and a highway. During the spring, these roads would become muddy and eventually start to washout the dirt and leave the stone. When the roads dried up in the summer, they would harden up, leaving little ridges which were like the ridges in a washboard.

Driving on these washboard roads with any speed was impossible, unless you wanted to shake the car to pieces. They were usually graded during the summer when it was good and dry, and it took a couple of days after the grading work to clean up all of the dust in the house caused by the grader. After the grading was done, most of the roads were covered with a thin layer of tar or oil to keep the dust down. All of us kids had to be careful for a couple of days after the tar and oil was applied to Crockett Highway because we were barefooted, and walking near the road usually meant that we got tar or oil on the bottoms or our feet. If we tracked this into the house, Mom was not pleased.

Some of the more traveled roads were blacktop roads, and these roads were quite narrow and crowned in the middle for drainage. Pa referred to these roads as hump-backed roads. He had a low opinion of the roads in Michigan, having driven an over-the-road truck for a number of years, in a number of states.

My first memories of a presidential election came in the fall of 1948. This is when I first became aware that most of my family members were Roosevelt Democrats who believed that all wars and recessions were caused by Republicans. Mom and Pa did not discuss politics in any detail that I remember, nor did my aunts, uncles, and grandparents. But they did seem to have strong feelings about what was right and wrong with respect to the responsibility of an individual.

The whole family valued hard work as a measure of a person's worth. They were against any type of assistance from the government when it came to providing for their families. I can remember Pa saying, "It's a damn poor man who cannot hold a job and support his own family," and, "When you take a job and agree on a wage, you owe your boss a full day's work for a full day's pay." I can also remember Grandpa saying, "I'll go out and pick shit with the chickens before I'll take one dollar of welfare." All of the family favored Harry Truman over Thomas Dewey, and they all referred to Truman as "Give 'em hell Harry." They would say things like "Give 'em hell Harry will stand up to them Communists," and "Give em hell Harry will keep us out of another war." I did not know that much about what all this meant, but I did know that whatever was happening was important.

I heard Pa tell a joke after the election that was one of the first adult jokes I understood. The joke went like this: On the day of the election, Thomas Dewey said to his wife, "Tomorrow night you will be sleeping with the next President of the United States." On the day after the election, Thomas Dewey's wife said to her husband, "Is Harry coming here or am I going there?"

In the fall of 1948 Dr. Tubbs sold the farm. This brought an end to the farming influence on my life. There would be no more summer visits and sharing times with Grandma and Grandpa and all the other family members on the farm that had played such an important part of my life to this point. Grandma and Grandpa Myerholtz moved to Canton, Ohio to live with my Aunt Irene and Uncle Slim, and I missed them very much.

When Pa was dating Mom, he was driving a semi-truck for a living, and that is when he met my Uncle Slim who was working for the same trucking company. Pa invited Slim home to Grandma and Grandpa's house one weekend and introduced him to Irene. Slim and Irene were married shortly after Mom and Pa, and eventually moved to Canton. Irene and Slim had four children by this time: Larry, Ginny, Ken and Bob. Irene was a redhead like Pa, she was very slim and pretty, and she smoked. Slim was slender, he was almost bald, he also smoked and liked to drink beer, and he did not seem to have much ambition. Pa used to say, "Slim will never have to worry about working himself to death." No matter when I saw Slim, he always looked a little unkempt and needed a shave. Slim and Irene lived first in Canton, then Punxsutawney, Pennsylvania, and then they moved back to Canton, so we did not see them very often. They made the trip to the Tubbs farm about once each year, and I remember visiting them only once in Punxsutawney and couple of times in Canton.

That Christmas the school did the play, *A Christmas Carol,* and everyone in the school had a part. Louise in the fourth grade, me in the third grade, Janet in the first grade, and Caroline, the only student in kindergarten. I was one of the Cratchit children, as were Janet and Caroline. Louise had a small speaking part, but I do not remember what character she played.

CHAPTER 18

THE HOUSE ON LIME STREET

1949

Third Grade Class: University School

Top Row, Last person on the right: Jerry Sparks
Middle Row: First student on the left: Me
Middle Row: Last two on right: Evelyn Sautter and
Wayne Garvey

My Uncle Harmie had taken a job with Libby Owens Ford in Toledo and convinced Pa to put in his application for a job there. Pa did and eventually was hired. Since Pa had quit his job at the Peale Mill to take the job at LOF, it became necessary for us to move from the house on Peale's farm. Pa started to look for a house closer to Toledo, and when my Aunt Carrie found out that we were looking for a house, she contacted Pa and asked if he would be interested in her house on Lime Street in Bowling Green, Ohio. They had purchased the house in 1946, but their family had outgrown it, and they were having some financial difficulties. They decided to sell the house, and so they contacted Pa. He agreed to buy it, and the Lime Street house became the first house my parents, along with the bank, ever owned. They paid $3,600.00 for the house and four lots, and early in March of 1949, we moved to Bowling Green. Frank and Carrie moved to nearby Portage with their family.

I have a number of ironic connections with the Lime Street house. In addition to the early adventures with my Reyome cousins there, the Lime Street house was also the place where my Great Grandpa David Myerholtz died in May of 1929. A number of years before the Reyomes bought the house, Gertrude, Grandpa's sister, and her husband, Esta Wentz, owned it. After my Great Grandmother Mary died in February of 1929, my Great Grandpa spent some time visiting each of his children. The last child he visited was Gertrude, and that is where he died in May.

When we moved to Bowling Green from Michigan, Pa hired a man with a truck to help us, and we loaded up everything we owned in his truck. Then we all packed into the '39 Plymouth with a few boxes of clothing and headed for Ohio. There was not room for my dog, Mike, in either the truck or the car, and I was very upset about leaving him behind. Pa assured me that Mike would hang around the house, and when we came back in a couple of days, we would pick him up.

I worried throughout the next week, afraid that I would never see Mike again. Finally we went back to the house in Michigan, and as we approached the house I did not see him anywhere. Suddenly there he was, running through the field along the side of the road. I don't know if Mike had recognized the appearance of the car or the sound of that old Plymouth, but I barely had my feet on the ground when Mike jumped into my arms and started licking my face. I don't know which of us was the happiest, Mike or me. We put Mike in the backseat, picked up a couple of left behind items, and headed back to Bowling Green. All the way home, Mike kept whining and trying to get into the front seat with me.

Today there is no Lime Street in Bowling Green. In 1949, Manville Avenue ran south from East Wooster Street and made a slight jog to the right at the intersection of First Street, and from that point on to Napoleon Road, the street was named Lime Street. 525 Lime Street, our address, was on the northeast corner of the intersection of Fifth and Lime Streets.

I am not sure when the house was built, probably the late 1800s, but the original structure was basically a four-room, story-and-a-half house with two rooms downstairs and two rooms upstairs. Over the years, two additional rooms were added on the south side of the house. One room was a kitchen and the other room, a dining room. Each new room had a gable end facing Fifth Street and each had its own pitched roof. Eventually, a shed-roofed, concrete block addition on the east side, provided a back porch area and a pump room that was also used as a laundry room. The rest of the house was covered with white asbestos shingles.

The house was the first house I can remember living in that had running water, thanks to a well and electric pump. The property included four small lots with the house sitting on the corner lot. There was an outhouse at the rear of the property, and a stone drive approach along Fifth Street. A number of large trees were growing on the property, including a very large cottonwood tree that stood by the corner of the back porch. A large wild rose bush, covered with bright yellow roses during the late spring and summer, grew right in front of the house and almost on the edge of Lime Street. In addition to the yellow roses, the bush was covered with thorns and bees. We all had to be careful when walking or running barefoot near this bush because the grass around it usually hid thorns and bees, and we would often end up with one or the other stuck in our foot.

When we first moved into the house, there was an old upright piano in the living room that Aunt Carrie had left. All of us kids thought this was great. We had never had a musical instrument of any kind, so we were all taking turns trying to play it. Pa didn't put up with the piano playing for very long. One evening, as we were banging away on the piano, he entered the living room with an axe, and afterwards, all of us kids helped carry pieces of the piano out of the house.

I soon came to know that this section of Bowling Green was considered to be the poor side of town. In fact, it was referred to by most of the other town residents as Hog Town. The area of Hog Town was bounded by Lime Street on the west, First Street on the north, South College Drive on the east, and Napoleon Road on the south. All of the lots in this area were small, and the houses were of older and poorer construction. Some had been built before the turn of the century, some shortly after World War I, and others during the depression. The ones built during the depression were little more than clapboard shacks with shed roofs and in some cases, dirt floors. There were no sewers, no city water, no curbs on the streets, and no sidewalks. Most of the people who lived in the area were common laborers who kept chickens and other farm animals on their property.

All of our neighbors had some form of livestock. Bill Brown and his wife, Juanita, lived directly across from us on Fifth Street. They were both elderly and raised chickens in their backyard. Next door to them lived Merle Reyome and his wife, Midge. They were both slightly older than my parents and had two sons living at home, Ray and Bill. Ray was the oldest, and Bill was a few years older than me. Ray and Bill had a coop full of pigeons. Merle was the brother of my Uncle Frank Reyome, and was also the knuckle ball pitcher who had broken Grandpa Myerholtz's finger while playing baseball in Woodville.

Clyde Hainer and his wife, Elsie, lived next door to the Reyomes. They raised chickens and had three daughters living at home at that time. Erma was my age and in my class. The two older daughters were Thelma and Joyce. Next to Clyde lived his brother, Charlie Hainer, and his wife, Cora. They had rabbits and chickens and were both retired. The property east of our property on Fifth Street was owned by Mr. and Mrs. Henschen who had retired from their farm west of Bowling Green. They had sheep, chickens, and a horse. Mr. and Mrs. Bordner lived behind us on Fourth Street, and they had chickens. John Goodman lived on the corner of Fifth and Elm Street, and he had chickens and rabbits. Early every morning, the sounds of roosters crowing away could be heard throughout the neighborhood.

Another neighbor who lived on Fifth Street was Clyde Stoner. In the Hog Town area, most of the houses had either an outhouse or a septic tank which needed to be cleaned periodically. Clyde operated the only outhouse cleaning business in town. He had a truck with a large tank and a pumping system that he used to clean them. We all referred to Clyde as, 'The Honey Dipper.'

I soon learned that all of the men in the neighborhood referred to other men in the neighborhood as 'old man.' Bill Brown would refer to either of the Hainers or John Goodman as Old Man Hainer or Old Man Goodman. And the others would refer to Bill Brown as Old Man Brown. I think that Pa was the only man in the neighborhood who was not referred to as old man.

It wasn't too long after we moved in that someone noticed that John Goodman had not been seen for a couple of days. Pa went to his house and knocked on the door, and when he didn't get an answer, Pa opened the door. He found John dead, sitting at the kitchen table. Pa told us that he had been dead for at least a day, and it appeared that John had been eating and just died.

I soon found out that the sounds and sights associated with living in the country were much different than those in town. I have mentioned that the Daybrook plant was directly across the street from the house. Actually, the entire plant, including the parking lot, ran from First Street to just past Sixth Street on the east side of Lime Street. The main manufactured product of the plant was truck bodies, and because of the demand, the plant operated around the clock with three shifts of workers. The sound of grinding, welding and other loud banging that was a part of the process could be heard in the house at any time of the day, and especially during the summer nights when it was hot and the windows of the house were opened. The other nightly occurrence was the light from the electric welding arcs and the cutting torches. They were like little flashes of lightning that lit up the ceiling and walls through the window of my darkened upstairs bedroom. The New York Central Railroad line ran north and south on the west side of the Daybrook plant, and the sounds of trains were heard every few hours, night and day throughout the neighborhood. They were especially loud when the occasional steam engine trains came through.

Downtown Bowling Green at that time was a typical farming community. A large grain elevator and feed mill were located on South Main Street where the Huntington Bank now stands, and there was another grain elevator located beside the New York Central Railroad tracks on Ridge Street. It was not unusual to see tractors and wagons and an occasional horse and wagon on Main Street, especially during the harvest season. There was a very large H.J. Heinz plant located on North Enterprise Street, and once the tomato crop came in from late August until the end of September, the whole town smelled like catsup. At that time the Wood County Fair was held in the City Park, and so again during Fair week, tractors and various pieces of farm equipment and live stock were common sights on the streets of BG.

We moved into town in March and started school immediately at the University Elementary School located in BGSU's Hanna Hall on East Wooster Street. We had to walk the one-half mile to school. Because the school was part of the University, there was a number of student teachers and teaching assistants in each class, in addition to the permanent teachers.

Louise was in the fourth grade, Janet was in the first grade, Caroline was in kindergarten, and I was in the third grade.

Louise was fourteen months older than me, but at that time we were about the same height, and from day one, we looked very much alike. Because of this and the fact that we were starting at a new school, most of the kids, and even some of the teachers, just assumed that we were twins, and that I had failed a grade at some point. I don't know how many times I had to explain that we were not twins, and that I had not failed a grade.

My teacher's name was Miss Lorenzen, an older lady with blue-gray hair and glasses and a no-nonsense approach to teaching. I soon learned that the one thing she could not tolerate was chewing gum in class. If a student was caught chewing gum, he had to take the gum out of his mouth and stick it on the end of his nose, leaving it there until she told him to remove it and throw it in the wastebasket. I never got caught with chewing gum because chewing gum usually gave me a toothache.

We had recess in a large playground area on the east side of Hanna Hall, directly in front of the campus heating plant. This was the first school since Woodville that had a real playground for recess activities. Best of all, it had a ball diamond, and as spring came around, we got to play baseball. Another great advantage of attending the University School was that we had access to the University indoor swimming pool in the Natatorium. One day a week, each of the different grades had an assigned time to walk over to the Natatorium building on campus and have recess in the pool. We got to use the locker rooms and the showers, and we all learned how to swim. I cannot think of any of my University School classmates who did not learn to swim by the time we finished the sixth grade.

One of my first new friends was a boy named Jerry Sparks who lived at the end of Fifth Street near South College Drive. Jerry had been hit by a car a number of years before I met him. The accident happened when Jerry was walking across an alley, now the present day walkway beside Sam B's Restaurant on Main Street, and was struck by a car coming out of the alley. He was not hurt seriously, but he lost about half of his right ear.

Jerry was the first boy I had ever met that was my age and swore like an adult. He was about my size and, like me, was not one of the better students in our class. I also became friends with Wayne Garvey who lived on Troup Avenue just past First Street. Wayne was smaller than me, and he was the fastest runner in our class and could throw a football better than anyone. Wayne made sure that I knew he did not live in Hog Town. He lived north of First Street so he felt that he and his family were better than Jerry and me, and he used to kid us about living in Hog Town.

I was not the only David in our class. David Wulff lived near the university and we became good friends. I often stopped at his house on the way home from school to play, and one of the things that David and I did was cook. His mother had started to teach him how to cook simple things, like grilled cheese sandwiches, chipped beef on toast and, best of all, cupcakes.

There was a large junk yard on the corner of Elm and Seventh Streets which was run by Scotty Reynolds and his son Pooch. I am sure that Pooch had another name, but if he did, I never knew what it was. Scotty's junk yard was mainly old junk cars that were piled one on top of another in a lot that ran from Seventh Street to Eighth Street on the east side of Elm Street. The junk yard was a great place to play war games, something Jerry and I and other neighborhood kids liked to do. We hid among the junk cars, lobbing imaginary grenades at invisible enemy soldiers. We also climbed up into one or two of the junk cars that were sitting on the top of another junk car and pretended that we were flying fighter planes in the war. We sat behind the steering wheels and yelled out such things as, "Bombs away over Tokyo because the Jap's feet stink!" or "Hotsy totsy, we're gonna bomb the Nazis." We would play these games until Scotty caught us and ran us off.

There was a large vacant lot on the corner of Third and Elm Streets across from the Pentecostal Church that had a back stop and a ball diamond. There was a ball game there just about every night from spring to fall, and most every boy in the neighborhood was a part of the game. We would choose up sides using the old tossed-bat, hand-over-hand method to see who got to choose first. Whoever was the one catching the tossed bat had to be sure to call "Chicken claws" or "No chicken claws" when catching the bat in order to have an extra advantage in winning the first pick. "Chicken claws" meant that you could grab the knob of the bat on the last turn, and "No chicken claws" meant that you could not grab the knob on the last turn. The teams were always different and sometimes, if there were not enough boys, we did let any girl who wanted to play, join the boys' team. Usually the only girl that wanted to play was Diana Ducat, who lived across Third Street from the field and was in my class. Often we would play until it was too dark to see the ball.

When fall came, the ball game changed to football, and we usually played touch football. Sometimes we did play tackle, but when we played that, the girls could not play. When there were only a couple of us, we would just pass the ball around. Wayne and I played a game that we concocted ourselves. Since Wayne liked the Detroit Lions football team, and I liked the Cleveland Browns football team, he would be Bobby Lane. He would throw the ball to me, and I would be Otto Graham when I threw the ball back to him. The object of the game was to complete a pass to the other person and see how many passes we could complete. The one with the most completions was the winner. As a receiver, you were supposed to make every effort to catch the thrown pass, which I did, but after playing this game a couple of times with Wayne, I began to think that he was more interested in winning than in trying to catch all of my passes.

There was a number of Mom and Pop grocery stores in Bowling Green at that time, and the one nearest to us was Evans' Market which was owned by Goldie and Harold Evans. They had a small grocery store in a building on Summit Street just off Georgia Avenue that we called Goldie's. To get there, we went down Lime Street to Derby Avenue to Enterprise Street to Georgia Avenue and around the corner to the store on Summit. Goldie and Harold would let my parents charge groceries over the week, and my parents would pay the grocery bill when Pa got paid at the end of week. I would often go the store after school to pick up whatever Mom needed to fix supper or school lunches the next day. It was fun to go in to Goldie's, get what I came for, and then just say, "Charge it." Another advantage of shopping at Goldie's was she would let customers turn in food coupons from the paper for whatever they wanted to buy. I could get a five cent coupon for canned beans and take it to the store and get a five cent candy bar.

I found out later in life that the Evans' helped out my Mom and Pa in another way. When we moved to Bowling Green, we still had an ice box, and Mom very much wanted a refrigerator which in those days cost about $150. Goldie and Harold made a deal with my parents. The Evanses would buy a new refrigerator at Franks Sales and Services and have it delivered to our house. Mom and Pa would then make weekly payments until the refrigerator was paid off.

That summer I spent a couple of weeks at my Cousin Carl's house in Blissfield, Michigan. Aunt Gusty and Uncle Melvin lived on Maple Street, and the Raisin River ran through their backyard. Carl had been given a Red Rider BB gun for Christmas, and we spent most of our time finding targets to shoot. Our favorite pastime was to take a number of old tin cans and empty glass bottles upstream from Carl's house and drop them into the river. We would run back to the yard and wait for the cans and bottles to come drifting slowly down river. When they arrived, we would take turns shooting the BB gun at the floating targets until we sank them all. We then walked back up stream and dropped in more cans and bottles for the next round of target practice. With all the broken glass and tin cans we added to the river, it was a good thing that no one was allowed to swim in the Raisin River here.

Sometimes when I stayed with Carl, Aunt Gusty would load us all in the car and take us to the YMCA and YWCA in Adrian, Michigan to swim in the pools. The thing I found unusual about this was that the boys all swam totally nude at the YMCA, while the girls all wore swim suits and swim caps at the YWCA. The first time I swam nude I did feel a bit strange because I was one of the younger boys, and there were teenage boys swimming in the pool. A naked teenage boy can be pretty intimidating to a skinny, naked eight-year-old.

The YMCA was not the only place that Carl and I swam in the nude. The Raisin River runs through the City Park in Blissfield. No one was suppose to swim in the Raisin River within the Village limits, and it said so on a sign posted in the park. But that did not keep the young boys of the neighborhood from swimming on a hot summer day. Carl and I used to tell my Aunt Gusty that we wanted to go play at the park, and she would say we could go as long as we did not swim in the river. We would then go to the park, but we would continue walking up stream through the park to an area just around the river bend that put the park out of sight.

This place along the river had a small level grassy area with a large tree growing near the river bank. Hanging from one of the tree branches was a long thick rope. There were always a number of boys swimming there on hot days, all naked, and all taking turns swinging out on the rope and dropping into the river. Carl and I would strip off our clothes and join them. I could never understand how so many boys could be told not to swim in the river and still do so without some parent knowing about the tree and the rope and the fact that at any time on a hot day there would be ten to fifteen naked boys in the river just around the bend from the City Park.

When we went back to Carl's house, the first thing that we would do was go to the pump in the backyard and pump water over our heads, We would tell everyone that we were so hot from playing in the park that we needed to cool off. All the while, we were just trying to hide the fact that our hair was wet from swimming in the river. During the years that I went to stay with Carl, I remember that two boys did drown while swimming in the Raisin River.

Neither Carl nor I received an allowance from our parents, but Carl and his sisters did get money to spend every Saturday night. My Aunt Gusty worked as a bartender at the Blissfield Hotel Bar, and my Uncle Melvin would join her there every Saturday night. They would give Carl money to go to Shawachers Store to buy a six pack of Pepsi, a bag of Potato Chips, a bag of candy, and six comic books. This happened every Saturday, and the kids were expected to stay in the house and have their treats and read comic books while their parents were at the Blissfield Hotel Bar. My cousins Shirley and Carl were in charge, and Linda, Betty, and the newest member of the family, Sharon, were to behave and do what they were told. When we got tired, we would go to bed, and Gusty and Melvin would come home after the bar closed.

One story that Carl told me about his family was that on one particular Friday night, Gusty and Melvin decided to go to a dance at a bar in Onsted, Michigan, and they took all of the kids with them. They stayed at the dance quite late and drove home with the kids asleep in the back seat. When they were carrying in the sleeping kids, they discovered they did not have the baby, Sharon, in the car. They loaded everyone back in the car and returned to the bar in Onsted to find Sharon still asleep on the bench where they had been sitting.

Sometime that summer, Mom and Pa took us to Canton to visit Irene and Slim and Grandma and Grandpa Myerholtz. Slim took a number of us, including Pa and me, down to the basement to show us the mementos he had brought back from the war which included a German Luger pistol. He had this gun since the end of the war, but for some reason, he had never totally checked it out. As he pointed the gun at the ceiling of the basement and pulled the trigger, the gun fired, sending a bullet through the floor of the living room above, just missing the rocking chair where Grandma was sitting.

Shortly after this visit, Grandma and Grandpa left Irene and Slim's house and moved in with us. Grandma had pneumonia during that winter and did not like being so far from all of her family. They stayed with us for a couple of weeks while Grandpa worked out a deal with one of our neighbors, Mrs. Welsh, to move into her house. Mrs. Welsh lived alone on the corner of Sixth and Lime streets, and she also had a farm out on Hammanburg Road, southwest of BG. The deal was that Grandma and Grandpa and my Uncle Bob would move in with her in her Sixth Street house, and Grandpa would work on her farm to pay the rent. In addition, Grandpa and Grandma got jobs at the Heinz plant when the tomato crop came in. Grandpa was in charge of the Chili line during one of the shifts, and Grandma peeled tomatoes. Both jobs were seasonal so they only lasted during the tomato season.

I did not have a brother that was near my age. My sisters Louise, Janet, and Caroline, were always around, and my brother Ray was seven years younger than me. Louise was the one I spent the most time with, and the one I could talk to about how I felt about things. We often shared the problems that we were having with school and classmates, as well as problems that we were having with our parents and other family members. She always seemed to understand what I was going through, and she could make me feel better. But she was a girl.

I had some male cousins that I would see occasionally, and my cousin Carl was the one I spent the most time with, but that was mainly in the summers. The cousins that I saw the most were Cathy, Marie, Barbara, and Laura, the children of my Aunt Kate and Uncle Esty. All girls.

So when my Uncle Bob moved to Bowling Green, it was like I had an older brother. We started doing things together. I had pieced together a bicycle and Bob had an old bike, so we would sometimes ride our bikes out Napoleon Road to the North Branch of the Portage River and go fishing behind the old folks home. Occasionally, we would pack up some blankets, food, and a kerosene lantern on a Saturday afternoon and fish all night, or until we fell asleep on our bed of blankets. We would come back home during the day on Sunday.

I started going to movies whenever I had the money to buy a ticket, and I usually went with Bob to the Lyric Theater. I remember that I saw a showing of the original versions of both *Frankenstein*, and *Uncle Tom's Cabin* at the Lyric with Uncle Bob.

The Lyric Theater was located on the north side of East Wooster Street and it featured mostly B-Movies. At that time it was common practice to make low budget movies featuring unknown actors to be shown in lower cost movie theaters. The Lyric Theater was near the Greyhound Bus Station where we could buy just about any penny candy that was made. We would first stop at the Bus Station, buy a pocket full of penny candy, and then go watch the movies at the Lyric.

The Saturday matinee double feature typically was two western movies, three or four cartoons, and an episode of the latest serial. Some days there was a bonus with a *Three Stooges* feature. The main movie was one staring either Roy Rogers or Gene Autry. The second movie featured one of the popular B-Western movie stars of the day, and among my favorites were Lash LaRue, The Durango Kid, The Cisco Kid, and Johnny Mack Brown. If we were really lucky, the main feature stared Randolph Scott. Of course, Randolph Scott was not a B-Movie star, but he did make a lot of western movies. Besides the western double features, the Lyric would often have a Bowery Boys double feature. These movies were always funny and featured the Dead End Kids in modern day New York City out-smarting either gangsters or crooked politicians. I especially liked the Tarzan and Jungle Jim movies. It really did not matter to me that both Tarzan and Jungle Jim were played by Johnny Weissmuller or that a Jungle Jim movie was just a Tarzan movie with clothes on.

The serial was usually either Tarzan, Dick Tracy, Flash Gordon, or some cowboy that I had never heard of. The one being shown was usually episode five or six, and I did not always know what had happened in the previous episodes. It typically started with the hero escaping from some form of certain death and ended with the hero going into some other form of certain death, so I never knew how he would escape until I was lucky enough to catch the next episode.

The Lyric was one of the two movie theaters in Bowling Green at that time. The Cla-Zel was the other theater, and it featured only first rate and first run movies. It cost thirty-five cents to go to the movie at the Cla-Zel, while it cost only fourteen cents to go to a movie at the Lyric. I did not go to the Cla-Zel very often, but I did go if a Gene Kelly musical was showing. I loved to watch Gene Kelly dance and wished I could dance like him. I also went to the Cla-Zel whenever they were showing a John Wayne Movie. If John Wayne was in the movie, I had to see it.

One time when we were at the Lyric seeing a movie, Bob learned there was an opening for an usher, and he applied and was hired. This proved to be a bonus for me. When I went to the first movie after my Uncle Bob had the job, I bought my fourteen cent ticket and handed it to my uncle who pretended to tear it in two. He then handed me back the whole ticket. The next time I went to the Lyric, I handed him the same ticket, and again he pretended to tear it in two and handed me back the whole ticket. The Lyric's manager, Mr. Hopper, usually kept the same color tickets until he needed to order more, and then he would change from blue tickets to red tickets. I do not know how many movies I saw with that first ticket, but it was quite a few. When the Lyric went to red tickets, I bought one and continued to use it whenever my Uncle Bob was the usher. Since I was not buying a ticket, I had an additional fourteen cents to spend on penny candy so I usually split the extra candy with Uncle Bob.

In September my brother Dan was born at Wood County Hospital. He was the third one of my siblings to be born in September. Caroline was born on September 11, Ray was born on September 13, and Dan was born on September 15. I used to think that it was a little unusual for three children in one family to be born so near to the same day of the same month. When I was old enough to figure out that Pa's birthday was January 7, it became clear that these three siblings were Mom's "Happy Birthday" present to Pa. Later, Louise and I and my other sisters and brothers would kid Mom by asking her, "So what are you giving Pa for his birthday this year?"

Pa was working at Libby Owens Ford full time. There were three shifts: the 7-3 shift, the 3-11 shift, and the 11-7 shift. Every two weeks, he would change shifts. He was adjusting to working in a factory for the first time in his life, and he was also adjusting to shift-work which he did not particularly care for. However, he was making over two dollars an hour at the LOF job, which was the first time he was paid that much money. He was forced to join a union for his job at LOF, and he was not fond of them. He often said that the only thing that a union was good for was,

"Helping guys who didn't want to work keep their jobs." He also said, "I don't know why I should pay the union to keep my job when I can keep it myself by the work I do."

Pa bought a different car, a 1941 Ford, and he shared the drive to work with two other men who lived in BG who also worked at LOF. One was John Bissele, who lived on Napoleon Road, and the other was, George Rhine, who lived on Pearl Street. One night on the way home from the 3-11 shift there was a thunderstorm, and Pa hit a tree that was blown over in the middle of the road. He damaged the grill and the front fenders of the Ford, but no one was hurt. I can't remember what happened exactly, but shortly after the accident, for some reason, the bank repossessed the '41 Ford, and Pa was forced to come up with a car on short notice. He found a 1939 Lincoln Zephyr at Baron's Junk Yard. The Lincoln needed some engine work which he quickly fixed, and we had a car again. He took the Lincoln out for a test drive after he got it fixed, and when he returned to the house, he told Mom that the Lincoln would go 100 miles an hour. When Mom asked how he knew that, he said, "Because I just drove it that fast." The Lincoln had a twelve-cylinder engine and the longest hood of any car I had ever seen. It was a coupe and trying to haul all six kids plus Mom and Pa at the same time was very difficult. We did not go many places as a family for a while.

In the fall of 1949, I started the fourth grade and found that Miss Lorenzen had also moved to the fourth grade so I had her as a teacher for a second year. The good thing about this year in school was that Miss Lorenzen read aloud, and she chose to read a number of books by Marguerite Henry, including *King of the Wind*, *Misty of Chincoteaque*, and *Stormy, Misty's Foal*. I loved all of them. The bad thing about this year in school was spelling bees. Miss Lorenzen had a deep-seated love for either spelling bees or watching young boys sweat and struggle to spell a word orally, while the girls in the class watched and giggled. It seemed that every other week or so we would have a spelling bee, and by far, I was the worst speller in the class. She kept telling me that all I had to do was visualize the word in my head, and then spell it as I saw it in my mind. I guess my mind didn't spell very well either. I was usually the first one to sit down for misspelling a word.

CHAPTER 19

SPRING AND A YOUNG MAN'S FANCY TURNS TO . . .

1950

Myerholtz Cousins at Reyome's House in Portage

Top Row: Shirley holding Bill, Janet, Linda, Marie, Kathy, Me,
Louise, Carl and Jerry
3rd row: Raymond, Laura, Barb, Butch, Mike, Betty
2nd Row: Caroline, Pug holding Sandy and Rory
1st Row: Kitty, Sharon, Cookie

Every spring as a boy, there were certain things that I had to do because it was spring. As soon as the weather started to change in March, I had to have a new kite. A new kite cost anywhere from ten cents to twenty-five cents, and the string was another twenty-five cents. A kite could be bought at any of the hardware stores, the five and dime stores, or at Harry's Auto

Store. A kite usually lasted only a couple of weeks or until the first time I tried to fly it, but I had to have one because every other boy had one, and March was the best time to fly a kite.

I had to buy at least one new bag of marbles. Shooting marbles during recess was something that all the boys did. Most of the marbles I had won over the last year were long gone because my younger sisters had lost most of them.

I also had to get out my pocket knife and clean it up and sharpen the blade because someone was bound to challenge me to a game of Mumbly Peg. Mumbly Peg was a game played with a pocket knife and a peg in the ground. The skill of the game included a number of different ways to hold, throw, and stick the pocket knife in the ground near the peg. In those days, all boys carried a pocket knife.

Most boys also had a homemade scooter that either needed to be repaired or totally re-made. To make a scooter I needed a piece of wood, usually a two-by-six or a two-by-eight about three feet long, a pair of old roller skates, a wooden fruit crate which I could get at Goldie's store, and a piece of one-by-two wood about two feet long. All I had to do was nail the skates to the bottom of the two-by-eight, nail the fruit crate to the top of this board, nail the one-by-two to the top of the crate for a handle bar, and I had my new scooter. The fruit crate was placed on end with the open side facing the rear and was used to carry anything that I took with me on the scooter. These scooters hardly ever lasted more than a few months, but when spring came and the snow was gone, I just had to have a scooter to race against the other boys in the neighborhood.

No self respecting Cleveland Indians fan could start a new baseball season without a copy of the *Sketch Book*. The bus station was one of the newsstands in Bowling Green, and it was the only one that always had copies of the *Cleveland Indians Sketch Book*. It had pictures of all of the players with a write-up about each player. It also described any new players that the Indians had acquired from trades, and it gave fans information on the rookies that were moving up from the minor leagues.

Another spring requirement was a trip to the hardware store to buy a new baseball. The one from the year before was either lost, or water-logged from being left out in the rain, or little more than a ball of string with a lose cover. In addition, a new bat was usually needed because the one from last year had been cracked and nailed back together, or the tape on the handle was all loose, or the bat was pitted from hitting rocks, or

I had grown a couple of inches taller so naturally I needed a longer bat. Whatever the reason, a new bat was something every boy needed, and I knew the minute I picked up the right one from the rack that it was made for me. New gloves were a different story. Every boy wanted a new glove but few could afford one. I always went down to the hardware store and tried out all of the new gloves, pounding my fist into the natural pocket of the genuine cowhide major league model, autographed by some big leaguer like Ted Williams, Joe DiMaggio or in my case, Larry Doby. I would leave the store with the smell of leather and Neat's-foot oil still in my nostrils and dream of the day I would be shagging fly balls with that beautiful new glove.

In the spring of 1950, Pa rented the vacant lots that were behind our house, and we planted a garden. This was not just a little garden; it was a quarter of the block in size. Pa hired a local man, Cy Capell, to plow up the ground. Cy had a horse, a hand plow, and an old wagon that he used to haul trash and whatever someone was willing to pay him to haul. We started in the spring with the planting, and we planted every vegetable that was available. From spring on, every couple of days, I was in the garden hoeing and pulling weeds. That spring I also started mowing the lawn with an old push-type reel lawnmower. Up to this point I would sometimes help with the mowing, but I was now expected to do it all by myself. The garden and the mowing kept me busy all summer. From that summer on, Pa rented this property for a garden. One thing that Pa and I both learned that first year was we should not plant cantaloupe and cucumbers where their vines could intertwine, unless we wanted the cantaloupe to taste a little like cucumbers.

As I mentioned, I did not receive a weekly allowance as a child. In fact, I did not even know what an allowance was until one of my more affluent classmates explained it to me. I did on occasion have a little money because sometimes Mom or Pa would give me a quarter or fifty cents for doing some kind of work in the yard or for helping Pa work on a car. But usually it was because I gathered junk. Local junk dealers would buy scrap metals by the pound. I used to walk the railroad tracks from East Wooster Street to Napoleon Road and pick up any loose pieces of metal that had fallen off the many trains that ran on the New York Central Railroad. I was also on the lookout for any junk or metal that I could find along the streets in the neighborhood. I would save tin cans, and once in a while when I helped Pa with a car repair, he would give me the old car parts for my collection of junk. If I were really lucky, Pa would give me an old car battery which was worth more money because of the lead in the battery. Once I had a wagon load of this junk, I would head off for the Baron Junk Yard. Scotty Reynolds had a junk yard just two blocks from our house, but he only paid about half of what I could get when I took the junk to the Baron Junk Yard. The only problem with Baron's was that it was located on North Summit Street out near the Heinz Plant so it was about a mile from our house. The extra money was worth the longer walk.

There were a number of dogs in the neighborhood, and most people did not keep their dog tied-up. The dogs that were tied-up quite often got loose and ran around the neighborhood looking for any of the other dogs that were loose, and soon a dog fight would break out. My dog, Mike, was not tied-up, and for the most part, he stayed in our yard, but whenever other dogs appeared on the street in front of our house, Mike was right there to challenge them so he often ended up in a fight with another dog. Whenever this happened, all of us became quite concerned for Mike's safety and frightened by the viciousness of the fight. Some of the older boys in the neighborhood encouraged their dogs to fight and sicked their dogs unto other dogs, just to watch the dogs fight. I never understood why anyone would want to watch a dog fight, especially if they cared at all about their dog. I tried to keep Mike from getting out of the yard and sometimes even grabbed hold of his collar, but if he really wanted to go after another dog, I usually wasn't able hold him back.

Whenever a dog fight broke out near the house, and if Mike was involved, Mom came out of the house with either a broom or a bucket of water. If she had a broom, she swatted the other dog on the hind-end with the bristle end of the broom and chased him off, and then she swatted Mike on the hind-end and told him to get back in the yard. If she had a bucket of water, she threw the water at both of the dogs, and they both were so surprised by the sudden deluge of water that the fight was over immediately. I soon learned from watching Mom how to break-up a dog fight.

I don't know if Mike got into a dog fight somewhere, of if he was hit by a car, but one day he came limping into the yard with a large chunk of skin ripped off his back leg and hip. He was bleeding very badly and was in pain. We loaded him into the car, and Pa and I took him to the vet. The vet told us that he did not have any broken bones, but he had lost a lot of blood, and he would need to be kept off his feet and indoors for a couple of weeks to heal. He gave us some purple medication to wash the wound and gave Mike a shot. We brought Mike home and made a bed for him in the washroom. Every day I would wash his wound with the purple stuff and make sure that he had food and water.

After about a week, when I went to the washroom to check on Mike, he was standing by the door, and he wanted to come outside. It was the first time I had seen him on his feet in a couple of days so I told myself that he must be getting better. I let him out and he walked very slowly to the yard where he lay down under the cottonwood tree. I sat down on the ground beside him and started to pet him. He laid his head on my lap, and I knew that he was not getting better. His breathing was slow and ragged, and he seemed very tired. We sat there only a few minutes when he closed his eyes and died. We buried Mike under the Box Elder tree in the back yard, and I cried often for the next few days.

It was then that I found a place to be by myself and think about Mike. I crawled out the upstairs bedroom window onto the roof over the washroom and walked up the pitched roof over the kitchen into the valley area between the two gables. I could sit there under the cottonwood tree and be totally out of sight of everyone. I sometimes went up and stayed there for an hour or more and just thought about Mike or whatever else was on my mind.

I also found that I could climb up on the roof of the Henschen's chicken coop which was attached to a small barn. I could sit in between the barn and the coop in a valley area and not be seen by anyone. Whenever I was feeling sad or upset that I was in trouble with Pa for some reason, I went to one roof or the other and was alone to think about what I needed to do to make myself feel better. I could often hear my sisters or my mother calling me, but I usually did not respond because I did not want them to discover my special hiding place.

At some point in late spring, Grandma and Grandpa decided to move out to Mrs. Welsh's farm on Hammansburg Road. The main problem with this move was that Grandpa did not have a car, and neither the farm or our house had a telephone. We had to depend on Mrs. Welsh to tell us if Grandma or Grandpa needed something or needed someone to take them somewhere. The other problem was that my Uncle Bob also moved away, so he had to give up his job as an usher at the Lyric Theater and my magic ticket to the movies was gone.

Mom took a job cleaning the office of Dr. Huffman, a dentist in town, and at one point he asked her what had happened to her teeth. After they talked about this, they worked out a deal where Mom would clean the office as before, but the dentist would pay her with a new set of false teeth. I am not sure how long Mom had to work to pay for the teeth. I only know that she was very happy to have teeth, look more her age, and be able to smile again.

During the summer us kids were allowed for the first time to go to the City Park to the swimming pool by ourselves. It only cost ten cents to swim and five cents more if we rented a basket for our clothes. The only problem was that we had to walk to get there. The City Park was a little over a mile and a half from our house, and we had to walk through downtown Bowling Green on the way. Louise and I were in charge, and Janet and Caroline were allowed to go with us as long as they did what Louise told them to do. Sometimes we would even take sandwiches and eat lunch there before walking home. It was the time when polio was a real concern, and people thought that it could be spread in pools. Rules required us to shower before and after swimming in the pool and wade through a foot bath with chemicals in the water before we entered the pool.

I don't know what started it, or when it started, but I seemed to be getting into more trouble with Pa when we were working together. He was still working at LOF and doing shift work, so we would only see each other when he wasn't at work or asleep. Pa would tell me that he wanted certain things done in the garden or the yard and I would help him whenever he worked on cars. It just seemed that he was often upset, and he would get mad at me for not doing things the way he wanted them done or for not getting them done quicker. He would yell at me, and if he were really angry, he would tell me, "You don't have the brains that God gave a duck," or he would ask, "How stupid can you be?" Sometimes he would slap me across the face.

At times growing up, I misbehaved, and Mom handled it by telling me to go out and get a switch. She gave me a couple of swats with the switch, and it would be over. I knew what I had done, I knew I was in trouble for doing it, and Mom had punished me. But with Pa, I did not always know what I had done to get into trouble, and in some cases, it seemed that even if I did exactly what he told me to do, he was still angry at me. Occasionally, after getting really upset, he would tell me that he was sorry for yelling at me or for hitting me, but usually he did not say anything.

Pa was also starting to be sick quite a bit. He would have bouts of stomach problems, and he would get overly upset about things. He would also have what the doctor called anxiety attacks. I had no idea what an anxiety attack was, and I sometimes wondered if this was the reason that Pa was upset with me, or if I was the reason for his anxiety.

Sometime in the summer I was talking to one of the boys in the neighborhood, and he told me that he was going to give up his paper route with the *Toledo Blade*. I asked Mom and Pa if I could take over the route, and they told me that if I did, it would be my responsibility totally, for both the delivery of the papers and the collecting of the money. I went downtown to the place where the *Toledo Blade* papers were delivered daily and met the Bowling Green representative of the *Blade*, Mr. Capriotti. His first name was Marion, but all of the paperboys called him Cap. He told me that he thought I might be a little young for the job, but that he was willing to give me a chance for a couple of weeks to see how I would do.

I started with thirty-seven customers on a route that included Manville Avenue, Troup Avenue, and South College Drive from Wooster Street to First Street. Every day the *Blade* papers would be delivered to a small building in the alley behind Henderson's' Sporting Goods Store at about 2:30 in the afternoon. I would ride my bike downtown with my canvas paper bag, pick up my thirty-seven papers and then ride down Wooster Street to where my route began. I delivered the papers and rode on home.

On Saturday mornings, I would take my ring of customer cards and collect. The ring of cards had the name and address of each customer on the route, and each customer had a similar card. The way it worked was, I would go to each house and collect for the papers delivered that week and punch out the amount paid on both cards. The customer and I both kept track of the payments. At that time the daily paper was ten cents a day, and the Sunday paper was fifteen cents. Each week after collecting for my route, I would take all of the money down to the *Blade* station, and Cap would count out the money, taking out what I owed for the papers and giving me the rest of the money. I can't remember how much of this money was mine, but it seemed like a lot the first time that I got paid.

When Cap counted out the money, he kept two jars of coins on the table. As he went through the coins that I brought in, he sometimes picked out a dime or a quarter or whatever and put it in one jar, and then he took a similar coin out of the other jar and put it with my money. It took me a while to realize that he was looking for old coins and that he was culling them out of all of the coins that the paperboys collected. I often wondered how many old coins he found and how much these coins might have been worth.

I only had one problem with a customer giving me a hassle about paying for the paper. Right after I started the route, I had one customer who had not paid me for a period of over a month, and when I tried to collect one Saturday, he spoke to me through the closed door. He told me, "Get the hell off my porch." I told Cap what had happened, and Cap immediately told me to get into his car, and he drove me to the customer's house. Cap had me ring the bell, and when the man asked who was there, I told him I was there to collect for the *Blade*, and again, he told me to

"Get the hell off of my porch." Now Cap was not a big man; in fact he was only about 5'6"tall. But he yelled back at the man inside of the house, "Get your ass out here and pay this paperboy!" The man came out and paid me and apologized to me and to Cap for being rude, saying that he had been trying to get some sleep.

Having a paper route provided immediate rewards. I now could afford to buy a movie ticket anytime I wanted. I just needed to collect for my papers on Saturday morning, pay my bill, and then head for the Lyric Theater to see the matinee double feature. I was surprised by another reward at Christmas time. Almost every customer gave me a one dollar tip.

The Anderson Funeral Home was one of the three funeral homes in Bowling Green at that time. The owners had just purchased a new 1950 Cadillac Limousine, and they traded in a 1939 Packard Limousine which was for sale at the local Cadillac dealer. The Packard had a row of jump seats that folded into the back of the front seat, but with the jump seats in position, it was possible to seat six adults in the back of the car. The Packard was used to take the pall bearers to the cemetery. It had very low mileage because it was only used to go to the cemetery and back, and it had had very good care as it was used only for funerals. Pa bought the Packard, and for the first time he was able to haul all six of his kid at one time without someone having to sit on the floor or on someone's lap.

Now that Pa had a car with a seat for everyone, he started taking us to the Portage Drive-In theater. Portage was only about three mile south of Bowling Green, and once a week there was a dollar night and it only cost one dollar for the car, no matter how many people were in it. Mom would pop up a big bag of popcorn, make a jug of Kool-Aid, and we would head for the drive-in on dollar night. Us kids usually got out of the car and played on the playground equipment at the front of the parking area and watched the movie from there. As we got tired, we would one by one return to the car, and usually we would all be asleep in our seats by the time the movie ended.

I started the fifth grade with a new teacher, Mrs. Sima. I also started to see a trend. Each new school year my new teacher would immediately compare me as a student to my sister Louise, who was in the same class the previous year. Louise was a good student, and I have to admit she worked at it more than I did. I didn't think that she was smarter than me, but as I got older and each year there was the comparison, I began to wonder.

In fifth grade I developed a strong attraction for a classmate, Evelyn Sautter, and she was the first girl who seemed to be interested in me. We would be matched up often by Mrs. Sima whenever we had activities that were boy-girl oriented. We were also partners when we had dance lessons as a part of our gym class, and we learned some ballroom and square dances. Of course I already knew how to square dance because of the dancing we did at Grandma's house. I had always liked to dance, and I was about the only boy in the class who thought dancing was fun and not a punishment. Evelyn and I would sometimes spend recess talking to each other instead of playing with the rest of the class.

I had never been the target of a bully until the fifth grade. There were a couple of sixth grade boys who lived in the Hog Town area that also went to the University School. These boys had a couple of younger boys that they hung out with, and sometimes the group would bully some of us especially if we were alone. Usually it would start with one of the younger boys being dared by one of the older boys to pick a fight with me. The younger boy would call me names, or call me "chicken" to try to get me to fight. I knew that if I did anything with the younger boy, the older boys would join in, so I usually just kept walking and did not say too much. Sometimes one of the older boys would grab me by the front of the shirt and threaten to hit me, and again, I would refuse to get into a fight with them. Usually they were satisfied with calling me "chicken" as I walked away. The one thing that I never did was run. I also started having a bit of a problem with Wayne Garvey. Wayne could run faster than anyone in the class, so he always felt that he could out-run any trouble that he started. On a couple of occasions when we were playing, Wayne would get mad for some reason and would reach out and slap me in the face, and then he would take off running knowing that I could not catch him. One time when he slapped me, we were in front of Sharon Panning's house, and he started running around the Panning house. I chased him around the house a couple of times then I turned and ran in the opposite direction around the house, and I caught Wayne as he came around the corner. I tackled him and was sitting on his chest with my fist drawn back to hit him. I became aware that a number of our classmates who were walking home from school had gathered around to watch, and a number of the kids were saying "hit him, hit him." Wayne was saying, "please don't hit me, please don't hit me". I finally got up off him and remembering a line form a John Wayne movie, I told him he wasn't worth the effort, and I walked home. It did seem to make a difference. Wayne did not slap me in the face anymore.

Chapter 20

FIFTH GRADE

1950-1951

Watching TV at Uncle Harmie's

Caroline, Pa and Ray, Mom and Dan, Janet, Me, and Louise

We always had at least one radio in the house for as long as I can remember. Pa listened to country music and just about every Indians game that he could tune in over the static, and Mom listened to soap operas. I was amazed at the number of soap operas that were on the radio at that time. It seemed that no matter what time of the day it was, she could find a soap opera to listen to, and Mom listened to most of them. *Our Gal Sunday, One Man's Family, The Guiding Light, Portia Faces Life, The Romance of Helen Trent,* and *The Goldbergs* were some of the ones that I remember, but I am sure there were more. Mom also liked to listen to *Don McNeal's Breakfast Club, The Art Linkletter Show,* and *The Arthur Godfry Show.*

For me, there were a number of radio programs that I listened to most every evening. I would start with *The Adventures of Sergeant Preston and His Dog Yukon King*, followed by *Straight Arrow* and *The Lone Ranger*, and sometimes, I would listen to *Fiber McGee and Molly, Amos and Andy, Red Skelton*, and *The Jack Benny Show*. Other shows I listened to occasionally included, *The Inner Sanctum, The Shadow*, and *Mr. Kean, Tracer of Lost Persons*, which were all mysteries.

The other form of entertainment that I really got into was the comics in the newspaper. Up to this time, I can't remember that we ever had a daily newspaper. I would sometimes look at the funny papers in *The Toledo Blade* when we were visiting Grandma and Grandpa Dickerson on a Sunday, but once I had a paper route, reading the comics became a daily activity. My favorites were *Dick Tracy, Terry and the Pirates, Steve Canyon, Steve Roper, Li'l Abner* and *Pogo*. The older I got the more I enjoyed the humor of Pogo. Pogo was one of the first daily comics that made political statements that were also very funny. I read just about every other comic that was in the paper, and at that time, the Sunday comic section was about eight pages long.

Comic books which cost ten cents at that time were another great source of entertainment. My favorites were *Roy Rogers, Red Rider, Archie*, and an action comic called *Black Hawk*. Comics were sold at every newsstand in Bowling Green, and also at the Greyhound Bus Station. Most of the boys that I knew got their comic books at Hale's News and Magazine Store on South Main Street. The shop had just about every comic and magazine that was printed in those days. When I went into the store, Mr. Hale would be behind the counter, but about every ten to fifteen minutes, he would go into the backroom for a break. While he was in the backroom, a few of the boys would grab a couple of comics or magazines and run out the door before Mr. Hale came back to the front of the store. None of my friends or I ever did this, but it still bothered me.

We were all aware of television, and some of my friends in school had TV sets. Sometimes I would go to Wayne Garvey's house on Tuesday night to watch the *Milton Berle Show*. My Aunt Gusty and Uncle Melvin were the first family members to get a TV, so spending time at their house was even more enjoyable. Grandma and Grandpa Dickerson also had a TV early on. They had moved to Toledo, and were living in an apartment on Lagrange Street near Michigan Avenue, and whenever we visited, we looked forward to seeing what was on the TV. It was usually a Sunday, and TV programs did not start until sometime in the afternoon or early evening. When there were no shows to watch, we turned on the test pattern which was the TV station logo. Sometimes we were there when the station was broadcasting a program, and if we were lucky, we watched the *Kukla, Fran, and Ollie Show.* Many TV shows were only fifteen minutes long, so it was possible to watch four different programs in an hour. None of the programs were complicated, and a number of the shows were little more than a travel log that could be seen at the movies.

In addition to watching TV at Grandma and Grandpa Dickerson's house, we enjoyed going to their house because the Wonder Bakery was on Summit Street, right at the end of Lagrange Street. We used to walk down to the Wonder Bakery and go into the Day Old Shop and buy pastries. We could buy day old Hostess Cup Cakes for two cents a package. There was no expiration date on the pastries at that time, and the Hostess Cup Cakes had been sent out to some store where they had been on the shelf for some undetermined amount of time before being returned to the Wonder Bakery. I knew they were more than a day old, but again, they only cost two cents and always tasted good.

In the spring of 1951, the *Toledo Blade* had a contest with the prize being a trip to New York City. Any boy with a paper route could win a trip to New York by signing up fifteen new customers for his route. I immediately started going door-to-door in the area of my route, and to my great surprise, I was able to get fifteen new customers, and I was on my way to New York.

All of the paperboys gathered at the newly opened Central Station in Toledo, and boarded a New York Central Railroad passenger train on a Friday evening. The train traveled all night as we slept in our seats as best as we could. We arrived in New York about eight o'clock on Saturday morning. The boys were split up into four groups and went in different directions. The group that I was with first went to The Rockefeller Center, visited a television station, and then we went to the Radio City Music Hall where we watched the new movie, *Kim,* and a short live program by the Rockettes dancing group. The older boys seemed to enjoy this dance show more than I did. We saw the Empire State Building from the sidewalk looking up, and the next place we visited was Chinatown. We ended our sightseeing bus trip with a visit to the Bowery. I have to admit that I was disappointed with the Bowery. I had seen many Bowery Boys movies and this didn't look anything like the movies, and I did not see even one of the Bowery Boys walking down the street. We boarded the train late Saturday evening for the trip home, again sleeping in our seats, and we arrived in Toledo late Sunday afternoon. New York City in less than a day! My only souvenir was a pair of wooden chop sticks from Chinatown.

Late in May of my fifth-grade school year, our class took a trip to Greenfield Village in Dearborn, Michigan. I can't remember the circumstances that led to this trip. I can only remember that everyone was very excited about going. To this point, except for my trip to New York, I had never visited anything or any place other than attending family gatherings. I had no idea what Greenfield Village and the Henry Ford Museum were, but from what I heard the teachers saying and the excitement that I saw in the rest of the class, I knew that this was a special place. We rode on buses to Dearborn, and I sat with Evelyn on the ride there and back. I got a lot of kidding from the rest of the guys because of that, but I didn't mind. I came home thinking that Greenfield Village and the Henry Ford Museum were wonderful.

At that time in Bowling Green there was a man named Bud Gallier who sponsored a number of youth activities. Actually, his name was Monroe Gallier, but every one called him Bud. Bud was associated with the YMCA and a number of other organizations that catered to youth activities, including a summer camp program. Every year, a Bud Gallier Ice Cream Social was held at the City Park to raise money to finance the summer camp program and other activities that Bud sponsored. Bud would personally serve ice cream and talk to everyone that he could in an effort to raise money to pay for a summer camp trip for children who could not afford to go.

That summer, Louise and I were chosen to take part in Bud Gallier's summer camp program. He, along with another driver, took Louise and I and three other kids from Bowling Green to the YMCA Camp, Fort Hendrick, which was located on Lake Erie near Mentor on the Lake, east of Cleveland. We were at camp for a week, and it was something that I had never experienced before. We swam in Lake Erie, took canoe rides, did archery, played basketball and softball, and also took part in a number of craft projects. The only time I had been away from my parents this long was when I stayed with relatives, so again, it was totally different for me to be basically on my own at camp.

One of the things that I specifically remember was the first time I went into the boys' restroom. As I have mentioned before, I was accustomed to outhouses, so walking into a large modern restroom with a centrally located round washbasin that would accommodate about twelve people at a time was something that I had never encountered. When I walked up to the washbasin, there were three or four other boys washing their hands and a circular stream of water was flowing into the washbasin from the center. As I started to wash my hands, the other boys left, and the water stopped flowing. I looked all over to find out what would turn the water back on, but never found anything that looked like a spigot. All at once another boy walked up to the washbasin, and the water started flowing again. It was then that I realized that the washbasin had a pedal around the base that I had to push with my foot in order to turn the water on. I discovered one more miracle of modern plumbing that day.

By now Pa was having even more problems with his job at LOF. He did not like working in a factory setting, and he definitely did not like working for the union. His main complaint with the union was that the foreman was always getting on him for working too fast and for doing too much work. Pa was working on a line that made gas mask lenses, and he was told he could only make so many lenses per hour. Whenever he made more lenses than he was supposed to, the foreman would get on his case, and he would sometimes tell Pa he needed to take a break or slow down. This upset Pa who could not understand the concept that he had to follow what the union said about working at its pace and not at his own pace. Pa was also working at that time with Bob Ries, who married his sister, Lois, in the fall of 1948. Sometimes when Pa was told to take a break, he would go into the restroom and find Bob asleep in the stall. He could never understand why he was in trouble for working too fast, and Bob never got into trouble for sleeping in the restroom. Bob Ries eventually left LOF and joined the Air Force, and he and my Aunt Lois were stationed for a number of years in Europe.

Pa was also having more stomach aches and started seeing Dr. Rothe about these problems. After a number of tests and discussions with Pa, Dr. Rothe determined Pa's physical complaints were due to the fact that he did not like working in a factory. In addition, he wasn't sleeping properly due to changing shifts so often. Dr. Rothe suggested that he needed to get an 8-to-5 job that would allow him to work outside.

That was when Pa took a job working for the Averys Coal and Supply Company located on West Wooster Street in Bowling Green. Averys consisted of a coal yard, a building supply yard, and a burial vault company, and it was owned and operated by the partnership of Ed Richard and Bill Schuler. Pa was hired to work in the coal and builders' supply part of the operation. The down-side of this change of jobs was that Pa had been making about $2.20 per hour at LOF, and he took the job at Averys for $1.35 per hour. The up-side was that within a very short time, Pa's stomach problems were gone and he was feeling great.

CHAPTER 21

SIXTH GRADE

1951-1952

Photo by Shelby Schooner Myerholtz

Me in My Whitehouse Hamburger Baseball Uniform

I started the sixth grade in September with a new teacher named Mr. Carroll, and it was the first time that I had a male teacher. Shortly after school started, I was told that I had a speech problem; I was not pronouncing the S sound correctly. I knew that on some occasions, a couple of the older boys in the neighborhood had called me slush mouth, but no one else had ever suggested that I had a problem. I have mentioned that the elementary school I was attending was on the campus of Bowling Green State University, so the school had a number of student teachers in and out of the classroom every day. The school also had access to the special facilities available at the university so I was soon taking speech classes with a therapist from the university staff. I was not the only one in the class; Lois Blinn was there also. Lois once had non-paralytic polio and spent time in an iron lung. A tracheotomy left her with damage to her voice box. Lois and I became good friends during these speech sessions.

In the sixth grade, I became a school crossing guard. Certain members of the sixth grade were chosen by the teacher to help other children cross the streets in front of Hanna Hall in the morning and again in the afternoon when school let out for the day. East Wooster Street was in the front of the school, and at that time it was also State Route 6, so it had truck traffic as well as the busy Bowling Green University traffic. University Drive went north from East Wooster along the west side of Hanna Hall, and it was one of the main accesses to the center of the university. There was a stop light at the intersection, but it was up to the student crossing-guard to determine when it was safe for the children to cross the street. Each of the crossing-guards had to be at school one-half hour early to put on our crossing guard belts and get our crossing flags. The flags were poles about four feet long with a white flag that had a large red *STOP* printed on it. There were four crossing guards, with one guard on each side of the two streets, and we would hold our poles across the crosswalk to keep the children from stepping into the street. When the light changed, and there were no cars making a turn onto the street, we held our poles in front of the traffic and allowed the children to cross the street. We also needed to stay after school for one-half hour and do the same thing when the children left school for the day. I think that there were a total of eight crossing guards so we were a guard for a week and then we were off a week.

Two things made being a crossing guard a good thing. One was that Evelyn and I were on the same weekly schedule of guard duty, and the other was that at the end of the school year, the crossing guards were taken to a baseball game in Cleveland to see the Indians play. It was my first time to see a major league ballgame. That year, Cleveland played the Detroit Tigers, and as I remember it, Cleveland won. It was also another time to take a long bus ride sitting beside Evelyn.

In the sixth grade, the university sponsored a music program for the elementary students with lessons on band instruments. I asked to take lessons on the drums, but I was told there already were too many students taking drum lessons so I had to choose a different instrument. At that time big band music was something that I liked to listen to on the radio, and I thought maybe I could learn to play the trumpet and become the next Harry James. My trumpet teacher was Mr. Glassmeyer, and I tried my best for about a month to play three correct notes in a row. Finally, Mr. Glassmeyer and I agreed that he would have to look elsewhere to find the next Harry James, and I should look for some other form of musical outlet.

One of the boys in my class was named Ross Austin, and his father had started a Boy Scout Troop for boys in the sixth grade. I was asked to join and went to a few meetings and attended a campout at Camp Miakonda. I did not have a sleeping bag or any camping gear so Mr. Austin arranged to borrow some gear from one of the other troops. I enjoyed the hiking, canoeing, archery, and swimming in the Ottawa River. There was no swimming pool at the camp, only a concrete wall on each side of the river bank which formed an area where we could swim.

I really liked being in the Boy Scouts. However, I did not continue for two reasons. First, it cost money for the campouts and the gear that went with camping out. Secondly, the meeting often fell on an evening that Pa wanted me to help him work on a car. My Boy Scout life was limited to about three meetings and one campout.

My friend Jerry Sparks had an older brother, Bob, who had a job at the local bowling alley setting pins. One day he told us that the owner of the bowling alley was looking for some more boys to set pins on the weekends so Jerry and I went down to the bowling alley to see if we could get a job. The bowling alley was called Al-Mar Lanes, named after owners, Al and Marge Stevens. Al was a big man with a mostly bald head and bushy moustache, and Marge was a tiny little gray-haired lady who used a lot of make-up and had glasses that went up to a peak where the bows fastened to the frame. Marge also tended to be a little short with most of the pinsetters.

Al said that he would let us try setting pins for a couple of games to see if we could do it. The bowling alleys were set up with a box at the end of each lane where the ball and the knocked-down pins would end up after the ball was thrown. As a pinsetter, I would sit up on a bench above the lane box to stay out of the way of the flying pins and the ball. Once the first ball had knocked down the pins, I would jump into the box and pick up the pins and place them into a pin rack that had an opening for each individual pin in the ten-pin pattern. After I had picked up the pins knocked down by the first ball, I would place the ball on the ball return and send it back to the front of the lane. After the second ball was thrown, I would pick up the rest of the pins to fill the rack, and then I would pull a cord that caused the rack to reset a full rack of ten pins onto the alley. The alleys were arranged with an opening between the boxes of two side-by-side lanes so that one boy could work two alleys without having to climb out of the box. I started out working one alley until I got the hang of it, then eventually, I got to work two alleys at the same time. Working two alleys was what I wanted to do because I was paid $.15 cents a game, and if I worked two alleys I could double my money.

The bowling alley scheduled bowling leagues every week night with open bowling on the weekends. There was a law that a pinsetter had to be sixteen-years-old to set pins in leagues. Setting pins for the leagues was where the big money was because pinsetters were paid twenty-five cents per game. There were two leagues per night for a total of six games, and setting two lanes for three games, a pinsetter could earn three dollars. In addition, most of the bowling teams gave tips to the good pinsetters after the games were over by throwing pocket change down the alley to the pinsetter.

I was hired to set pins on the week-end. A disadvantage with setting pins on the weekends was that at times there were not enough bowlers to fill all of the lanes, so sometimes my lanes did not have a game going and I did not make any money. The good thing about setting pins on the weekend was that Al would let the pinsetters come in and bowl for free one hour before the lanes opened. I just needed to take my turn setting pins for the other pinsetters to bowl.

I set pins for a couple of months during the winter, but eventually I quit because I started helping Pa more on Saturday afternoons. When I told Mr. Stevens that I was quitting, he told me he was disappointed because I was one of the fastest pinsetters he had, and he had hoped that I would stay on. He also told me if I changed my mind to let him know, and he would take me back anytime I wanted to come back.

By taking the job at Averys, Pa had an opportunity to make some extra money in the evenings and on weekends. Averys sold concrete block, and Pa was asked to make block in the evenings for which he was paid so-much per block for all that he made. The block making machine consisted of a concrete mixer where ground stone (screenings) and cement were mixed, a conveyor to transfer the concrete mix to a hopper, and a block mold machine where the actual block was made. Pa usually took me and sometimes Louise to help whenever he made block. At first I just shoveled the screenings into the mixer, twenty shovels full, and added the cement, five shovels full, from a bag that Pa placed near the mixer. I would add the water and start the mixer. When the concrete was mixed, Pa would come back and open the chute on the mixer to let the concrete flow into the conveyor and fill the hopper above the block machine. He would operate the block machine while I mixed up the next batch of concrete. I soon learned how to wrestle the ninety-four pound bags of cement over to the mixer and how to operate the conveyor, so Pa could keep operating the block machine. When we made block, we usually worked from about 6:30 to 9:30 in the evenings.

At 8:15 a B&O passenger train would stop at the railroad station which was located on the opposite side of the tracks that ran through Averys. I would see this train every night that we worked in the block plant. I could see the people on the train especially in the winter when it was dark outside and all of the train lights were on. The passengers were in the dining car eating and drinking and looking like they were having such a good time. I often fantasized about getting on a train some night and going wherever it was going.

For years, Pa had made extra money by fixing cars, and up to this point he usually did this work outside on the ground. Averys had a maintenance garage and part of Pa's responsibility was to do the maintenance on all of the company trucks and equipment. He worked out an arrangement with the owners of Averys to use the garage to do car repairs on weekends and sometimes in the evenings. And when he did car repairs, I usually went along to hand him wrenches and help with the repairs. I don't think that Pa had a hard and fast rule for how he paid me when I helped make block or work on cars, but he did give me some money most of the time. More importantly, I eventually learned how to repair most anything on a car.

My paper route had grown to over seventy customers because I had taken over the route that was in our neighborhood. I sometimes had a problem delivering the Sunday papers because of the size of the paper.

The Sunday papers were always over 100 pages so the papers were big and heavy. Cap delivered the Sunday edition to my house, and when I woke up on Sunday mornings, the papers would be waiting for me on the porch. I could not handle all of the papers on the bike at one time, and when it snowed, I sometimes had to deliver the papers with a sled. On one snowy Sunday morning, Pa got up with me, had me load the papers in the back of the Packard, and he drove me around the route. I jumped in and out of the back seat and ran each paper up to the porch of customer's houses. Pa did not do this every week, but he did do it when it snowed or when it rained hard.

Snow got me and a number of the boys in the sixth grade in trouble that winter. We were walking back to class from the swimming pool one day after a big snow fall. A number of us made snowballs as we walked along and threw them at signs and trees and such, but not at each other. One of the snowballs missed the target and ended up hitting one of the windows of a college classroom. When we got back to our classroom, Mr. Carroll had already been told that a snowball had hit a classroom window, and he was not happy. As a result, he called each boy in the class to the front of the room where he took us by the right hand, bent our hand back, and smacked us on the palm of the hand three times with a wooden spoon that he kept in the drawer of his desk. It was tough holding back the tears because it really hurt, but none of the boys ahead of me cried, and I was determined not to be the first to do so.

In February of 1952 my youngest brother, Art, was born. I remember at that time candy cigarettes and bubble gum cigars were big items for kids to buy, and I bought a bunch of bubble gum cigars and passed them out to my friends at school in honor of my brother's birth. I heard Pa tell a number of people that he was trying to decide what to name the new baby and that he was considering "Eeny, Meeny or Miny, because there ain't gonna to be no Moe." It took me a while to figure out what he was saying.

In the spring of 1952, Little League Baseball came to Bowling Green for the first time. There were four elementary schools in Bowling Green: the University School, South Main School, Church Street School, and Ridge Street School. Each of these schools was to be the base for a Little League baseball team. All of the boys in the fifth and sixth grades were eligible to try out for the team, but only fifteen boys were going to be accepted on each team. Just like today, every boy who liked baseball dreamed of the day that he would play in the big leagues, and I was sure that someday I would be playing for the Cleveland Indians.

I made the team sponsored by Whitehouse Hamburger and wanted to play second base. Gary Kathrens was in my class and his father, Harold Kathrens, was our coach. He owned the White House Hamburger Restaurant on the corner of East Wooster Street and South Prospect. Everyone called Mr. Kathrens, Skinny Kathrens, but we just called him Coach. The other teams were sponsored by Bowling Green Banking Co., Louie's Friendly Service, (a gas station), and Millers-Saunders Hardware.

When we got our uniforms, I was hoping to get the number fourteen which was Larry Doby's number, but by the time my turn came to get a uniform, it was already gone. I took the number eight, which was Ray Boone's number. Ray Boone played shortstop for the Indians, and Pa didn't think Ray Boone was very good, but his number was one of the few numbers left. When the season started, I was in right field and played most of the year there. We played our games after school at one of the school fields, and since it was after school, neither Mom nor Pa came to any of the games. I can't remember how many games we won or lost, but we ended up in third place. I got a few hits that year, but not many, and my dream of playing for the Indians faded into the dust of the field. I found that I could not hit a baseball all that well, and my throwing arm was no better than average.

In mid-summer the circus came to town. I had not seen a circus up to this time in my life, and when I heard that the circus was offering free admission to any local boy who would help set up the big top, I made up my mind that I was going to be one of the first boys in line to help. The circus had moved in with its trucks and moving vans the night before at the corner of South Main Street and Napoleon Road, not that far from my house. Early that morning Jerry Sparks and I rode our bikes over to where they would be setting up and found that there was already a large number of boys waiting to be picked to help. We quickly got in line and when the circus supervisor started picking boys, he seemed to be choosing only the bigger and older boys. He walked by us at least two or three times before he finally said, "And you two," as he pointed at Jerry and me. We were in!

Our job was pretty much the same as the other boys, carrying ropes and poles and stakes and such and placing these items where we were told by one of the circus roustabouts. We also helped spread out the top of the tent and the side walls for the big top. Once all of the parts of the tent were in place and some preliminary assembly of the poles and ropes and canvas was completed, the elephants were brought in. I had never been to the zoo before, and as I mentioned, I had never seen a circus before, so when the elephants came walking in very near us, about thirty boys collectively caught their breath at the sight. Certain ropes were attached to each elephant's harness, and as the elephants walked slowly in the same direction, the big top rose slowly off the ground and in a matter of seconds, the whole big top tent was fluttering softly in the breeze as the roustabout secured each tent pole rope.

Once the main tent was set up, all of us boys were given other fetch-and-tote type jobs involving other smaller tents for side shows and games of chance. Jerry and I helped set up the tent for one of the side shows. As we helped to unroll the banner for this particular side show, we discovered that we were setting up the tent for "Dirty Gerty, The Wild Woman From Borneo." The banner included painted scenes of a wild woman living in the trees like an ape. There were also descriptions of how she lived in the wild as an "almost animal" and the dangers of getting too close or looking her in the eye. As we helped set up the tent, Jerry and I both agreed that we had to come back to see Dirty Gerty.

Once everything was ready for the circus to open, all of us boys were given a ticket for the show later that evening. We were also allowed to take one walk through the cages and look at the circus animals. Some of the boys had seen most of the animals before, but for me it was the first time to actually see live animals like lions, zebras, tigers, and monkeys of all types.

Jerry and I came back that evening and the first place we went was to the side show tent to see Dirty Gerty. We had a free ticket to see the circus, but it cost an additional twenty-five cents each to see Gerty. I had brought some money from my paper route collections which I planned to use to buy cotton candy. However, the chance to see a real live wild woman was more important than a ball of spun sugar, so we paid our money and entered the tent. We could see that a large cage was set up on some bales of straw in the back of the dimly lit tent. We had to walk between some ropes that formed a walkway toward the cage, and as we approached, a large sign about ten feet from the cage, read, "Danger, Stay Behind This Sign." I could not see anything in the cage except for the straw on the floor and an old army blanket spread over something lying on the floor of the cage. Just as we reached the danger sign, the form on the floor suddenly threw off the army blanket and began jumping around the inside of the cage, wildly rattling the bars of the cage door.

It was Dirty Gerty, and she was really a wild woman. She had long, black, stringy hair that looked like it had never seen a comb. She was wearing what appeared to be a grass skirt and a dirty old white T-shirt that was full of holes and covered with dried mud. Over top of the T-shirt she wore a bra that was made out of two half coconuts, held together with a piece of string and tied around her with some more string. She was barefoot and her feet and legs were also caked with dried mud. She kept hopping around and making sounds like a monkey and strange jesters at us. She put her hands down the front of her grass skirt, and every so often, she would point at one of the men customers and cup her hands around the coconuts. I watched for about five minutes, wondering what it was that I was looking at, when the circus man in the tent told Jerry and me that we were not supposed to be there because we were too young, and that we had to leave.

We reluctantly left and went over to the big top and watched the circus acts until the last show was over. As we left, we decided to take one last walk past the Dirty Gerty tent, only to find a "Closed for the Evening" sign on the side of the tent. We continued walking around the circus tents as they were all closing down for the night. As we walked behind some of the house-trailers where the circus people were staying, we saw a familiar form sitting on a bail of straw behind one of the trailers. There in the moonlight, smoking a cigarette and still wearing the grass skirt and the coconut bra, sat Dirty Gerty. The only thing missing was her stringy, black, hair, clearly revealing that Dirty Gerty was a man. He was just one of the roustabouts, not a wild woman from Borneo at all. Somehow I could not help but wonder if the cotton candy would have been money better spent.

Later that summer, Louise and I were again selected to go to the YMCA camp courtesy of Bud Gallier.

CHAPTER 22

SEVENTH GRADE

1952-1953

We had an old china cupboard with glass doors that was not in very good condition. There wasn't room for it in the house so it sat on the back porch by the washroom door and held some extra pots, pans, and canning jars. Also on the porch was a bundle of asbestos shingles. The house was covered with asbestos shingles, and when us kids played ball in the side yard we sometimes would hit a ball against the side of the house and break a couple of the shingles. Pa had brought home the bundle of shingles to replace the broken ones.

One day when my brothers, Ray and Dan, were having some sort of argument about something or other, Ray took Dan's graham cracker away from him and put it up on the old china cupboard. At this time Ray was five and Dan was three. Dan tried to reach the cracker but couldn't, so he pulled out the drawers near the bottom and started to climb up the front of the cupboard. As he climbed, his weight caused the cupboard to tip forward, and Dan and the cupboard fell onto the bundle of shingles and the concrete floor of the porch.

Dan had a cut on his forehead, but the most serious injury was to the index finger of his left hand. It was badly cut from either the glass in the cupboard or the edges of the asbestos shingles. Mom and Pa took Dan to Wood County Hospital where the doctor did his best to sew Dan's finger back together. He was able to save the finger, but after that Dan was never able to bend the last knuckle, and he lost most of the finger nail. Because of his age, and the extent of his injury, Dan received a lot of intention from Mom and Pa and other family members during his recovery. Up to that point in my life, I do not remember feeling that either one of my parents had ever treated any of us kids differently. After this accident, it seemed that Dan continued to receive special attention from Pa.

About this time, Grandpa got a letter from Heinz that he was being called back to work so he told my Uncle Bob to ride his bike into Bowling Green to tell Pa that he and Grandma needed to move back into town. It was about a fifteen mile bike trip for my uncle on a very old bike, but he made it, and soon Grandma and Grandpa moved back to the Lime Street house with us. Grandpa went back to the Heinz plant as the foreman of the Chili line during the tomato season. Heinz also promised him a full time job once the season was over. So Grandpa and Grandma needed to have a house in Bowling Green.

There was an old Victorian house for rent on Gypsy Lane Road next to the New York Central Railroad tracks which interested Pa. He thought it would be a good house to buy either to fix up for future sale or to move our family into, since it was larger than the Lime Street house. After much discussion (Mom was not convinced), it was decided that Grandpa and Grandma would rent the Lime Street house from Mom and Pa, and we would rent and move into the Gypsy Lane Road house. We moved into this house just before the start of my seventh grade school year. It was in fair shape but needed to have work done to save the cracking plastered walls, and it needed a good coat of paint both inside and out. The house was heated by coal stoves, and the windows were starting to have air leakage. There were no storm windows so heating the house was difficult.

There were new places for us kids to explore, and the woods across Gypsy Lane Road was one of the places where we spent much of our free time. The Wood County Farm Bureau facility was just across the New York Central tracks from the house, and once a month there was a livestock auction that attracted crowds of people. I would often go and watch the cattle auction.

One Friday evening, shortly after we moved into the house on Gypsy Lane Road, a car pulled into the driveway. I was on the back porch, and Pa was just walking up the steps from work. The driver got out and told Pa he was there to see a certain woman. When Pa told him that there was no one there by that name, the man became angry and began to swear. He demanded that the woman come out and see him. He insisted she would know why he was there. Pa again told the man that the woman was not there, and that he should get back into his car and leave. The man did not give up. He said that he had been there before, and he did not intend to leave until he had what he came for. It frightened me to realize that the man was drunk was not going to leave quietly.

There was an old iron skillet sitting on the back porch which I had been using to leave food scraps for a stray dog that was hanging around the house. Pa picked up that iron skillet and started down the steps toward the man, telling him to "get the hell out of here." The stranger repeated that he was not leaving until he got what he came for. By this time, Pa was getting close enough that the man suddenly understood that he meant business. The man hurried back to his car, just as Pa threw the skillet and bounced it off of the hood of this intruder's car. The man quickly started his car and backed out of the drive, squealing his tires as he sped off down the road. We never had another man stop by and ask for that woman again.

Whenever one of my aunts or uncles needed to move, Pa often was the one who came up with a truck to do the moving. I guess it was because Pa usually had jobs that involved access to a truck. Whenever Pa helped someone move, I went along to help. My Aunt Annie and Uncle Bill had been living in Bradner, Ohio with their two boys, Mike and Rory. Bill was offered a job running a Red and White Grocery store in Saginaw, Michigan so Pa rented a flat bed truck from Averys. We all pitched in and loaded up Annie and Bill's furniture and belongings and headed for Saginaw. I did not even know where Saginaw was, but I quickly learned that it was a long way away. I think I slept more than I was awake on the trip to Saginaw and back.

Shortly after we moved Bill and Annie, Kate and Esty moved into the Gypsy Lane house with us for a short while before they found another house to rent farther down Gypsy Lane Road. Pa and I helped them move both times. When school started, all ten of Pa's and Esty's kids rode the same bus to school.

The Junior High School was located on South Grove Street, across the street from the Senior High School. The school building was built in the early twenties, so it was starting to be old and out-dated. The main first floor was up a flight of steps from grade-level with the basement half-way below grade-level. All seventh grade classes were held on the first floor which also had Room 5, the main study hall. The gym in the basement was originally designed to serve not only as a gym, but also as a swimming pool. It could be filled with water, but it had not been used as a swimming pool in quite some time, perhaps because when there was an unusually heavy rain, the sewers backed-up and started to fill the gym basin with water. Playing basketball in the gym was a real challenge because the baskets were hung on the end walls of the old swimming pool so there was no space between the basket and the end wall and nobody ever made a driving lay-up in that gym.

My seventh grade homeroom teacher was Miss Inman, and all of the Junior High students referred to her as Granny Inman. I am not sure how old Miss Inman was, but she looked like she could have been anywhere from 80-100 years old. She was very short, about five feet tall, quite thin, and she had very gray hair. She had a habit of bouncing up and down with her weight on one foot when she was upset. This bouncing up and down usually took place at the beginning of the class when we did the daily weather report. Each student in the class was assigned a day of the month to give the weather report. There was a thermometer, a wind speed indicator, and a humidity indicator mounted outside of the window of the classroom. The student would read the various devices aloud and another student would record the reading. Miss Inman's bouncing began when a student, usually a boy, incorrectly stated the sky conditions. For instance, if it were partly cloudy, they would report that it was totally sunny or totally cloudy. The bouncing would begin, and she would give a lecture on what constituted partly cloudy or whatever sky condition was reported. This happened at least two to three times a week. Miss Inman taught science and used the same outlines and quizzes that she had used for years. Many students had older sisters and brothers who passed on their old papers to their younger siblings.

My English teacher was Miss Galvin, and the kids referred to her as 'Galvanized Galvin' because she was so strict and set in her ways. She used to walk between the rows of student desks with two rulers in her hands, and she would rub the rulers on each other as if she were sharpening a knife. She was big on memorization and penmanship. We all had to memorize a number of poems, including, "The High Road," "Rex is a Gentleman," and "The Pheasant." I can still recite "Rex" completely and most of the other two poems. We all had to have a fountain pen and our own bottle of black ink, and we had to do cursive writing exercises.

My history teacher was Mr. Morse and all of the kids referred to him as Monk. I always liked history, and I have to say I did enjoy Mr. Morse's class. Mrs. Weston taught the math class, Miss Mooney taught the art class, and Mr. Cook taught the gym class. Mr. Cook was well into his sixties and was short, skinny, and bald. All of the boys were required to wear white gym shorts and a white T-shirt to gym class, and Mr. Cook did the same. He was quite a site with his skinny little legs that were actually whiter than his shorts and T-shirt.

There were only a couple of my classmates from University School in my homeroom so I had to meet and make friends with kids that I had not known before. I met Jim Berry who had gone to Ridge Street School and Gail Nicely who had gone to South Main Street School. I soon became friends with both of them.

The Junior High School did not have a cafeteria so most of the kids brought their lunch. If I wanted to buy my lunch, I had to cross the street and eat in the cafeteria in the High School. The kids who brought their lunch to school, which included me, ate in Room 21. This room was used as an assembly room for special programs. There were tables and chairs in the back of the room, and there was a large open area at the front. The best part of eating in Room 21 was that there was a record player, and the teacher on lunch duty played current hit records and allowed us to dance. Gail and I danced quite well together, and I soon met a number of other girls because I was one of the few boys who wanted to dance.

After the start of school, all seventh grade boys were told that they could try out for the seventh grade football team so I decided that I would try out. We were given a football uniform and told to run from the Junior High School to the City Park for practice. I attended that first practice and when I got home that evening after I finished my paper route, I told Mom that I was trying out for the football team. She told me that she had signed me up for Catechism starting the next week at the Lutheran Church and that between the paper route and Catechism I would not have time for football.

Up to this point, our family had not been members of a church. However, after we moved to Bowling Green, we started attending St. Mark's Lutheran Church on holidays and occasionally for Sunday Services. Grandma and Grandpa were Lutherans, and most of their children had attended Catechism classes, but none of the family attended church on a regular basis. Mom and Pa were determined to have all of us kids confirmed into the Lutheran Church, and Louise and I were the first to reach the age for attending Catechism. The class was taught by Pastor Smith, and in addition to Louise and me, the other seventh grade class members were David Wulff, Nancy Klotz, Winston Richard, Larry Kindler, and Laura Osborn. The only other member from Louise's class was Dewayne Lohmann.

During the Catechism classes, we were taught we were all sinners and that we committed sins by thought, word, and deed. We had to take notes on the Sunday sermons and during one sermon on sin, I became convinced that I was surely going to hell for all of my sins. I broke out in a cold sweat and thought I was going to pass out. I was in the youth choir at that time, and the choir director saw me and came over and sat beside me and asked if I was alright. He continued to sit beside me for the remainder of the sermon, and the feeling eventually passed. For about a week after that I would wake up and have a hard time getting back to sleep because I was afraid that if I went back to sleep, I would die and go directly to hell. I am not sure what made me quit thinking these thoughts, but the fear that I was bound for hell did pass.

As far as my dreams of playing football, Mom proved to be right. Between homework for school, Catechism, my paper route, and helping Pa, I did not have time for football. It was just as well because at that time I was barely five feet tall and weighed all of 115 pounds.

One thing that I did find time for was Rec Hall. Every Tuesday and Saturday night, the school sponsored a dance at the High School in the Recreation Hall. In addition to dancing, the Rec Hall had ping pong tables, a shuffle board game, and various board games to play. I started going to Rec Hall with Louise and her friend, Charlene. Louise and I had started to dance together at home to the radio, and we were pretty good at dancing the jitter bug. We even got to the point that we could do some of the lifts and tosses that we had seen in some of the movies. I did not go every week, but I went often enough to meet more people from my class. I met a girl named Pat Lambert who was in the seventh grade and lived near Goldie's Grocery Store. Pat was the first girl that I walked home after one of the Tuesday night Rec Hall dances.

It turned out that Grandpa's fulltime job with Heinz was as a night watchman. It was his responsibility to make rounds every hour to check and record the temperatures of the hot beds where new tomato plants were growing. Heinz was always developing new varieties of tomatoes and pickles, and a part of the factory operation was to grow plants for the coming year's crop of tomatoes. I would sometimes go with Grandpa on a Saturday evening, and we would listen to a ballgame on the radio or to country music, and I would go with him as he walked his route through the greenhouses and hotbeds. On the nights that I went with Grandpa, I would remind myself that I was going to keep him company, and I needed to stay awake. But, I would usually fall asleep at some point, and Grandpa would wake me up in the morning to walk home with him.

Late in the year I had a bad sore throat, and my doctor said that I needed to have my tonsils out. The accepted belief at that time was that tonsils served very little use and that they should be removed as soon as possible. Most kids my age knew that at some point they would have their tonsils out. All of the nurses reassured me that after the surgery, I could have all of the ice cream I wanted. The one thing that they did not tell me was that the ether in my body would make ice cream curdle in my mouth, and that throwing up half-swallowed ice cream with stitches in my throat would be no fun.

By now, my paper route had grown to over a hundred customers. I had picked up another route adjacent to mine, and I also picked up a number of new customers as part of the various contests that the *Blade* had to increase circulation. Delivering that many daily papers was manageable, except on Wednesdays, the day when all of the stores put in their advertising for the week. Stores were not open on Sundays, and Friday night was the one night that they stayed opened until 9 o'clock, and this made Wednesday the best weekday to load the paper with advertisements. Other weekdays the paper was only 20-30 pages, and I could fold the papers in such a way that I could throw them on the customers' porches as I rode by on my bike. But on Wednesdays, the papers were at least 30-50 pages, and I could not fold them so they could be thrown from my bike. Each paper had to be walked to the porch and hand-delivered. I added saddle bags to my bike to carry the papers that would not fit into the basket.

I had a couple of customers who would occasionally ask me to help them with some yard work or other chores, and this gave me a chance to make additional money. When the older widow women needed help, I would accept a couple of cookies in payment. One lady on my route, Mrs. Akenberger, would sometimes ask me to kill one of her chickens for her for so she could cook it for a Sunday dinner. The first time that she asked me to do this she handed me an old hatchet that had an edge about as thick as a nickel. When I tried to chop off the chicken's head, the hatchet was so dull that all it did was cause the chicken to make a choking sound. So I resorted to wringing the chicken's neck like Pa had taught me in Woodville. Another time she asked me to go up onto her roof and spray her chimney for wasps. She was living in a small one story house with a flat roof that was built during the depression. I got on the roof with a borrowed stepladder and sprayed the chimney opening with a can of wasp spray. All at once a whole swarm of wasps flew out of the chimney and came flying straight at me. I started running across the flat roof toward the stepladder, but I did not stop for the ladder. I just ran right off of the edge of the roof and hit the ground running. I did not stop until I was about a block down the street.

Next door to Mrs. Akenberger lived Mrs. Van Sickle, but everybody called her the Cat Lady. No one knew for sure how many cats she had, but it was a houseful. I remember whenever I went to collect, she would take a minute to answer the door because she had to chase cats out of the front room to make sure that none tried to escape. The minute she did open the door, I smelled the overwhelming odor of cat urine and found myself backing away. It was even worse in the wintertime because she heated the house with a kerosene heater, and the cat odors, along with the smell of the kerosene heater, was almost more than I could stand. I often wondered how she was able to live in the house.

Our Lime Street neighbor, Old Man Brown, was on my route, and every Saturday when I collected, he would greet we with the same line. He would always say "Hello you fart smeller, I mean you smart feller." He would then laugh like it was something new that he had just said for the first time, even though it was the same thing every week. I would laugh along with him like it was the first time I had heard him say it.

One of my customers on Napoleon Road was Mr. Webb, and he hired me to cut his grass. He had a push type reel mower like we had at home, so I was used to that type of mover. One Saturday when I showed up to cut his grass, he had just bought the first power lawn mower that I had ever seen. He told me that he was making it easier for me to mow his yard. As I said, I had never seen a power mower before, and I did not know that it was self-propelled. When I started it up and pulled back on the cutting control bar, the mower took off and mowed down two of his small Blue Spruce trees before I could disengage the cutting control. Mr. Webb was very understanding, and he let me continue to mow his yard.

Quite often I would ride the bus in the wintertime and walk my paper route because it was easier to walk in the snow than it was to ride a bike. When I did walk the route, I would finish on Napoleon Road and then walk the New York Central Railroad tracks from Napoleon Road to Gypsy Lane Road where the tracks ran by our house. Walking the tracks was something that I did quite often to get up town. It was shorter and easier to walk the tracks than it was to walk down Gypsy Lane to South Main Street and then downtown. When I walked the tracks, depending on the time of year, I could pick wild strawberries or wild asparagus. Walking toward the house, I would sometimes pickup coal that had fallen off the coal cars or pieces of scrap iron for my junk collection.

I continued working with Pa, making block a couple of evenings every week. One night in June of 1953, just after the end of the school year, we were making block at Averys when a semi-truck pulled into the yard. The driver got out of the truck and told us that he had just come through a really bad storm just south of Bowling Green and that there were many downed trees and considerable damage to buildings. We felt that this was strange since it had not even rained at Averys, and we wondered what might have happened on Gypsy Lane Road. We cleaned up and headed home to make sure that everyone was okay. When we arrived at the house, we discovered that it had not rained there either. However, we turned on the radio and soon found out that a tornado had passed through southern Wood County between Mermill and Cygnet, and that a number of houses and barns had been destroyed, and a couple of people had been killed.

The next day volunteers were asked to help with the cleanup of the area hit by the tornado. Mr. Richard, the owner of Averys, asked Pa to take one of the dump trucks and go out to help with the cleanup. Pa took me along, and for the first time in my life, I saw firsthand just what a tornado can do. The tornado touched down near the intersection of Jerry City Road and Liberty High Road and traveled northeast across Route 25, crossing Bays Road. We helped pick up trash and debris in a number of areas, and in the process, I saw things that I could have only imagined.

Walking through an open field, over a hundred yards from the nearest buildings, I picked up an unbroken egg and a number of unbroken dishes from someone's kitchen. I saw a man using a pair of pliers to remove coins from his coin collection that were imbedded in a tree beside what was left of his house. I saw dead pigs and a dead cow that were impaled with pieces of wood. And I saw the road bridge from the Bays Road crossing of the Rocky Ford River ripped intact from the road bed, lying in the river about 100 feet from its original location. Pa and I helped with the cleanup for two days.

The following week there was a severe storm warning one evening, and we were so afraid of another tornado that we all went down into the cellar to wait out the storm. I remember that my sisters, Louise, and especially Caroline, were so scared that they cried the whole time that we were in the cellar.

By late summer, Mom had had enough of the Gypsy Lane house, and we moved back to the Lime Street house, and Grandma and Grandpa moved into a small house on Sixth Street. The Sixth Street house was only four rooms, with a front room, a kitchen, and two small bedrooms. It was one of the depression-built homes and had a flat roof with the building walls and roof all covered with green tar paper. It was not much of a house.

The Lime Street house had become infested with cockroaches while Grandma and Grandpa were living there. We battled the little pests for a number of weeks before we finally bought a house bomb, a large canister of gas that was toxic to insects. We removed all of the food from the house, closed all of the windows and doors, set the bomb in the middle room of the house, lit the fuse on the can, and exited the house as quickly as we could. The bomb burned and released the insect killing gas into every room in the house. After a couple of hours, when it was safe to enter, we opened all of the windows to air out the rooms before we could reoccupy the house. We had to bomb the house at least twice more before we got rid of the cockroaches.

It was about this time that I became aware of the fact that my Uncle Bob had a girl friend. He was working at Averys with Pa, and he had bought a 1947 Ford. We were still doing things together, like playing ball and going to the movies. The only difference was that he drove us wherever we wanted to go. One day we were driving home from downtown, when we saw Shelby Schooner walking along the street, heading home. Shelby lived on Seventh Street and was sixteen-years-old. Bob stopped the car beside her and asked her if she wanted a ride home, and she said, "Yes." I was sitting in the front seat so I opened the door and slid over to the middle of the seat next to Bob, Shelby got in next to me, and we drove her home. As we drove away from her house, Bob warned me, "You damned fool, if you are ever in the car when I pick her up again, you better get your ass in the back seat!"

Shortly after we moved back to Lime Street, Pa decided that Grandma and Grandpa Myerholtz needed a home to call their own. He, along with his brothers and sisters, agreed to share the cost and the work needed to build a house for them on one of the lots that Mom and Pa owned. Our neighbor, Merle Reyome, was a mason, and he agreed to lay up the concrete blocks for the house at a reasonable cost, and Pa, his brothers, and Merle worked on weekends to build the house. They bought all of the building materials at Averys, and Mr. Richard agreed to sell the material at a reduced rate because Pa worked there. Everyone in the family pitched in and worked whenever they could to try to get the outside of the house finished by the end of summer so the inside construction could be done during the winter.

Pa decided that since he was putting a bathroom in the new house, he would put in a septic tank and leach bed for our Lime Street house at the same time. The rock level in the yard was about three feet below grade, and the depth required for the septic tank was about six feet. We had to dig out three feet of rock for each of the septic tank pits, and we had to dig out about a foot of rock for each of the leach bed trenches. Most of the rock had to be chipped out with pick axes by hand so it took us all the rest of the summer and into the fall to complete this work.

At Christmas time, Pa received his first bonus from the Averys Coal and Supply Co. I don't know how much money he was given. All I know is that Mom and Pa went to Franks Sales and Service and came home with our first television set. It was not a very big TV, and at first it only had Rabbit Ears for an antenna, but it was wonderful. We had two Toledo

Stations to choose from: CBS channel 11 and NBC channel 13. Friday night was a big night for Pa to watch television because the *Gillette Friday Night Fights* were on. Boxing was one of Pa's favorite sports, and he would not miss them. Grandpa usually came over to watch, and sometimes Bob would be there too. I became a fight fan and each of us had our own favorite fighters. Pa liked middle weight boxers more than he did heavy weights because he liked the speed of the middle weights. Pa thought that both Sugar Ray Robinson and Jake LaMatta were true boxers, but he thought Gene Fullmer was just a mauler. We did watch the heavy weights, especially Joe Louis who was the champion, but he did not fight that often. Jersey Joe Walcott was another of Pa's favorites.

On Saturday nights we watched *Big Time Wrestling*, and again Grandpa would usually come over and watch with us. We all had our favorite wrestler, with Verne Gagne being the most popular. Verne had a hold where he twisted his legs and arms around his opponent in what he called the Cobra Twist. Once he got into this hold, we knew that the match was over. We also were fans of Yukon Eric who was a very large man, wrestled barefoot, and wore bib-overalls and a flannel shirt. We did not like Gorgeous George, the Sheik, and The Mighty Atlas. We considered these wrestlers to be just fakers while we knew that Vern Gagne and Yukon Eric were real.

Us kids usually had to watch whatever Mom and Pa wanted to watch in the evenings, but we did get to watch what we wanted during the day on Saturday after our chores were done. For me, the best part of having a TV was being able to watch *The Milton Berle Show* and *The Ed Sullivan Show* without having to go to Wayne Garvey's house.

CHAPTER 23

EIGHTH GRADE

1953-1954

Pa in the Backyard of Lime Street Home
Outhouse and Rabbit Pens in Background

In the spring, Grandma and Grandpa's house was completed and they moved in. My Uncle Bob had already moved to a small rental house on Sand Ridge Road when he and Shelby suddenly decided to marry in January. We continued to work on the new bathroom in our house. We cut a doorway between Mom and Pa's bedroom into the washroom area, and closed in a portion of the washroom to make the new bathroom. To use the bathroom, we had to walk through Mom and Pa's bedroom, but going through their bedroom at night was still much better than going to the outhouse.

Pa decided he would get rid of the two gas stoves that heated the house and replace them with a gas furnace. To be able to get heat runs into each room of the house, we had to go under the house and dig out a space under the floor for each heat run. The house did not have a cellar, but it did have a small crawl space under Mom and Pa's bedroom that was accessible through a small window in the foundation. Up to this time we had used the crawl space as a root cellar to store potatoes and certain vegetables from our garden. I was the one who crawled in and out of the window to put in and take out vegetables because the opening was too small for Pa, and the girls did not like to go into the crawl space because of the spiders.

We cut an opening in the floor of Mom's bedroom to have access to the crawl space, and then we started tunneling under the floor from there to each point where a heat run would be installed. At first it was fun lying on my belly, digging dirt out in front of me with a small ash scoop and putting the dirt into a bucket. The bucket was handed up to someone in the bedroom who would take the dirt out and dump it. It was like so many of the war movies that I had seen where the prisoners of war were digging out of a German prison camp. But after awhile, all the dirt in my eyes, nose, and mouth made me aware that it was not fun; it was hard, dirty work. Between the bathroom and furnace the whole family kept busy most of the spring and summer.

That spring I completed my Catechism class, and on Palm Sunday I was confirmed into the Lutheran Church. But before my confirmation, I had to be baptized. I felt a little strange about this since I was the only one in my Confirmation class who had not been baptized as a baby.

During the summer, Louise and I were selected by the church to receive a free week at the Lutheran Church Mawana Summer Camp at Mansfield, Ohio. The camp was located in a very hilly and wooded area with a small stream and Fleming Falls waterfall. All of us were assigned to a tribe with an American Indian name. I was a Navajo. We took part in numerous competitions between tribes, including a scalping competition. Each tribe member was given a short piece of colored gauze bandage to wrap around his wrist. The object of the competition was to find someone from another tribe and to try to pull his scalp, the colored gauze, from his wrist. At the end of the time, the tribe with the most scalps was declared the winner. I came away without my scalp, wondering who thought up this game where a bunch of kids at a church camp would be out scalping each other.

The eighth grade was, without a doubt, my worst year of school. This was mainly because three girls in the class started giving me a lot of hassle and teasing me. I am not sure what started it, and whether it was because I was not one of the better students, or because I was from Hog Town, or because I did not dress very well. I also wondered if it was the fact that when I helped Pa work on cars, my hands would get greasy and I always had dirty finger nails. It seemed that these girls always whispered whenever I walked by them in the hall, and I would hear them laughing after I had passed. I became very self conscious and tried to avoid them.

Two of these girls were in my English class. That would have made the class challenging enough. However, my teacher was Miss Underhill, and again, Miss Underhill had had my sister, Louise, the year before and made it clear that she felt I was not as good a student as my sister. Giving oral presentations and speeches was a major part of the first semester grade, and I did not want to get up in front of the class. At one point we had to give an impromptu speech, and when Miss Underhill called on me, I refused to get up and give a speech. She told me to make a speech or take an *F*, and I said that I would take an *F*.

At that time one of the things that some of the kids did at school was to list the names of students that they did not care for in a book and then send the book around to their friends who would write a comment or state their opinion of the kids listed in the book. The book was called a *Slam Book,* and basically it gave whoever wrote in the book the opportunity to say some very nasty things about the kids that were listed in the book. I found one of these books on the floor in study hall one day and my name was in it. Most of the comments under my name were not very nice.

I started skipping school and decided I would quit school at sixteen. In those days, teenagers could apply for a work permit when they were sixteen and quit school to get a job. None of my male uncles had graduated from high school, and all of my older male cousins on the Myerholtz side had quit school when they were sixteen, and that became my plan. When I skipped school, I would walk down Wooster Street to Averys where Pa was working. I would tell him that I didn't feel good and wanted to lie down on the seat of the car, or I would tell him that I just needed to get out of the school for awhile. Sometimes Pa would let me ride along with him on a delivery or let me just hang around the garage, and he did not say too much.

But one day, Pa told me that I could not come to Averys anymore during school. He said that I had to stop skipping school, and I needed to start doing better in school because I was going to stay in school until I graduated, even if it took until I was twenty years old. Although neither of my parents had graduated from high school, they were determined that all of their children would. I now realized that I would have to tough it out, and I decided to try to do better in school although it took a while for that to happen.

Most everyone in the neighborhood had rabbits and at that time eating rabbit was fairly common. In fact, there were a couple of rabbit farms in and around Bowling Green that sold them for meat. I often helped Charlie Hainer feed his rabbits and clean the pens, and I learned a lot about raising rabbits from Charlie. One day my friend Jerry Sparks told me that he was going to move, and he needed to sell the two rabbits that he had. One of the rabbits was a New Zealand Gray buck, Gilbert, and the other rabbit was a doe. At about the same time, Charley Hainer told me that he was going to sell the four rabbits that he had because he was getting too old to take care of them. I decided that I would get into the rabbit business. I bought both Jerry and Charlie's rabbits, and then I had two males and four females. I built some cages under the Box Elder tree in the backyard and immediately bred Charlie's does with Gilbert, and Jerry's doe with Charlie's buck, and soon I had more than tripled my inventory of rabbits. The next time I bred the rabbits, I planned to have the does deliver about six weeks before Easter so that the new bunnies would be just weaned at Easter time. I sold over thirty bunnies that first Easter at a dollar apiece. After that, I always sold bunnies at Easter. I also developed a number of customers who would buy a rabbit every couple of weeks for a meal. The customer would stop by a couple of days ahead of time and tell me when he wanted a rabbit for dinner. The day of the dinner I would kill and dress out the rabbit so that it was good and fresh when it was picked up. Pa was the one who taught me how to skin and dress out a rabbit, and how to check the rabbit's liver to be sure it was in good health before it was sold for a meal. He had always hunted rabbits, and we often ate rabbit ourselves during hunting season.

Eventually I had more rabbits than I had cages. I dug a trench about a foot deep all around the cages to form an area about fifteen feet square. I fenced in this area by placing the bottom of the fence in the trench and burying it to keep the rabbits from digging out of the enclosure. I dug a shallow pit in the center of the enclosed area, covered the pit with boards, and covered the boards with dirt, leaving a couple of small areas that would allow the rabbits to go into the underground pit area. I let all of the does loose in the enclosed area and kept the bucks in the cages. The pen allowed the rabbits to have a more open living area and eliminated the need to clean so many cages since the waste from the rabbits was absorbed into the ground. At one time I had more than sixty rabbits in that pen.

It was about this time that all of my sisters began babysitting to earn a little money. Once in a while they would take a babysitting job, and then decide they wanted to go out with friends or on a date. If I wasn't doing anything, I would substitute for them and babysit. I didn't mind, except that it didn't pay much, usually only twenty-five to thirty-five cents per hour.

Growing up with three sisters was sometimes a challenge and sometimes just entertaining. Every night they went through the ritual of curling their hair. At that time it was common practice to use long strips of white rags. They would twist their hair around the rag, roll the rag and the hair into a curl, and then they would tie the rag in a knot to hold the curl in place. I thought they all looked like their heads fell out of a rag bag when they went to bed. Another thing I found to be entertaining about my sisters was the scramble they made to get their clothes ready for school each morning. None of us had a huge wardrobe, and we all needed to wash and iron our own clothes at times. Mom did the wash a couple of times a week, but if my sisters wanted to wear something that Mom had not recently washed, they needed to wash it out themselves and in most cases, iron it. Female apparel was always hanging in various parts of the house to dry, and each morning they raced to be the first to get to the iron.

Another memory of my sisters is they all liked to chew gum. They not only liked to chew gum, they liked to pop the gum while they chewed it. The problem was that Pa could not stand to hear anyone popping gum, and he was always scolding the girls for doing it, threatening, "You want that gum? Quit popping it!"

One Saturday I went up to Averys after I had finished my paper route to help Pa work on a car after Averys closed at noon. It was early in December, and when we were finished working on the car, Pa asked me," How's your bike was holding up?" At that time my bike was little more than a rusty frame without fenders but with a large metal basket on the handle bars and a rear carrier that held the saddle bags that I used to haul my papers. The chain was in bad shape and had broken a couple of times in the past month, and I had added some new links. The worst problem with my bike was that the Bendix brake had started slipping. At that time all bikes had Bendix brakes which were designed to engage when pedaled forward, and this would drive the rear wheel. When I wanted to stop, I pushed the pedals backward and the Bendix brake would lock in place and cause the rear tire to slide to a stop. When the brake slipped, the rear wheel didn't engage as I pedaled forward. This could be very painful for me because if the brake slipped while I was pedaling forward, the pedal would suddenly slip down, causing my pedaling leg to drop quickly. The rest of my body would follow and abruptly make contact with the crossbar of the bike. There was no way to know if the brake would slip so when it did there was nothing I could do except hope that I would not be permanently damaged by the crushing impact of the steel cross bar of the bike.

Pa knew that the bike was not in good shape. He told me to follow him into one of the truck garages where he started to pull back a tarp. As he pulled it back, I could see six new bicycles and one new tricycle all lined up in a row, one for each of us seven kids. My bike was black with white pin-striping and chrome fenders. It was the most beautiful bike I could ever hope for. He told me that he had received his bonus and bought a bike for each of us at Book's Bike Shop in Bowling Green. He made me promise not to tell anyone what he had shown me, and I kept my end of the bargain. I even managed to act really surprised on Christmas morning. It was a great Christmas.

CHAPTER 24

NINTH GRADE

1953-1954

Easter Sunday on Lime Street: Louise, Mom, Me,
Dan, Ray, and Art

Pa and I continued working on the house, making block some evenings, and working on cars on the other evenings. Along with the paper route, it seemed like I was working all of the time. My rabbit business was still doing well, and I sold a large number of bunnies at Easter. I managed to finish the eighth grade without failing a class. I even ended up with a *C* in English, much to everyone's surprise, especially mine.

The *Toledo Blade* changed its paper distribution station to a room located in the alley behind the Majestic Paint Store on South Main Street. The good thing about this move was that Ma Hubbard's Bakery was located next to the paint store. Every day most of the paper boys stopped at the bakery before they picked up their papers, and I became hooked on whole wheat applesauce donuts.

Late in the spring we had a snowstorm, and when I went down to pick up my papers, a number of the other paper boys were throwing snowballs at a stray kitten that was in the alley. I picked up the kitten and put her in the zipper pocket of my coat. I then took my papers and went on to deliver my route. When I got home, I took the kitten out of my pocket and showed her to Mom and my sisters. She was a little calico and barely old enough to wean. We did not have a dog at that time so Mom said I could keep her. I named her Tinker Bell. We did occasionally have a mouse in the house, and Tinker Bell turned out to be a good mouser.

There was one slight problem later that summer with Tinker Bell. When the weather got hot it was hard to sleep upstairs, even with the windows open. Sometimes I would crawl out of the upstairs window in the girls' room and climb out on the washroom roof, drop down to the ground, and sleep in the backyard under the pear tree. I had won a pup tent from the *Blade* for getting some new customers, so I pitched the tent under the pear tree and basically started sleeping outside most every night. Usually Tinker Bell slept in the tent with me. At that time, for some reason, Mom decided to get a canary and she kept it in a cage in the kitchen near the cabinet counter top.

One morning I woke up in the tent and found that there were a number of bright yellow feathers on the floor. I looked for Tinker Bell, but she was nowhere to be found. I went into the house and took the cover off the bird cage to find only an empty cage and Tinker Bell, sleeping on the couch in the living room, looking for all intent and purposes like the 'cat that swallowed the canary.' Needless to say, Mom was not happy, and Tinker Bell almost lost her happy home. Once we got a new canary and a new location for the cage away from the counter top, things smoothed out between my cat and my mother. Tinker Bell was basically an outdoor cat and came and went from the house on her own. One day she left and we never saw her again.

That summer for the first time our family took a vacation together. Pa's jobs had not included paid vacations with the exception of his job at Libby Owens Ford. But when he was there, he would usually work on cars or do other part-time jobs during his vacation time. Averys gave him a week of vacation days, and he and Mom decided that we would all go to Niagara Falls.

We left early one morning and drove all day and arrived at the falls late in the afternoon. The trip was not bad because all of us kids had a seat to ourselves in the Packard Limousine. We walked around the falls a bit and ate at a hotdog stand. When it got dark, Pa parked the Packard in a lot near a public restroom, and Mom got a blanket out of the trunk for each of us. We climbed into our seats in the Packard, locked the doors, and went to sleep as best as we could. We used the public rest room to wash up in the morning. We spent the better part of the morning walking around the falls and then headed home. We stopped at a White Castle Restaurant for a late lunch and continued driving, arriving home very late that night. Our first family vacation lasted two days.

If Pa had any free time, he usually wanted to go fishing. Often on Saturday afternoon after work, Pa would go and take me with him. One Saturday we drove over to Wier's Rapids on the Maumee River. Just as we got to the river it started to rain. Pa turned the Packard around and backed the car down the river bank until the rear of the car was right at the edge of the river. He opened the trunk and took the spare tire out and put it on the ground by the car. We both got into the trunk and sat down. The open trunk lid made a great shelter. We were each able to cast out our fishing lines into the river with me casting right-handed and Pa casting left-handed. We fished for a couple of hours, sitting in the trunk of the Packard while it rained, and we caught bullheads and channel cat fish without getting the least bit wet. It was truly one of the magic moments that I ever spent with my Dad.

Uncle Gordon, my Aunt Shirley's new husband, loved to fish even more than Pa did, and Pa and I started fishing with Gordon often. Gordon had done a lot of fishing in the Toledo and Lake Erie areas so he took us to a number of places that Pa and I had never fished before. He introduced us to The Superior Bait Shop in Toledo and Coolie Canal, a great place to catch yellow perch. Gordon, like all of my uncles, had a very colorful vocabulary and a great sense of humor.

From an early age, I had heard most every swear word used in every possible way from Pa, Grandpa, and my uncles, so I knew the difference between a swear word uttered in anger, a swear word used in a humorous or a kidding manner, or a swear word used without thought. My Uncle Gordon had an unusual nickname that he called me. For whatever reason, he called me the 'bug fucker.' I never once thought that Gordon was using the term in a derogatory manner or as a way of putting me down.

My Aunt Kate and Uncle Esty decided to get a divorce in 1954. It was difficult for all of us because Mom was Kate's sister, and Pa was Esty's brother. It was also hard for us kids, since we had probably spent more time with our double-cousins Kathy, Marie, Barbara, Laura, and Bill than we had spent with any of our other cousins.

There was a lot of conflict at this time, and just before the breakup, Kate and Esty and their family had stayed with us for a couple of weeks in the Lime Street house. When they were getting ready to leave, Esty went out and started the car and pulled into the drive along side of the house. He honked the horn and Kate and all of the kids said their good-byes and got into the car. Mom was standing beside the passenger side door talking to Kate, and she asked Esty if he could afford to give her a little money to help pay for the groceries that she and Pa had provided while they were staying with us. Esty mumbled a couple of swear words, rolled down his window, and as he was driving away, threw a few dollar bills out of the window. Mom immediately started crying and ran into the house. I picked up the dollar bills and took them in and put them on the kitchen table. I could not remember seeing my mother so upset.

That summer my Aunt Lois and Uncle Bob Reis came home from England, and we had a big yard party at our house, and most of my aunts, uncles and cousins were there. Lois and Bob had been in England with the Air Force for two years, and they returned with two children, Sandy and Jake. But the hit of the party for me was the car that Uncle Bob brought home with him. It was a bright red Austin Healy convertible. It was beautiful. Bob took me for a ride in it, and I knew then and there that someday I would own a convertible.

Late in the summer Pa agreed to do some work for the Wood County Fair Board on a property that the Board owned on Haskins Road near the fairgrounds. Pa told me that I was to go with him to help cleanup and mow the property to get it ready for the upcoming fair.

As we were working, Pa got upset with something that I was doing, and when I started to defend myself, he yelled, "Just get your ass out of here and go home." I stood there for a few minutes as Pa went back to mowing on the riding mower. I decided to do what he told me to do, and I started walking home. As I reached the corner of Haskins Road and West Wooster Street, Pa pulled up beside me in his car, rolled down the window, and told me, "Get your ass in the car." He asked me what I thought I was doing, and I told him that I was only doing what he had told me to do. He got very angry and told me that I needed to go back and work, and if I did not want to do that, he could arrange to put me in the children's home that was just across Wooster Street from where we were at that moment. I did not think that he really meant he would do that, but he did say it, and for a number of days after that I was worried that he might do it.

Pa was still drinking at the time, and I hoped that was the reason that he got so angry at times. After about a week, he seemed to be past his anger, and he never again threatened to put me in the children's home.

I started the ninth grade in the fall, and as usual, it didn't take long for Louise's reputation as a good student to catch up with me. I signed up for Algebra and the teacher was Mr. Gorman, the head football coach, and Louise had been in his class the year before. We were only a few weeks into the new school year when I didn't understand something he was explaining, and Mr. Gorman became impatient with me, and said in front of the rest of the class, "You're not as smart as your sister are you?" Needless to say, I did not do well in Mr. Gorman's class after that.

Despite Mr. Gorman, that school year was a turning point for me in several ways. I elected to take American History and ended up in the same class as Louise, who was taking the class as a sophomore. I learned a valuable lesson in that class. I found out that Louise was not smarter than me, she just worked harder at school than I did. In spite of her hard work, remembering dates and facts was easier for me, and I ended up with the *A* and she got an *A—*.

I had an English teacher who took more of an interest in me and my struggle with spelling and vocabulary. She took a personal approach, and I soon found that I did have some ability when it came to the English language. I am not sure that my spelling improved, but my confidence in verbalizing and writing did. Miss Robson was the Latin teacher, but because of an increase of freshmen students, she was also teaching one English Class. I was one of the lucky ones who had her that year.

As a freshman, I was able to take mechanical drawing as a part of Industrial Arts, and I found I had an ability to visualize shapes and angles in my mind which helped me develop a good skill level in drafting. My friend Jim Berry also was in the class, and we became even better friends. Jim's dad was a draftsman with the Ohio Department of Transportation, and he encouraged both of us to stick with the drafting as a possible future profession. I took every drafting class that was available during my years in high school.

I had developed a friendship with Evelyn Sautter in Elementary School, and with Gail Nicely and Pat Lambert in the seventh and eighth grades. I was now starting to make friends with a number of other girls, but to this point, I had not even considered asking a girl out on a date. My self esteem was pretty low, I had really bad teeth, and I was sure that I had bad breath. I thought that being face-to-face with a girl and trying to kiss her would only end up with her running and screaming into the night.

I did not take part in many school activities except for the football games and an occasional dance at the Rec Hall, but I did go to a Halloween party for the junior high school that year. I dressed as a hobo with a full rubber mask that I thought hid who I was very well. At one point, a girl dressed as a black cat with a rubber cat facemask, asked me to dance, and I said, "No." I was not sure who she was, and I thought she might be a certain girl in our class who had a questionable reputation. She asked me to dance a couple more times, and again I said, "No," convinced at this point that I knew who she was. When we all took off our masks later, I found that the girl was really Evelyn. She said that she knew who I was all along, and I could not convince her that I hadn't danced with her because I thought she was someone else. I don't think my relationship with Evelyn was ever the same after that. She soon started dating another boy who was a junior, and that relationship lasted all through high school.

I finally did have my first date. I asked Pat Lambert to go to a movie and she said, "Yes." I don't remember the name of the movie, but I did take her to the Cla-Zel because I wanted to impress her. After all, the Lyric was where all of the younger kids went, and we were freshmen. After the movie, we went across the street and had a milk shake at Raymond's Sweet Shoppe, and then I walked her home. I never thought about it at that time, but walking from my house to Pat's house, to the Cla-Zel, then back to her house and home was probably about a two-mile walk for me. I only mention this because at that age, walking was about the only way to get anywhere if it involved being with a girl.

One day, Cap asked me if I would be interested in helping him with the *Toledo Blade* Sunday Edition. Every Saturday morning the advertisement sections of the Sunday newspaper was delivered to the *Blade* office in Bowling Green. Then at about eleven o'clock Saturday night, the news sections would be delivered. He wanted me to help him put the newspapers together and deliver them to the porches of the boys who had Sunday paper routes and the newsstands and stores in BG that sold the Sunday paper. I accepted the job and found that it took from eleven o'clock at night till about six o'clock Sunday morning to stuff and deliver all of the papers. If the weather was bad, and the *Blade* truck was held up by snow, it sometimes took until mid-morning on Sunday. The last stop on the route was the Green Gables Restaurant on South Main Street where we would have a breakfast of donuts before we went home. At first I tried to go to bed early on Saturday evenings and get up at 10:30 for work, but that was hard to do, especially if there were things going on Saturday night. I found it was better to just stay up all night and sleep during the day on Sunday.

I now had a new source of income, and one of the first things that I bought with the extra money was a shot gun. I had started hunting with Pa when I was about thirteen, and I usually used a 410 shot gun that I borrowed from my neighbor, Bill Reyome. Hunting pheasants in Wood County was a big deal at that time because of the large pheasant population. In fact, even President Eisenhower came to Ohio to hunt pheasant near Lake Erie. All of the hotel and motel rooms in BG would be occupied by out-of-state hunters, and Miller-Saunders Hardware held a yearly 'Longest Tail-feather' contest. Everyone who bought a hunting license and shot gun shells at Millers-Saunders Hardware was automatically entered in the contest. Whoever brought in the longest feather to the hardware won a new shotgun. This contest happened every hunting season, so most local hunters bought their license and shells at Miller-Saunders.

Many high school boys and a large share of the junior high boys, would go hunting on the first day of hunting season. The first day was always November 15th, and all a boy had to do was bring in a note signed by a parent, stating he would be hunting on the first day, and he would be excused from school. Also, the week before hunting season, boys were allowed to bring their shotguns to school for gun safety instruction as a part of the Phys/Ed class. The gun had to be broken down with the barrel separated from the stock, but then it could be carried onto the bus and brought into school.

There was a lady on my paper route who had lost her husband about a year before, and one day I was collecting for the paper, and she asked me if I liked to hunt. I told her "Yes," and she asked me if I knew anyone who might be interested in buying her late husband's shotgun. I asked her if I could see the gun, and it turned out to be a Model 87 Winchester 16-gauge pump. I told her I would like to buy it if I could afford it. She said that she had no idea what it was worth, but if I were willing to give her fifteen dollars for it, she would sell it to me. I think I set a speed record on my bike going home to get the money.

Usually whenever Pa and I went hunting, my Uncle Harmie went with us. Harmie lived in Rossford and still worked at LOF, but he also worked a half-day at Averys every Saturday morning. Harmie smoked a pipe and always smelled like pipe tobacco. He had a '49 Mercury that he drove, but he also had a small motorcycle that he would drive during the summer, and he often took me for a ride on the back of the bike. In addition, he had a small go-cart that he would bring up to Averys on Saturdays, and he would let me drive the go-cart around the coal yard.

I developed a good relationship with Harmie because I was at Averys quite often. While Harmie was in the Marines he had done some boxing for the company that he was in, and he tried to teach me how to box. He would go into a boxing stance and jab the air in front of my head and stomach. One day he brought a pair of boxing gloves with him to Averys, and we put on the gloves. He was showing me how to bob and weave, and how to jab and protect myself from various punches. He was good at pulling his punches so I got to the point that I felt safe being a little more aggressive in my approach in boxing with him. My short lived boxing lesson ended when I bobbed my head at the same time that Uncle Harmie was bringing his right hand up to pull an upper-cut punch at my chin. The punch caught me square on the nose, knocking me down, and causing me to bleed like a stuck hog. I quickly lost all desire to learn more about the fine art of boxing. However, after that, whenever Uncle Harmie would go into a boxing stance and start sparring with me, I would grab hold of him and change the boxing match into a wrestling match.

Harmie was about 5'7" tall, and by this time I was about as tall as he was. I weighed about 125 pounds, and he weighed about 180 pounds. He was built like a concrete block, so when we wrestled, it was a real miss-match. Harmie had a slight resemblance to Lou Costello, and often went into one of Lou's routines which always made me laugh. Harmie liked to kid me about things, especially about how I reacted when I was upset. I guess that when I was upset, I would get a pouty look on my face where my lower lip stuck out. I'd cross my arms across my chest and angrily exclaim, "Oh well." Whenever I was upset, Harmie took great delight in folding his arms across his chest, thrusting out his lower lip, and spitting out the words, "Oh well." Then he would laugh, long and hard. My Uncle Harmie had been in the Iwo Jima invasion, and had taken part in the occupation of Japan, but he spoke very little of it. The older I got, the more that I wished that I knew about that part of his life.

Another uncle that hunted with us quite often was my Uncle Bill McDole. Bill and Annie had moved back from Saginaw and were again living in Bradner, Ohio. Bill was the first male member of the family that always greeted me with a handshake. He would also ask me personal questions about what was going on in my life, and he always seemed to be genuinely interested in my answers. My uncles Harmie, Bill, Gordon, and Bob, accepted me as one of the boys and never made me feel like I was just a tag along kid. Not having a brother close to my age, my younger uncles served somewhat as older brothers. They accepted me into their activities, including their horse play, and at times, there was a lot of horse play, accompanied by an equal amount of profanity.

Growing up, Mom had always said that her hope for me was that I would not smoke, I would not "swear like a drunken sailor," and most of all, that I would not drink. Up to that point, I had not disappointed her.

Pa loved to hunt for mushrooms, but not just any kind of mushroom. He only hunted for morels. They could be found in Northwest Ohio and Southern Michigan for about a month in the spring, especially around Mother's Day. Everyone in the family, including Grandma and Grandpa and all of us kids, loved to eat them and we usually never found enough morels to satisfy everyone's hunger. Whenever Pa went mushroom hunting, I went with him, and often Grandpa went along too. If we found enough morels, Pa would slice each one in half, and Mom would roll them in flour with a little salt and fry them in butter and we would all have a few. If we only found a few mushrooms, then none of us kids got any. Mom and Pa ate them all.

Grandpa Dickerson also liked to hunt for mushrooms, but he would pick a number of varieties. He would insist that Grandma Dickerson fry them up, but no one else in the family would eat them if they were not morels. Grandpa Dickerson must have known what he was doing, because he always ate them, and he never had any problems.

One day I had gone mushroom hunting with Pa, and as usual we had driven out to Dirlam Road to look along the banks of the north branch of the Portage River. When we started home, Pa asked me if I would like to try driving the car. Up to this point, I had been allowed to drive a tractor, but I had never been allowed to get behind the wheel of a car. I couldn't believe Pa was going to let me drive because I was still only fourteen, but I immediately said, "Sure."

Our current car was the 1939 Packard limousine with a standard transmission and a clutch with the gear shift lever mounted on the floor. The gear shift lever was about two-and-a-half feet long. To drive a tractor, I put it in gear, set the throttle, let out on the clutch, and I went forward in one gear. It was different with a car. I had to shift gears two times as I built-up speed, and I had to coordinate the pushing of the clutch and the shifting of the gears or I would get a very loud grinding of the gears. I also had to coordinate the control of the accelerator with the pushing of the clutch to keep from racing the engine when the clutch was pushed.

After stalling the car a couple of times because I did not give it enough gas, I finally got off to a jack-rabbit start and was surprised when I heard only a small grinding of the gears as I shifted into second and even less on the shift from second to third. I drove for about three miles on Napoleon Road before Pa had me pull over so he could drive into town. After that, Pa let me drive every so often, and he sometimes allowed me drive the car forward and backward in the drive area at Averys.

I finished the ninth grade with the best grades that I had received in junior high school. At that time, the ninth grade was still a part of the junior high, and there was a graduation ceremony where we received a diploma certifying that we had successfully completed junior high.

CHAPTER 25

SOPHOMORE YEAR

1955-1956

Me and Pa in the Lime Street Backyard

My taste in movies had changed by the end of junior high. I still enjoyed a good western movie, and there were plenty of them. But the Roy Rogers and Gene Autry movies on Saturday mornings at the Lyric Theater were a thing of the past. I started going to more of the movies at the Cla-Zel with some of my classmates. Late in the spring, Jim Berry and I went to the Cla-Zel Theater to see the movie *East of Eden* starring James Dean. We both had heard of James Dean and after seeing the movie, we were instant James Dean fans, and we could hardly wait for his next film. Jim started cutting his hair like James Dean, and I thought Jim did resemble the actor.

That spring and summer, Jim and I attended a number of movies together including *Mr. Roberts, Pete Kelly's Blues* and *Picnic*. While watching *Picnic*, I fell in love with Kim Novak and made it a point to see every movie she made. Another movie that we saw together was *Black Board Jungle*. The neat thing about this movie was the fact that the musical sound track was totally rock and roll, including the title track which was "Rock Around the Clock," by Bill Haley and the Comets.

Jim had a record player which played 45 RPM records, as well as LP albums at 33 1/3 RPM. The Bigelow Music Store on East Wooster Street had a large record selection and all of the kids bought their records there. The store had three small booths inside where we could take the record that we wanted to buy into the booth, close the door, and play the record on a turntable before we bought it. Jim and I would stop at Bigelow's and listen to a few records before going to his house to listen to records on his record player. We especially liked the Big Band sound and the sound track from *Pete Kelly's Blues* which was Dixieland Jazz. Jim had a bongo drum and a drum practice pad with a pair of drum sticks. One of us would take the bongo drum and one of us would take the drumsticks, and we would improvise percussion accompaniment to whatever was playing.

Throughout the spring and summer, Pa let me drive more and more. Whenever we went mushroom hunting or fishing off one of the country roads, he would pull over to the side of the road and let me drive for a few miles. I also got to drive cars in the driveway at Averys, and sometimes Pa would let me fill the gas tanks on the bosses' cars. Ed Richard had a '53 Ford and Bill Schuler had a '48 Chevy, and both of them filled their gas tanks from the gas pump in the supply yard. If I was around when one of them needed gas, Pa would let me drive the car back to the pump, fill the tank, and drive the car back to the office. This worked out well until I backed Bill's Chevy into a cement block pile and put a large dent in the back fender.

A couple of weeks later, Bill indicated that he was going to buy a different car so Pa offered to buy the Chevy. Bill agreed, and Pa bought the car and said that Louise, who had just received her license, would be the one driving it. Louise was working at Isaly's and had been walking to work. When school started, Louise drove Janet and Caroline to school, and sometimes she drove me, depending on the weather. One day, Louise started to drive home from school and heard a strange noise in the wheel of the car. She was concerned enough to park the car and walk home. When Pa got home from work, Louise told him about the noise in the wheel, and Pa started to laugh. He explained that he stopped by the car at the school, pulled off a hub cap, and put a handful of stones inside. When Louise had started the car and moved forward, the stones rolled around in the hub cap creating the noise. I am not sure Louise ever saw the humor in this.

On September 30, 1955 James Dean died in a car crash in California. Jim and I were devastated. We were anticipating the release of his newest movie, *Rebel Without a Cause*, and we had seen the movie trailers. Jim had already bought a red nylon jacket like the one James Dean wore in the movie, and in the jacket, Jim looked even move like James Dean. J.C. Penny had a window display of the red jackets, and before they all sold out, I bought one, too. I can't remember how many times I went to see *Rebel Without a Cause* once it opened at the Cla-Zel, but I know that I went almost every night that it was playing there.

The tenth grade was a mixed year for me. I did fairly well in most of my classes except for English. I again had a teacher who was not impressed with my abilities, and I sort of regressed. However, this was the first year that I realized that I might have some talent in the art of drawing. One day when I was in study hall with nothing to do but homework, I decided to draw a sketch of the study hall teacher who happened to be Miss Mercer, my not-so interested English Teacher. I drew a sketch of her face, showing the frown that she usually wore. It was quite a good likeness, and I was sitting there admiring the finished product when a hand reached over my shoulder and picked up the drawing. I turned, and John Montgomery was holding my drawing and chuckling softly to himself. John was a friend of mine in class and was sitting behind me in study hall. John was the tallest person in the school and was the center on the basketball team. He told me that he thought the drawing was really good and quickly passed the drawing to the boy sitting across from him. This boy looked at it, and he too smiled and passed it on to the person next to him. I sat there thinking for sure that Miss Mercer would at some point see what was going on, and that I would soon be on my way to see Mr. Parlette, the Principal. Somehow, the picture went up and down every row of seats in the study hall and made it back to my desk just before the bell ending class.

I learned to type that year. I could type as fast as anyone in the class. The only problem was that I was still a terrible speller, so most of the words that I typed were misspelled. I also did very well in mechanical drawing, and Mr. Swigart, the Industrial Arts teacher started encouraging me to consider pursuing a career in drafting.

I made a new friend that year, Blynn Gause, who I had been aware of since junior high. The reason I knew Blynn at that time was because he was dating Gail Nicely, and she wore his ID bracelet with his name engraved on it. I had a continuing crush on Gail and therefore I did not like Blynn. But when Blynn and I shared a table in Biology, I found that we had something in common, boredom. Mr. Clark was the Biology teacher, and although he had a good knowledge of the subject, he lectured in a very dry monotone, and sometimes it was hard to stay awake and alert. Both Blynn and I agreed that we would make sure that the other was not caught napping.

The two of us would sometimes have lunch together or go to a movie. At that time, lunch hour lasted a full hour so many kids left the school and walked downtown to eat at Isaly's, an ice cream diner. Isaly's was located on South Main Street where the Easy Street Café is now. The floor was covered with red and white tiles, tables and chairs lined one wall, and a counter and grill stood on the other wall. We could get a burger and fries with a coke for about fifty cents. There was a juke box on the back wall so rock and roll music was always playing and some kids even danced in front of the juke box. On occasion, we went to Rogers Drug Store for lunch. Rogers had a back entrance that made it a quick walk from the school, through the alley beside the telephone office, past the rear of the Cla-Zel and into the backdoor of Rogers. The thing about Rogers was that there was a soda fountain, and we could order a flavored coke. Cherry cokes and lime phosphates were my favorites at Rogers.

I started going to all of the home football games on Friday nights. Jim Berry played in the marching band, so I usually went to the game with Blynn. The games were played at the BGSU football stadium which was located on Ridge Street across from the cemetery. If we won the game, the band marched back to the school, down Ridge Street to Main Street, and then down Main Street to West Wooster to the high school. All of the kids fell in behind the band, and we walked back down Main Street like a parade, with the band playing the high school fight song.

Once football was over, basketball started, and again I would usually go to the home games. John played on the basketball team so Blynn and I would sometimes go together. After the Saturday night basketball game, Rec Hall was open and we would go and dance or play shuffleboard. We were still fifteen, and neither of us had a driver's license so we walked everywhere. I lived the farthest away from the school so I rode my bike to Blynn's house and then walked with him to wherever we were going. If there was not a home football or basketball game, we went to the Cla-Zel on Friday nights. Most of the kids in our class sat together on the left side of the theater, and at times we made funny comments about the movie to the point that the usher had to come down and tell us that we needed to settle down.

Early in the spring of 1956, I became aware that one of the downtown stores was looking for a stock boy. Henry Rappaport owned the Rappaport Variety Store which was located on South Main Street across from the old Bank of Wood County. The Rappaport Store sold everything from fine china and glassware, to wall paper, books, candy, cards, and general merchandise. In the fall the store sold flower bulbs and in the spring it sold bulk garden seeds. Rappaports also rented glassware and china for parties. I interviewed with Mr. Rappaport and he indicated that I would work after school each day and on Saturdays while school was in session, and during the summer I would work full time. He offered me fifty cents an hour, and I agreed to take the job. Taking the job meant that I could no longer continue to do the paper route. I went to the *Blade* station to talk to Cap, and I told him that I was going to take the job at Rappaports. He agreed that that was a good plan. He asked me if I would be willing to continue to work on the *Sunday Blade* each Saturday night, and I told him that I would.

Henry Rappaport was Jewish and he was the first Jewish person that I had ever known. Until that time, the only thing that I knew about Jewish people was that Grandma did not trust them. I had seen the *Life Magazine* pictures of the concentration camps, and I had heard the talk about how the Jews were treated in the war and even some talk about how the Jews were the cause of the war. So I was not sure what to expect when I started working at the store.

Working at Rappaports was a very good experience for me in a number of ways. It gave me an opportunity to work with some very nice adult people. Mr. Rappaport had an office which was actually a small loft area in the rear of the store. He usually was in his office most of the time, but would come down to the main floor whenever certain customers were in the store. He always made sure to say "Hello" to me whenever I came to work, and he always asked how I was doing. He would even sometimes ask about my family and seemed to be really interested in me as a person.

Mr. Rappaport employed one other male at the store; his name was Russell Smith. Russell was supposed to be the individual who gave me my orders for the day. Russell appeared to be in his late fifties or early sixties. Sometimes it was hard to find him in the store when I was looking for him. I soon discovered that Russell would go out the back door of the store and down the alley to the side door of Kaufman's Restaurant which allowed him to enter the bar area without being seen. I also soon learned to anticipate what needed to be done so that if Russell was not around, I did not just stand around waiting for his return. At that time in Bowling Green, downtown stores were opened from 9-5 on Monday, Tuesday, Thursday, and Saturday, and they were opened from 9-9 on Fridays. All stores were closed on Sunday because of the Blue Laws. On Wednesday, all stores closed at noon, as did all banks and doctors' offices. Most Wednesdays, I washed the windows of the store, rain or shine, even in the winter.

All the other employees at Rappaports were women ranging in age from their early forties to their late seventies, and most of them had blue hair that they had reset weekly. The oldest of the ladies was Virginia Jameson who we all called Ginny. She worked part-time, usually on Fridays and Saturdays. I was always amazed at Ginny's keen sense of humor. Virginia Haas worked fulltime and must have worked at the store longer than the others because she always gave the impression that she had some sort of seniority when it came to making decisions if Henry Rappaport was out of the store. Dolly Wilcox and Laura Thomas also worked fulltime as did Gladys McConnell. Gladys was probably in her forties and had a son, Bob, who was a couple of years older than me, and a daughter, Sharon, who was a year younger than me. The other person who worked there part-time was Geneva Strausbaugh. All of the ladies were very helpful in teaching me about fine china and stemware, and how to tie bows and do gift wrapping. Working with mostly women, I soon developed a habit of saying, "Yes, ma'am" and "no, ma'am" when I was talking with the ladies. I also started saying, "yes, sir" and "no, sir" when I was talking with Mr.

Rappaport or with Russell Smith. This carried over to the customers that I was dealing with. Mom had always told us kids that it did not cost anything to be polite, and I tried to follow her advice.

Rappaport's had a large variety of merchandise, and it was my job to unload, unpack, and stock the store shelves with this merchandise. There was a loading dock in the alley behind the store where trucks would make deliveries. I helped the truck driver with the unloading, and then I either unpacked the items and placed them directly on the store shelves or took the items up to the second floor and stored them in the various storage bins until they were needed in the store. There was an old counter-weight elevator in the back of the store where I placed the items to be taken upstairs. I gave a tug on the rope in the elevator to start the counter-weight moving, and the elevator would slowly move up to the second floor. It was the same process to move merchandise down from the second floor. I was also responsible for filling the candy bins at the front of the story. This task always included sampling one of whatever candy bin I was filing. I swept the floor every evening before I left for the day.

One of my other duties was to deliver purchased or rented items. At that time, many people still walked uptown to shop, and when they purchased items at Rappaports, they had the option of having the item delivered to their home. Rappaports had an old bicycle I could use for such delivers, but since I rode my own bike to work, I would usually use mine for the delivery. Rappaports also had a number of regular customers who were elderly ladies. These ladies would call down to the store and indicate that they had a need for some particular item such as a new canister set. I would then load up one of each of the canister sets that we had in the store, bike to their houses, and show them the sets that I had brought. They would pick out the one they wanted, pay me for it, and I would take the rest of the sets back to the store.

The most interesting request that I had to deal with involved one particular elderly lady who lived on North Main Street. Every couple of months she called down to the store to say that she needed a new hairnet. I gathered together one of each style of the hairnets that we had in stock and biked to her house. She looked them all over and picked out one or two. I know that the cost of the hairnets that she purchased at that time were no more than forty-nine cents each, and my wage was fifty-cents an hour. Mr. Rappaport certainly did not make any money on it, but he believed that it was his responsibility to make sure that he kept his customers happy.

Mr. Rappaport was a good friend of Max Leitman who owned Leitman's Men's Store on North Main Street, as well as the Corner Grill on the corner of North Main and Court Street. Mr. Rappaport was also a good friend with Dr. Jones, the local Veterinarian. All three were members of the Kiwanis Club. Mr. Rappaport introduced me to both of these men, as well as other local businessmen, the first time each of them came into the store after I started working there. He would say "I would like you to meet my newest employee," and he would introduce me. It made me feel important. Later that year, when the Kiwanis Club had their annual Father and Son Dinner, Mr. Rappaport asked me to be his guest at the supper, as all of his children were grown and living out of state. I had never attended such an event before, and eating a full course formal dinner was a new experience. We shared a table with Dr. Jones and his daughter and a couple of other businessmen I did not know. I bought a new white shirt and a necktie for the dinner so that I would be dressed appropriately, and I wanted Mr. Rappaport to be glad he had invited me to be his guest.

That summer, Mom and Pa took all of us to the Smoky Mountains. We piled into the Packard and headed south. We stopped at a tourist place in Kentucky called Dog Patch which was based on the Al Capp comic strip character, Li'l Abner, and featured all kinds of Li'l Abner and Yokum Family souvenirs. When we camped for a night at Norris Dam in Tennessee, Pa put a tarp across the top of the Packard and fastened the edge of the tarp to the ground, and we all slept in the car on the ground under this tarp. The next day we drove Route 441 through the Smoky Mountains, ending up in Cherokee, North Carolina where we camped for the night. Pa did not want to drive the same road back through the mountains so he took a road that basically wound its way through the lower levels of the range. It turned out this road was full of sharp turns and quick dips, to the point that most of us kids got carsick. Pa had to stop every few miles for one of us to step out of the car to be sick. We spent another night camped in Kentucky before returning home. Our second family vacation lasted four days.

There was a customer on my old paper route who lived down the street from us on Fifth Street where I noticed a 1947 Ford had been sitting in the side yard for awhile. One day I asked the lady who was living there if there was something wrong with the car. She told me that her husband had taken the engine out to overhaul it and had not been able to get it fixed. He had since bought another car so she did not know what he planned to do with the Ford. I told her if he was interested in selling it, to let me know.

I stopped to check on the car a few days later and she told me her husband wanted to sell the car as is for fifty dollars. I talked to Pa, indicating that I would like to buy the car and fix it up so when I turned sixteen, I would have a car. He informed me that if I bought a car, I would have to pay for the insurance and gas because he would not be able to afford to pay for these for me. He told me he would need to look at the car before he would let me buy it.

We met with the man and found that he had taken the engine apart in his garage and had not put it back together. He had all of the parts in a couple of boxes on the floor under his work bench. We checked the boxes and looked the car over and went home. Pa said he thought that we could fix the engine, but I would also have to pay for any parts we needed to buy, and I would have to save the money to pay for the car before we could do anything. I talked to the man and he agreed to hold onto the car until I had saved the fifty dollars.

From that day on, I started saving my Rappaport money, any money that I earned from helping Pa, and any money that I made from my rabbits. Later in the fall, when I had saved the money, Pa and I went down the street and hooked the Averys pickup onto the body of the '47 Ford, and we towed it to Averys and parked it in the back lot of the supply yard. We then loaded up all of the engine parts and took them up to the garage at Averys. Over the winter and into the spring as I had the money, Pa and I put the engine back together, overhauling the engine as we did. We eventually reinstalled the engine in the car.

The hardest part was installing the distributor in the engine and setting the timing. For some reason, Ford had designed the distributor so that it was located in the front of the engine block and under the fan which was mounted on the top of the engine block between the two flat heads of the V8 engine. To set the timing we needed to reach around the fan and between the radiator and the engine to adjust the distributor. The only way to do this with the engine running was to take the fan belt off to keep the fan from operating. Once we got the timing set, we drove the car home. I was now fifteen, with a car, waiting to turn sixteen.

On more than one occasion I had heard Pa indicate that the best car made was the car he was currently driving. He was driving a Packard at this time so a Packard was the best car made. I had also heard him say on more than one occasion that he would never own a Ford. Actually, he usually said, "I would never own a god-damned Ford." For some reason he did not like Fords.

At that time most of the cars were made in the United States. Each September the new car models came out, and this was a big deal to all fifteen and sixteen-year-old boys who would soon be driving. Each car manufacturer would advertise the date that the new model would be available for the public. When the new models arrived they would be kept covered or hidden until the advertised date of the first showing. A couple of days prior to the date, the new model would be on display in the dealer showroom, all covered by canvas, cloth or paper so the general shape of the car was visible, but the details of the car were still hidden. Most of the men and boys in town either drove by or stopped at the local dealers, just to try to get a glimpse at all of the new models.

On the day of the new model year, each dealer would make a grand display of the removal of the covers revealing the wonderful new Ford or Chevy or whatever, and for at least a week after that, men and boys alike would go from dealer to dealer, just to see the latest and greatest that the auto industry had to offer. Much time on the job and at school was dedicated to discussing these yearly, new-model extravaganzas. It was an important time in the life of all boys because owning a brand new car was every boy's dream and checking out the new models was like a rite of passage in becoming a man.

CHAPTER 26

JUNIOR YEAR

1956-1957

Sylvia Terrell and Me at the Lime Street Home
In the Background: Ray and the Daybrook Plant

In the winter of 1955, a new pastor, Loyal Bishop, arrived at St. Mark's Lutheran Church. He was just out of the Seminary at Wittenberg College, and showed up in Bowling Green driving a 1955 red and white Ford convertible. He had a crew haircut and looked like a fullback for the football team. One of the first things he did in the spring of 1956 was start a church league softball team, and Pa and I signed up to play. When we fielded our first team in the Bowling Green Church League, Pa was playing third base, my Uncle Bob was the pitcher, my Uncle Bill was the catcher, and I was the second baseman. The games were played at the University ball diamonds on Ridge Street, behind the football stadium. All church league teams were fast pitch, and Uncle Bob was the best pitcher in the league, and probably the best pitcher in Bowling Green. Our team won a lot of games that year, due in part to the advantage we had of taking batting practice against Uncle Bob. When we faced an opposing team, we could usually hit their pitcher. I know that I never got a hit off Bob in practice, but I did manage to get hits off other pitchers, not many, but a few. Pa was a good hitter as was Uncle Bob and Uncle Bill. Pa's main problem was that he had bad knees and sometimes when he started to run to first base or run in on a ground ball, his left knee would slip out of place, and he would fall down. He could put his knee back in place by having someone pull on his lower leg, but once he was on the ground, he could not get up until the leg was back in place. The biggest problem for me, besides not hitting very well, was that Pastor Bishop played short stop. The throw from short stop to second base is not very far, and unfortunately for me, Pastor Bishop had an arm like a cannon. I sometimes felt like I had been shot in the hand when Pastor threw the ball to me.

In fast pitch softball, a base runner on first base could lead off and steal second base, so I had to cover second base for all right-handed batters if there was a runner on first. This in itself is not that difficult. It's just that the runner usually slid into second base, and I was not very big, so when a larger runner decided to knock me off the bag, I was a sitting duck. And just to add to the challenge of covering the bag, if the runner trying to steal second, appeared to be a sure out, my Uncle Bill would throw me a curve ball from the catcher's position to "test out my reflexes," as he put it. I usually knew that the curve ball was coming because Uncle Bill would have a big smile on his face as he threw the ball.

Mr. Rappaport owned a large warehouse in the alley behind the store. The warehouse was used for the storage of various items of merchandise, and that spring Mr. Rappaport indicated that he needed to get someone to give him a price for painting it. The building had metal siding and a metal roof, and both were starting to rust. I asked him if he would let me paint it. After we talked about it a bit, he agreed, and we worked out a deal. I would do the work in the store that needed to be done each day, and I would be paid the usual fifty cents an hour. When I was all caught up, I would then work on painting the warehouse, and for that work I would be paid seventy-five cents an hour. It took most of the summer working part-time to get the building walls and the roof painted, but it ended up that I made some extra money, and Mr. Rappaport saved some money so we were both happy.

Pizza came to Bowling Green in the summer of 1956. A new restaurant Called Petti's Alpine Village opened on North Main Street next door to Klever's Jewelry Store. The new menu was Italian and included pizza. Most of the kids in Bowling Green had heard of pizza, but many, including me, had never eaten it because the closest Pizza place was in Toledo. Jim and I had to go to the grand opening of Petti's for the sole purpose of having our first slice of pizza. Since neither of us had ever eaten pizza before, we did not know how to respond to the waitress's question, "What would you like on your pizza?" We resorted to asking, "What can we have?" As the waitress ran down the list of available items, we responded "yes" or "no." When she came to anchovies, I did not know what an anchovy was, but it sounded Italian, and I was thinking that it was something like an olive so I said "sure." Needless to say, an anchovy is nothing like an olive, and after the first bite, I figured out a way to pick the anchovies off the pizza without everyone in the restaurant seeing me doing it. I moved all of the anchovies to one piece of pizza and left that piece on the tray. I left Petti's feeling a bit more worldly for having eaten pizza, a little smarter for knowing what an anchovy was, and quite convinced that I would never order anchovies on my pizza again.

At this time Gene Sharpe was working at Averys. Gene was from Kentucky and living in Custar, Ohio with his wife, Patsy, and four children, two of which were infant twins. Patsy had more than she could handle, and once school was out in Kentucky, Patsy's younger sister, Sylvia, came to Ohio to help take care of the kids. One day Gene asked me if I would be interested in meeting Sylvia and maybe spending some time helping her watch the kids on a Saturday evening while he took Patsy to a movie. I said that I would do this as long as he was willing to pick me up and take me home since I did not have a license yet.

Sylvia was fifteen. She was very cute, she was also easy to talk to, and I especially liked her southern accent. I went home with Gene a number of times that summer on weekends and babysat with Sylvia. To this point I had only had one date with a girl, so I am sure I was a bit shy and at times, a little uneasy about myself. We would watch TV and talk, and for the first time I held a girl's hand. In late August, Gene told me that they would be taking Sylvia home to start school. One week day evening shortly afterwards, I went to Custar with Gene to babysit with Sylvia for the last time. Louise was picking me up later that evening to take me home as Gene and Patsy were getting home late.

When Louise arrived, she was with her friend, Charlene. Louise honked the horn to let me know she was there. I had never kissed a girl, but as I said good-bye to Sylvia, I kissed her. I left the house, feeling good that I had kissed her and happy that she had let me. Unfortunately, both Louise and Charlene could see all of this through the front window so they gave me a hard time when I got into the car, kidding me about all the passion they had witnessed.

The next day Gene stopped at the house and asked me if I would like to go with Patsy and him and the kids to take Sylvia back to Kentucky over the weekend, and I said, "Yes." I took Friday and Saturday off work at Rappaports, and we left early Friday morning for London, Kentucky. As we left, both Sylvia and Patsy were holding a bottle and a baby, and they gave me the bottles and jokingly told me to keep them warm. I put a bottle under each of my legs and when we got to Cincinnati, and the babies were ready for their bottles, Sylvia and Patsy were surprised the bottles were still so warm. They asked how I had done it and were amused and impressed with my bottle-warming technique. We spent Saturday at Sylvia's house, and I kissed her good-bye again as we left for Ohio on Sunday morning.

It had been my plan to ask Sylvia for a date, and I wanted to take her to see *Love Me Tender*. All the kids were looking forward to Elvis Presley's first movie, and Sylvia was a big Elvis fan. However, it came time to take her home before the movie arrived in Bowling Green. When it did finally come in November, the general response to it was that the girls thought it was a great movie, but the boys did not like it much. Myself, I enjoyed listening to Elvis when he sang, but I thought that he was not much of an actor. He was no James Dean.

Charlene Szabo had been Louise's best friend since junior high school. She lived in an apartment on South Main Street with her divorced mother and her younger brother Chuck. Charlene always seemed at least four or five years older than her actual age. She developed physically early, and she was one of the most shapely and attractive girls in her class. She usually dated older boys, including some college boys, while she was in high school. Some of the boys in my class would ask me about her and infer that I knew her better than I really did. The week after I got back from Kentucky, Charlene was at the house one day and started teasing me about kissing Sylvia. We were out in the yard, and as she teased me, she started to run away. I caught her and bent her over a bit like I had seen many a movie star leading man do, and I planted a long kiss on her lips. As she stepped back, she said, "Davy boy, today you are a man!" I have to admit that at that moment, I did feel quite manly. I had done what just about every other boy in high school wished they could do. I had kissed Charlene Szabo.

Over the years, Pa had, on a number of occasions, promised Mom to quit drinking. He had also, on a number of occasions, announced to us kids that he was going to quit drinking. I am not sure when he did, but he did stop. It was one of those things that just sort of happened. After he quit, he seemed easier to get along with and did not get as angry. But he still did get angry with me for little or no reason when we were working together. I began to think that he had always felt some kind of competition with me. I know that when we were playing ball or shooting a basketball, or even shooting marbles, no matter how old I was at the time, he could not just let me win. He seemed to have to do me one better. He loved to play cards, and when he played, he had to win. He also liked to arm wrestle and would challenge me to a competition, and then quickly pin my hand to the table. I am sure he knew that he was stronger than me, but he seemed to need to prove it either to me or to himself. I never did figure out why he had to prove he was stronger than me.

In August, when I got my temporary driving permit, I started driving with Pa in town for the first time. We would drive a couple of times a week and usually on Sunday. Every time Pa needed to go somewhere, I would ask if I could drive. By the end of September, I felt that I was ready to take my driver's test. I made an appointment for a Saturday morning in mid-October with the License Bureau. My Uncle Harmie had a '49 Mercury, and he offered to let me use it to take my test because driving and parking his Mercury would be easier than the Packard limousine. The only problem was his Mercury had a stick shift on the column, and the Packard had the stick shift on the floor. But I managed fine and passed the first time.

I now had a license. Pa said from the very beginning that if I was going to drive my own car, I needed to pay for my own insurance and gas. At that time gas was twenty-two cents a gallon, so a dollar's worth of gas went a long way. I stopped by Jackson Miller's State Farm Insurance Office and applied for insurance. At that time I needed to get approved by the insurance company. When I finally was approved, I started driving myself to school. Louise was driving her car, and she usually took Janet and Caroline to school with her. Sometimes I had to drive the girls, and if I did, I would take the girls to school, and then I would go pick up Blynn. At noon we could leave school for lunch, and with a car we started eating lunch at one of the drive-in burger places in town.

Jack Kinney was Blynn's neighbor and two years younger than us and in Janet's class. Jack's house was around the corner on Buttonwood Avenue and Blynn's house was on Ordway Avenue The backyard of Jack's house was just across the alley that ran beside Blynn's house. Blynn had strung wires through the trees between his upstairs bedroom and Jack's upstairs bedroom, and they had a two way radio set up so they could talk to each other without using the telephone. Jack became a member of our group, and when I picked up Blynn, Jack came along.

One Saturday night when I was getting the Sunday paper ready with Cap, he asked me if I would be interested in another job. Every day when the *Toledo Blade* was delivered to Bowling Green, Cap would take the papers around to the various drug stores and grocery stores. He indicated that since I now had a driver's license, he would like me to do this job. The papers usually were delivered at about 2:30 PM and he suggested that I go to the school counselor to see if I could get a permit to drop my last period study hall and leave the school at 2:30 PM to deliver the papers, and I could still be at my job at Rappaports at 3:30 PM as usual. With a car, gas and insurance to buy, the new job was just what I needed.

By this time, I was buying most of my own clothes, as well as whatever else I needed. Louise also bought most of her own clothes after she started working. This caused a bit of a problem because Mom and Pa still bought Janet and Caroline's clothes which were mainly functional and not necessarily the latest style. Caroline would sometimes wait until Louise had left for school and then she would change into one of Louise's outfits and ride to school with me. Louise did not always take kindly to this, especially when Caroline chose to wear an outfit that she was planning to wear the next day. Mom started checking Caroline before she left the house to be sure that she was wearing her own clothes.

In early October the World Series started, and somehow, our World History teacher, Mr. Powers, arranged to have a TV set in his classroom. He was a big New York Yankee fan, as was Oscar Ogg, a classmate. For several years, I had had an ongoing debate with both Mr. Powers and Oscar about who was the best team, the Cleveland Indians or the New York Yankees. Every year between 1950-1955, New York had won the American League Pennant with Cleveland ending up in second place, except for 1954 when Cleveland finished in first place with New York in second place. It was now 1956, and the Yankees had won the pennant with Cleveland in second place, and the Yankees were playing the Brooklyn Dodgers in the World Series. At that time, all series games were on television in the afternoon. One of the highlights of this series was the perfect game pitched by Yankee pitcher, Don Larson, and I was able to see a part of Game 5 and that perfect game thanks to Mr. Powers.

Addison Atkins moved from Texas to BG after school had started. He developed a friendship with Blynn in the advanced algebra class, and I met him through Blynn and he joined our group. Blynn and Jack were the first friends I had who smoked. They would often kid me about not smoking, and sometimes they would try to get me to smoke a cigarette, but I always refused. They also occasionally had a beer that Blynn would sneak out of his dad's or his neighbor's supply. Again, they would kid me because I never wanted to have a beer. I just told them that my mother had a very strong opinion about smoking and drinking, and I did not want to disappoint her. After a time, they realized that I was serious about not drinking or smoking, and they quit hassling me about it.

Jim Berry's parents were members of the Masonic Temple. His father was a Mason, and his mother was a member of the Eastern Star. Jim himself was a member of the DeMolay Club which was sponsored by the Masonic Temple. The Temple also sponsored a club for high school girls called the Rainbow Girls. Every Halloween, the DeMolays and the Rainbow Girls held a parade and dance called The Calithumpian which took place on the Saturday night before Halloween.

The night of the Calithumpian Parade and Dance, I picked up Jim Berry and we drove downtown to see what was going on with the parade. On the way, we passed a house with a number of pumpkins on the front porch, and Jim asked me to stop in front of the house. He quickly ran up to the porch and grabbed one of the pumpkins. As we drove slowly passed the Cla-Zel Theater, there were a number of classmates standing outside. Jim rolled down the window and leaned out, holding the pumpkin. He called someone's name and threw the pumpkin in the direction of the theater. The pumpkin was followed by Jim's watch which flew off his arm as he tossed the pumpkin. I am not sure which was in more pieces, the pumpkin or the watch.

We parked the car and took part in the parade and dance, and afterwards I invited as many friends as we could get into the car to go with us to get a hamburger at Mac's Drive-in. We ended up with nine people in the car. Jim, Jon Klever, and I were in the front seat, and six girls were in the back seat. Jon Klever was in Demolay and was the Calithumpian King, and Gail Nicely was in Rainbow Girls, and she was the Calithumpian Queen. As I mentioned earlier, I had had a crush on Gail since the seventh grade, but it seemed that she was always dating someone else, and that someone else was usually a friend of mine. I also believed that she considered me more of a friend than a prospective date so I had never asked her out. But this night, when it came time to take everyone home, I made sure that Gail was the last person I dropped off so we at least had a few minutes to talk.

Just before Thanksgiving when I was picking up Blynn for school one morning, he suggested that we skip school and go into Toledo for the day. Jack immediately agreed that this was a good idea. We picked up Addie, and he liked the idea, too, so we set off for Toledo. I asked myself, "What could possibly go wrong with this plan?"

We drove downtown and parked at the Tiedtke's parking lot. At that time Tiedtke's was the largest department store in the city of Toledo. The parking lot was big and free and located in the downtown area where all of the movie theaters were. We had no sooner walked into the store when I ran into my Grandmother Dickerson who was shopping there. Her first question was, "Why aren't you in school?" I left Grandma hoping she would forget that she had seen me by the next time we visited her. We wandered around the store for a while and then decided to see if one of the movie theaters was opened. As we walked out the front door of Tiedtke's onto Summit Street, I immediately ran into my Uncle Richard selling the *Toledo Times* newspaper. He asked me "What are you doing in Toledo?" Again, I hoped that Richard would forget he had seen me on a school day.

We found that the Rivoli Theater was opened for an early double feature. We were in the theater for about three hours, and when we came out we were greeted by a snowstorm.

Apparently, it had started snowing about five minutes after we went into the theatre, about four inches of snow had accumulated so far, and it was still snowing at a fast rate. At that time, the expressway system around Toledo did not exist, so getting back to BG meant that we needed to go home through Rossford on River Road and Perrysburg on Route 25. The snowplows were not out yet, and driving was very slow going. When we got to Perrysburg, we found that there had been a truck accident on Route 25 and traffic was backed up into town. We decided to try to get to BG by taking River Road to Waterville and then taking Route 64 home. This did work.

However, by the time I got home, it was getting dark. There was no way I could explain where I had been and make it believable, and with both Grandma and Richard seeing me in Toledo, I knew that Mom would soon know the truth anyway. So I confessed to skipping school, hoping that telling the truth might buy me some forgiveness. I had to give Pa my car keys, and I was not allowed to drive my car or go out at night for two weeks. I went back to riding my bike to work.

Later that evening, Louise told me that one of the teachers asked her if I was sick that day so she knew that I had skipped. When I was late coming home that evening, Pa and Mom had asked her if she knew where I was, but although she knew I had skipped school, she did not tell them. I also had to give my apologies to Cap, as he had to deliver the *Toledo Blade* to the newsstands when I did not show up after school. Fortunately, this happened on a Wednesday, so I did not miss working at Rappaports since the store was closed on Wednesday afternoons. As I said, "What could go wrong with this Plan?"

As Christmas time approached, Mr. Rappaport decided that the store needed some help, and he hired Judy Herbert to work at the store. Judy was in my class and was one of the more popular girls in school. She was from a well-to-do family in town so she and I had very little in common socially or economically. Because of this, I was concerned that I would feel a little intimidated working with her. But as we worked together, I was quite pleased to find that she was a very nice girl with no real hang-ups about our differences. We had many good discussions about school and other topics, and she would smile and say "Hi" when she saw me in school.

There was a presentation of the *Messiah* at Bowling Green State University just before Christmas, and Louise and her friend Charlene had tickets to go see the performance. Charlene had been dating college boys throughout her senior year, and as it turned out, there was a boy in the row behind them that Charlene knew. This boy was with a couple of his friends, including one named Larry Noon. Larry was sitting behind Louise and before the night was over, he asked Louise out on a date, and she said "Yes."

For a number of years I had thought that I would like to learn how to play the guitar so when it got close to Christmas, I started talking to Pa and Mom about how I would really like to have a guitar. Our family always opened presents on Christmas Eve so after supper that Christmas Eve, I was anxious to get started opening presents. There was a package in back of the tree that looked suspiciously like it could be a guitar. Pa usually handed out the presents so when he called my name and reached back to get the present behind the tree, I could not contain myself. I called out, "It's a guitar!" As soon as Pa handed me the package, I knew it was not a guitar. Mom and Pa had wrapped up a scoop shovel to look like a guitar, but I had handled a scoop shovel enough to recognize what it was the minute I touched it. Everyone had a good laugh at the look on my face as I ripped off the wrapping paper to reveal the shovel. Pa went into his bedroom and returned with a guitar in his hand. And while it was not an expensive guitar, he had bought it at Bigelow's Music Shop, and I now owned my first guitar. I had visions of playing in a rock band and spent the rest of the evening trying to make the guitar sound like I knew how to play it,

In January I was driving my car home from school one wintry day, and Blynn and Addie were with me. We were heading to my house, and the streets were slippery with snow and ice from a recent storm. As we approached the railroad crossing on Lehman Avenue near the Daybrook Plant, the crossing warning lights started flashing, indicating that a train was approaching. I started to apply the brakes, and the car went into a skid on the ice, and the right side front wheel slammed into the curb. At this point, the steering wheel began spinning in my hand, and all of my efforts to straighten out the direction of the car had no effect. We finally came to a stop about five feet from the train which was now speeding across the tracks in front of us.

After the train passed and we all were able to breathe again, I got out and looked to see what had happened to the steering. I found that when the wheel hit the curb, the impact had broken the steering tie rod where it connected to the wheel hub. The steering wheel would control the left front wheel, but had no control of the right front wheel. To get the car the rest of the way home, I slowly drove the car forward and Blynn and Addie walked beside the right front wheel of the car. Whenever the right wheel started to turn one way or the other, they would kick the tire to move the wheel back into place. This took a little doing, as we had to turn two corners to get to the house, but we eventually made it home. Pa and I had the car fixed by the next day.

I had a new English Teacher named Miss Grabill who was fresh out of college and in her first teaching job. She was probably no more than twenty-two years old so she was closer to my age than any teacher I had ever had. She was also the most attractive. Straight skirts were popular with all of the girls in high school and also with Miss Grabill. Miss Grabill used to sit on the edge of the desk at the front of the room in her straight skirt with one leg hanging over the front corner of the desk. It was impossible not to notice the curve of her leg. She would be explaining something about verbs, or *Silas Marner*, or whatever, and as she talked, she would swing her leg back and forth, back and forth. I am sure that the eyes of every boy in the class were locked in on her legs, and their ears and brains had quit working.

One Friday night after a football game, I was driving around with a bunch of my friends and we happened to drive by Miss Grabill's house. She was living with Miss Randall, another teacher at the high school. As we drove by, we noticed that Miss Grabill was sitting in a car in the driveway with a man. Naturally we were concerned enough to go around the block and pull into the drive behind the car just to make sure that Miss Grabill was alright. We all got out of the car, surrounded the car she was sitting in, talked with her awhile, gave her a little hassle about setting an example for her students, and then we went on our way.

Miss Grabill stressed the importance of being able to get up in front of the class and give a speech. This was one of my biggest fears, as I have mentioned, and on more than one occasion, I had taken an *F* rather than give a speech. I did not want to disappoint Miss Grabill, so somehow I worked up the nerve to give a speech in her class and discovered that I could live through it.

Chemistry was also a good class that year. We had a new Chemistry teacher, Mr. Shaffer. At some point in his life, Mr. Shaffer had an accident that required plastic surgery on his face, and he had a noticeable scar on his nose and forehead. John Montgomery was in my chemistry class, and he managed to evacuate the classroom on more than one occasion. The chemistry class lasted two periods with about a four minute break in between each class period. Most students would leave the classroom on the break and go out into the hall to talk or whatever. There were a series of small recessed areas along one wall of the chemistry room which were arranged for conducting chemical experiments. Each recessed area had a sliding glass door so that the experiment could be somewhat separated from the class room.

During the class breaks, John had a habit of waiting until everyone was out of the room. Then he would go back to one of the experiment areas and pour a little nitric acid in a beaker and toss in a couple of pennies. He then pulled the glass door of the experiment area almost shut, and as the bell rang he quickly took his seat. In a matter of minutes, the chemistry room would start to turn a copper shade as the nitrous oxide gas from the copper melting in the nitric acid filled the room. Mr. Shaffer would order all of us out of the room and into the hallway, open the windows, and turn on the fans to clear up the air in the room. Once we were all back in class, he would give us the same lecture he gave each time this happened on the dangers of playing with chemicals.

There was another prank that caused disruption of the chemistry class. All of the chemicals were kept in a separate room off the front of the classroom. Sometimes when Mr. Shaffer went into the chemical room to get some additional chemicals that were needed for the experiment, one of the boys would quickly shut and lock the door with Mr. Shaffer still inside searching for whatever chemicals he was looking for. Soon there would be a rattling of the door knob, and Mr. Shaffer would ask for someone to open the door. Usually one of the girls opened the door, and we received the same speech we always got whenever he was locked in the chemical room on the importance of showing respect.

That summer I drove up to Blissfield to visit my cousin Carl on a couple of occasions. Carl also had his own car and was dating Diane Phifer. I often went up to see Carl on a Saturday night, and we would end up going to a dance either at the Sportsmen's Club, located off Route 223 just north of Sylvania, or the Blissfield American Legion Post. Diane would always go with us and sometimes, if Carl knew that I was coming, Diane would have a blind date for me. Carl told me that he planned to quit school that fall and get a fulltime job because he wanted to marry Diane as soon as he could.

CHAPTER 27
SPRING AND SUMMER OF '57

East Harbor State Park

Bottom row left: Dave Titus, Blynn Gause,
Jim Berry, Jack Kinney

Middle row left: Dave Titus' Girl Friend,
Caroline, Dianna Kithcart

Top: Sylvia Terrell
(I am taking the picture)

In the spring of the year, Bowling Green college girls were out in great numbers, either walking around in shorts or sunbathing on the lawns of the campus dormitories, and high school boys enjoyed cruising around the University to admire the scenery. One warm spring evening as Blinn,

Addison, and I were driving around, we headed out to the University just as it was getting dark. We drove down Ridge Street and into one of the parking areas behind the old football stadium.

All at once Blynn said, "Stop the car." I did and he jumped out and grabbed a sign mounted on a pedestal that indicated a university parking permit was needed to park in that area. He put the sign on the floor of the back seat, and we continued on our way. We had driven only a short distance from the parking lot when a university police car came up behind us and the policeman turned on his flashing light. I pulled over, and he walked up to the side of the car and told us to step out. He asked to see my driver's license and then asked why we had stopped in the parking lot. Blynn immediately answered, "I had to take a Piss." The policeman responded that we should find a better place to do that, and he suggested that we get into the car and go somewhere else. We left quickly with the sign still in the backseat. We drove around downtown for a while, and just before I took everyone home, we drove back to the university parking lot and quickly replaced the sign.

Early in the spring of 1957, I decided that I wanted to have a different car so I started looking around at the various used car lots in Bowling Green. I found a 1950 Mercury at the Close Buick Lot. The Mercury was a four-door, metallic green, with a sun visor and a spotlight. It had a whip antenna mounted on the rear bumper, and the previous owner had coated the head-liner with a fabric paint so the interior was also green. The asking price was $250.00, and the salesman offered me $60.00 for my '47 Ford. Pa agreed to sign papers for me so that I could pay off the car in $20.00 monthly installments for the next year. Although he agreed to sign, Pa also told me, "A Mercury is just a god-damned Ford with all the bolts tightened."

As I drove the Mercury home, I noticed that the steering wheel had a steering knob. I had seen steering knobs on most of the trucks at Averys so I knew what they were for. Most cars and trucks did not have power steering so a steering knob made it easier to turn the wheel, especially if you were parking or turning sharply at low speeds. The thing about this steering knob was that it was mounted on the left side of the steering wheel so I assumed it meant the previous driver was left-handed. It wasn't until I started going out with girls that I realized the steering knob on the left side made it possible to drive the car and still have your arm around the girl sitting next to you in the front seat.

At that time, two other boys in my class were driving '50 Mercs. Bill Brigham and Don Bullis both had black '50 Mercurys, and each morning we would try to park our cars in a line along the curb on South Grove Street. Sometimes when I came out of school to go to lunch or go home from school, I would grab hold of the door handle to open the door, and I would find that Pa had passed by in a truck and stopped to put a finger full of grease on my door handle.

During my junior year, I got into the first and only fight I ever had. There had been times when it appeared that I might be involved in some kind of physical contact with a number of boys who were either trying to bully me or push me into a fight, but I had never actually laid hands on anyone other than Wayne Garvey. I had friendly wrestling matches with a number of my cousins and with my uncles, and even with Blynn and Addie. But I had never actually grabbed hold of someone in anger or tried to harm anyone before this. There was a boy named Bob in the sophomore class who worked as an usher at the Cla-Zel theater. One Friday night Blynn, Addison, and I were at the movie theater, and we were more than a little noisy. We ended up being asked to leave the theater by Bob, who was doing his job as an usher. Of course we did not take kindly to being asked to leave, and we were convinced that it was all Bob's fault so we did not have a warm and fuzzy feeling for him when we walked out of the Cla-Zel.

For whatever reason, a number of our male friends at school began giving us a hard time for allowing a sophomore usher to kick us out of the Cla-Zel. One thing lead to another, and it was decided that someone had to set Bob straight about kicking upper classmen out of the theater. Since Bob and I were about the same size and weight, it was decided that I would champion our cause. It was arranged that Bob and I would have a show-down after school in the vacant lot next to the junior high school. We met at the appointed hour, and I was amazed at the number of onlookers that gathered to witness this event. Bob and I exchanged a number of threats and insults to set the stage for the fight and then we had at it.

Now, as I mentioned I had never been in a fight before, so I made several mistakes. The first mistake I made was that I did not take off the jacket I was wearing. My Uncle Gordon had given me a number of items of clothing that he no longer wore or had out grown, including a brown, leather jacket with a fur collar. I wore this jacket most of the time even if it was warm because a guy wearing a leather jacket had to look cool or so I thought. Bob did not make the same mistake; he took off his jacket. At first the fight was really just a wrestling match where I would grab him, he would grab me, and then we would roll around on the ground muttering at each other, trying to get on top of one another. But neither of us was making much headway.

Then I made mistake number two. We had each other in a headlock as we rolled around in the dirt, and I was trying to get my left arm under one of Bob's arms to go from a headlock to a full nelson, a wrestling hold that I had seen on TV. Bob kept me from doing this by grabbing the cuff of my jacket sleeve, and I tried to pull my left arm away as he held onto the sleeve. Suddenly my left arm pulled out of the sleeve and was inside of the jacket. I had Bob around the neck with my right arm, and my left arm was inside my jacket, and the jacket was totally zipped shut. Bob had me in a headlock with his right arm, and he pulled the left sleeve of my jacket up over my face and locked his left hand behind the back of my head, covering my face with his arm and the jacket sleeve.

Mistake number three was my decision to try to slip my left arm out of the bottom of the jacket so I would again have two arms in the struggle. As I tried to get my left arm out of the bottom of the jacket and tried to reach up to get hold of Bob in any way I could, I suddenly realized that I was pushing the jacket up toward my face, just as Bob was pulling up on the sleeve of the jacket. This all resulted in the thick fur collar being pushed and pulled into a position directly over my mouth and nose, and breathing became quite difficult and in a matter of moments, it was painfully clear to me that I just might be losing this fight.

As I realized that whatever I did only made matters worse, Laura Osborne's mother came out of her house, which was next door to the vacant lot, and started yelling at all of us and telling us to break it up. Everyone who was watching scattered, and Bob told me that he would let me go, if I agreed to also let go. I agreed without hesitation, and we both got to our feet. We took one more look at each other without saying a word, and we left the field of battle in opposite directions. I remember being very upset with myself for not thinking about taking off the jacket, but I was even more upset for getting into a situation where I was actually trying to hurt someone. I told myself that as long as I could take control of what I was doing, I would never get into that kind of a situation again.

Louise had her date with Larry Noon, and soon he became a regular at our house. Larry was from Akron where his dad worked in the office of the Goodyear Rubber Company. Larry was a freshman at BGSU and living in Rogers Quad. It soon became obvious that Larry had led somewhat of a sheltered life compared to what we had experienced as kids growing up. It seemed that whatever we were doing, Larry would take part, but he would usually indicate that he had never done it before. Whether it was fishing, playing softball, hunting mushrooms, digging a hole with a shovel, swinging a hammer, or helping us work on a car, Larry always took part and tried his best.

I remember on a number of occasions Pa would say he couldn't believe that Larry was in college and had never done whatever it was that we were doing, and he worried that Larry might hurt himself trying to do it. The main thing was that whatever we were doing as a family, Larry wanted to be included, and Louise wanted him to be there. I am not sure if his relationship with Louise was an influence on his college efforts, but he was in serious scholastic trouble at the end of his freshmen year. He decided that he would drop out of college and pursue a career in the military, and it was at that time that he joined the Air Force. Louise had graduated from high school and taken a job at the local telephone office, working as a telephone operator. Louise and Larry became engaged that summer.

Pa decided it was time to get another car. The '39 Packard was getting old, and since Louise and I were both driving our own cars, he did not need the Packard Limo to haul all of his children. He traded in the old Packard for a 1949 Packard.

As soon as school was out, Mom and Pa decided to take the family and drive to Denver, Colorado to visit her brother Frank and his family. At that time Mom's cousin, Martha, was living in Denver so we would be seeing her family also. My Aunt Juanita and her son, Johnny, were going with us and with them, Mom and Pa and all seven kids, we needed to drive two cars.

This meant that I would be driving my '50 Mercury to Denver. We left Bowling Green heading west on Route 6 which ran all the way to the west coast by way of Denver. Louise, Juanita, Johnny, and one of my brothers were in my car, and the rest of the kids were with Mom and Pa in the Packard. We camped two nights on the way to Denver, once near the Mississippi River and once in Nebraska. As we had done with the trip to the Smokys, Pa put a large tarp over the roof of the Packard and made a lean-to type tent on the passenger side of the car. We could either sleep in the car or on the ground under the tarp beside the Packard.

Mom and Pa brought lunch meat, cereal, and snacks for most of the meals on the road. However, at lunch time on the third day out, Pa decided to get a quick lunch on the road, hoping that we would get to Denver that day. We stopped at a little restaurant in the middle of nowhere in the western part of Nebraska. When the waitress came to our table, the first thing she said to us was, "Do you know who is sitting at that table over there?" We all looked in the direction where she was pointing and saw two good-looking young men sitting at the table talking to a couple of teenage girls. Before we could say anything, the waitress said, "It's the Everly Brothers." Of course all of us had heard of the Everly Brothers and their first hit song, *By By Love*, was playing on every rock radio station that we had been listening to for the past three days. In fact, it was playing on the juke box when we entered the restaurant. My sisters immediately went over to their table to get an autograph. When the Everly brothers got up to leave, I followed them to the door of the restaurant and watched to see what they were driving. They drove off in a new '56 Chevy convertible. Later that evening, we arrived at my uncle's house, eager to tell our story of meeting the Everly Brothers.

After the end of the war, my Uncle Frank had gone to Greenland to work on the construction of the Thule Greenland Air Force Base. I can't remember how long he was in Greenland, but he saved most of the money that he made while working there, and when he returned to Toledo, he and his wife Innis, moved to Denver into a new home. Frank and Innis had a set of twins, a boy named Frank Jr. and a girl named Francis; however, Frank Jr. was stillborn. Until this time, I had only seen my uncle on a couple of occasions, and I could not remember too much about him or his family. The only thing that I can remember about seeing him this time was I thought that he looked a little like the actor Dick Powell.

Mom's cousin, Martha, was the daughter of Grandpa Dickerson's sister, Irene. When Martha was thirteen, her mother died, and Martha went to live with Grandma Polley and stayed there until she met and married Paul Wallis Jackson. Martha had a son, Paul Wallis "Jackie" Jackson, Jr., but the marriage did not last. Martha was now remarried to a man named Lyle Yance, and Martha and Lyle had two young sons at that time.

Jackie, was about my age, so at least I had someone to talk to and spend some time with. On Wednesday night, Jackie asked me if I wanted to go out with his friends and him. Mom and Pa said that I could go, and we headed out to explore the wonders of Denver in Jackie's car. He picked up another boy before he picked up three girls. It was obvious that one of the girls was Jackie's girlfriend and another was his friend's girlfriend so the third girl was there to be with me.

I can't remember her name, but I do remember a few things about her. She was attractive and wore quite a bit of make-up. She also seemed to be a little more free with her language than I was used to hearing from the girls that I knew. We went to a drive-in and had burgers and fries, and then we headed out to the Red Rock Theater. I learned that it was an outdoor amphitheater located about fifteen miles west of Denver. It was carved out of the natural red sandstone of the mountain.

It was dark when we arrived and the park was closed so I wondered what we were going to do there. We all got out of the car and followed Jackie as he led us up a path into the rocks around the back of the stage area where he started to climb up between two rocks to a small ledge. Once he got to the top, he leaned over and held his hand down to help the girls up to the ledge. After Jackie's friend and their girlfriends were lifted up, it was time for the girl with me to go up. She was shorter than the rest of us so she could not reach Jackie's out-stretched hand. She was wearing a tight-fitting straight skirt, and she could not bend her legs very much. She reached down and pulled up her skirt to a point well above her knees. She placed her foot against the side of the rock, and said, "Give me a boost."

I was standing behind and about two feet below her and I asked, "What is the best way to give you a boost?"

She replied, "When I start to step up, put both hands on my ass and push up!" Now remember, I was from little Bowling Green, Ohio. I had had one date, I had kissed two girls, and I had never seen a girl's bare thigh, except if she were wearing a bathing suit. And here I was with a girl that I did not know, telling me to put both hands on her ass and push up.

So I did.

Once we were all up on the ledge, we walked a short distance through the rocks and came out into the amphitheater. There was no lighting in the stage area, however there was enough moonlight to safely walk around the amphitheater without tripping over something. The view of the lights of Denver was breathtaking from this point, and the stars overhead were even more spectacular. Although I was enjoying the view, I was concerned that we would be caught inside of the theater when it was closed. Jackie told me that he and his friends would come here on nights when there were no scheduled shows and just sit and talk and whatever. He said that others were usually there, and it was a popular meeting place for kids his age. We left the same way we got in, and I was the first one down off the ledge, followed by Jackie's friend and then the girls.

As I helped the girl with me down from the ledge above me she asked, "Well, did you get a good view?"

I assumed she was referring to the lights of Denver, and I said, "Yes."

The next day we all drove out to Lookout Mountain and Buffalo Bill's grave, and then to a place called Berthed Pass for our first real look at the Rocky Mountains. That was the day that I fell in love with mountains.

We packed up and headed east early the next day. As we neared Lincoln, Nebraska, we heard on the radio that there was a tornado warning for the Lincoln area. It was getting dark, and Mom did not want to chance camping with the tornado warning so we drove into Lincoln and checked into the first hotel we came to. It was an older hotel, and I think that it was called the Silver Dollar Hotel. It had silver dollars embedded in the floor all around the perimeter of the hotel lobby. We got three rooms and a couple of roll-a-way beds, and we were set for the night. There was no tornado, and we were up early and on the road. We got home very late that night. I was not yet seventeen, and I had driven to Denver and back to Bowling Green in eight days.

Driving cross-country gave me the opportunity to see just about every Burma Shave sign slogan that was ever made. I knew most of them, but I did find one new set of signs that said, "The big blue tube is like Louise, you get a thrill each time you squeeze." I started saying that little rhyme whenever I saw Louise and Larry holding hands or kissing or whatever. The dirty looks I got from Louise did not stop me.

I was still working on Saturday nights for the *Toledo Blade*. The only difference was that every other week, Cap would take a night off, and I needed someone to help on those weeks. Jim Berry agreed to help me. On some summer Sunday mornings, when we were done with the papers, Jim and I drove to the City Park, parked the car on Fairview Avenue, and walked across the golf course to the city swimming pool. We made sure no one was in the area, and we quickly climbed the fence around the pool and took a quick swim. It was usually about 5:30 AM when we finished the papers, so not many people were up and around to see us swimming in the pool in our underwear.

At this time, I was the only one in my group of friends that had a car. Blynn could sometimes get his father's '55 Ford for a special night only, and Jim sometimes drove his father's Chevy. Addison's mother did not have a car that I recall, and Jack Kinney was too young to have a license. When we went anywhere, it was usually in my Mercury, and I did the driving.

Sylvia Terrell came back from Kentucky to spend the summer with her sister, and we started dating again occasionally. Patsy and her family had moved to the Defiance area, and the distance made seeing each other more difficult. Blynn had started dating my sister, Caroline, so she became a part of my group of friends, and often Janet would come along, too. That summer we spent most of our free time going to the Portage Drive-in or to the beach at East Harbor. The East Harbor beach was the best swimming beach in our area and many of my friends from school would gather there on the weekend.

One Sunday morning after I had worked all night for the *Blade*, I went to the beach at East Harbor State Park with Blynn, Caroline, Addie, and some other friends. It was a hot day, and I was very tired because I had been awake for more than twenty-four hours. I soon fell asleep on the beach as the rest of my friends were swimming and playing around. I don't know how long I lay in the sun sleeping on my stomach, but when they woke me up to go home, my back and the back of my legs were very sunburned. I had Blynn drive us home in my car, as I had a hard time just sitting, let alone trying to drive. By the time I got home, I was having muscle spasms in my legs. I tried to get comfortable enough that night to be able to sleep, but no matter what I did, I was in great pain. The next morning Pa took me to the emergency room where the doctor told me that I had second degree burns on the back of my legs and back. I was given some salve and sent home, with directions to bathe the sunburned area with an oatmeal water mix. Mom also mixed up a paste of baking soda and water and rubbed it gently over the burned area. It was the better part of the week before I could wear long pants and return to work.

A couple of weeks later, I again went to East Harbor with Blynn and Addison but this time I kept my clothes on and did not swim at all. On the way home, we stopped at a fireworks stand and bought some cherry bombs. At that time, all fireworks were considered dangerous, and it was against the law to sell them in Ohio. But anytime we were in the area of

Lake Erie, there would always be at least one or two stands set up along the road to sell fireworks out of the trunk of a car.

Cherry bombs were one of the more powerful firecrackers that we could buy, and the special thing about them was that the fuse and the firecracker itself was water proof. We bought a full box, a gross, and for the next week we had fun setting off the cherry bombs in different ways. We first went out to Ducay Quarry which was located off Route 281 to the south of Bowling Green. We tied cherry bombs to small rocks and then dropped a lit rock bomb into the water and watched it sink out of sight. A few seconds later there would be an underwater explosion that was basically an up-surge of water, followed by a number of fish floating to the water surface.

One night we went out to the Wood County Stone Quarry next to the Portage Drive-in. We pulled into the stone storage yard and climbed up on one of the huge stone piles where we could look down on the drive-in theater parking area. Blynn had brought along his hunting style sling-shot. He put a cherry bomb into the sling shot pouch and pulled back the sling shot to the firing position. He held this position as Addison lit the cherry bomb, and then he fired the cherry bomb out over the cars parked in the drive-in. The first cherry bomb exploded about twenty feet above the cars. We took turns firing the next ten to twelve shots in rapid order and then decided that we had better get out of there.

Two nights later, we revisited the drive-in and again shot off about a dozen bombs. We then drove around Bowling Green, tossing cherry bombs in the yards of our friends. We were driving down Buttonwood Avenue, and Jack Kinney was with us, and he decided that he wanted to toss a fire cracker at his folk's house. Jack was in the backseat and held the cherry bomb as Blynn lit it from the front seat. Jack started to throw the cherry bomb out of the window as I drove the car. Unfortunately, when he tried to toss the firecracker out the window, he hit his hand on the top of the window frame and dropped the lit bomb on the floor inside of the backseat. Jack tried to climb quickly over the front seat as it exploded in the backseat under his feet. The sound of a cherry bomb exploding inside of a car is pretty intense for anyone inside of the car. Fortunately there was no damage to Jack and only a little powder burn on the floor mat.

Our cherry bomb fun ended one Friday night. We were driving around town and drove through the City Park. There was a public restroom just to the left of the park entrance, and as I drove into the park, Blynn told me to stop the car so he could go to the restroom. Addison and Jack got out of the car with Blynn, and I stayed in the car and talked through the window to a couple of girls who were walking in the park. All at once there was a loud explosion, and Blynn, Jack and Addison came running out of the building. As they jumped into the car, Blynn yelled "Get the hell out of here."

I drove quickly out of the park and down Maple Street as Blynn was telling me that he had tossed a cherry bomb into the commode, and the explosion had blown the commode to pieces. We did not light off any more fireworks that night, and I took everyone home. The next day, a Bowling Green policeman stopped at the house and told me that I needed to come downtown to the Police Department and answer some questions. When I got there, I was taken to see Chief Spitler. He told me that he knew everything that had happened, but he wanted to hear my side of the story. At first I pleaded ignorance. He told me that I might as well tell the truth, as he had already spoken to the others involved, and repeated that he knew everything. He just wanted the hear my account.

At this point I told him what had happened, being sure to say several times that I never left the car, and that I did not know what went on in the restroom or who threw the cherry bomb. He told me that all of us would have to share in the cost of replacing the toilet and whatever other damage there might be. He then asked if I had any more fireworks, and I told him the only one who had any was Blynn. He assured me that Blynn had surrendered the remaining fireworks, and he gave me a lecture on fireworks, and on picking my friends and staying out of trouble.

When I got home Blynn and Jack were there and asked me what had gone on. After I told them what I said, Blynn told me some things that I did not know. Blynn had gotten into some trouble in the past, and the Chief warned him that he might get sent to the detention home if he did not cooperate and tell the truth. The girls I had been talking to the night before had told the police what they knew. They reported who was in the bathroom and explained that I was sitting in the car talking when the bomb exploded. The police had talked to Blynn, Jack, and Addison before talking to me, and Blynn confessed when the police talked to him. He was glad that all of us told the truth because he was afraid that if there had been four different stories, he might be in more trouble. It cost each of us forty dollars as our share of the repair to the restroom.

The Mercury had a standard transmission, so I naturally thought that the car would be good in a drag race. It only took a couple of tries at drag racing to convince me that the Mercury was not very quick off the line. A standard transmission had an advantage over an automatic transmission in that the driver did the shifting and could determine from the sound of the engine the best time to shift from first to second gear and from second gear to third gear. The automatic transmission relied on oil pressure to do the shifting. With an automatic transmission, I would start in drive and the transmission would shift from a low gear to a second gear and finally to the third gear, based mainly on the speed of the vehicle. The first shift came at about twenty-five miles per hour and the second shift came at about forty miles per hour. The automatic transmission had a separate low drive position, but it would stay in low drive till it was shifted into drive.

Boys who were driving cars with automatic transmissions soon learned that by starting the car in low drive and running the car up to about twenty miles an hour, they could shift the transmission into drive and then quickly back into low, fooling the automatic transmission into running up to about fifty miles per hour before they shifted the automatic into drive. All of this resulted in a much quicker start off the line.

A number of boys from the high school would sometimes gather out on East Poe Road, and they would race each other starting from Dunbridge Road and racing east on Poe Road or north from Poe Road on Dunbridge Road. Usually they would race a quarter of a mile or until the first car reached sixty miles per hour.

I tried this a few times, but the Mercury was not that fast, and I was always a little concerned about speed, especially on Poe Road because of the deep ditch that paralleled the road. I did manage to cause some damage to the Mercury's transmission one night when I was trying to speed shift from first to second, and as a result I had a loud knocking sound in the transmission in first gear and in reverse. I took the car to the garage at Avery's, and Pa and I took out the transmission to fix it.

It turned out that the transmission also had a crack in the casing, so I had to find a used transmission at a junk yard. Since I had the transmission out, I decided to overhaul the engine. On the trip to Denver, the Mercury used about a quart of oil for every two tanks of gas, so it was in need of some work. I had helped Pa work on cars for a number of years so I had the knowledge I needed to do the work, and for the first time I did most of the work myself with Pa helping me when I needed it. Afterwards, the Mercury ran fine, but it was not any faster.

One problem with the Mercury was the fact that the fuel pump was a diaphragm type. It was mounted on the side of the engine block and in hot weather the heat of the engine would cause the gasoline in the fuel pump to vaporize to the point that the pressure of the vaporized gas on the diaphragm would cause the fuel pump to quit pumping gasoline, and the engine would stop running. This was called a vapor lock. I started carrying a gallon jug of water in the trunk of the car, and when the engine would quit running because of a vapor lock, I would pour cold water on the fuel pump to condense the vapor. This relieved the pressure on the diaphragm, and the fuel pump would again pump gasoline, and I could drive until the vapor lock struck again.

We were going to the Portage Drive-In quite often that summer. Usually Blynn, Addison, Jack Kinney and sometimes Jim Berry and I would go either in my car or in Blynn's '55 Ford. Most nights that we went, at least one or two of us entered the drive-in in the trunk of the car. When we did this, the driver of the car would pull into the back part of the theater and sit for a few minutes to be sure that no one was close or watching. When it got dark enough for the show to start, the driver would get out of the car and open the trunk to let out whoever was hiding there.

One time Blynn and I went with Jim Berry in Jim's car, so Blynn and I hid in the trunk. When we got there, the theater was just about full so Jim had to park farther up toward the front of the theater. The drive-in manager was well aware that people came into the drive-in in the trunk, and he would drive around the theater in his car, trying to catch someone getting out of the trunk of a car. Jim got out and walked around to the trunk, just as the drive-in manager stopped beside him. We heard the manager ask Jim why he was opening the trunk of the car. Jim quickly replied that he thought the trunk lid was rattling, and he was not opening the trunk but making sure that the trunk was closed. The manger then asked Jim to open his trunk, to which Jim said, "I don't have to," and he walked over to the concession stand.

We heard Jim walk away, and then we heard a car park next to us. A few minutes later Jim came back to the car, and turned on the movie speaker. He told us through the back seat that the manager had parked next to us. The manager stayed parked next to Jim for the whole first feature, and he finally left just before the intermission to go work in the concession stand. Once he left, Jim was able to slip out of the car and unlock the trunk, and he told us to wait a few minutes to get out and meet him at the concession stand. When we got out of the trunk and walked to the concession stand, Jim was standing within a few feet of the manager. As we walked in, Jim acted like he had just spotted us, and we all made quite a show of greeting each other as if we had not seen each other in awhile. Then Jim said in a loud voice so the manager could hear, "Why don't you guys come and sit in my car for the next movie?" We agreed that we would do that and went back to Jim's car.

Blynn got a job as a bag boy at the A&P Store, and soon after he started, he told me that A&P was looking for another bagboy. I went down to the store and filled out an application form, and a couple of days later I received a call to come in for an interview. I didn't know if I had a chance for the job, but the same day of the interview, I told Mr. Rappaport that if the job was offered, I was going to take it. He told me that he knew that he could not offer me as much money as the A&P could, and he knew that I would leave at some point. He reassured me that I had a job with him until that time came. At the A&P interview, I was told I had the job and I could start the first of October. I finished September working at Rappaport's and had a chance to say good-bye to all of the ladies that worked there.

A&P required employees to wear a white shirt and a black bowtie. I had to get my own white shirts, and the Great Atlantic and Pacific Tea Company gave me the black plastic bowties. I also had to join a union. I didn't know too much about the union; I just knew that Pa did not have a very high opinion of unions in general. Clay Reed was the store manager, and Virginia Garner was the assistant manager. There were a number of high school boys working there at the time, and I knew most of them including Blynn's older brother, Richard, and Terry Smith from our class.

I started as a bagboy, bagging groceries and sweeping the floor. At that time, it was store policy to have the bag boy take all groceries to the customer's car and place the groceries in the car. I was expected to bag the groceries so that each bag weighed about the same, and all soft foods were on top. I even had to take a short class on how to fill a grocery bag. The A&P store was closed on Sundays and opened until 9:00 PM on Monday and Friday nights, and until 6:00 PM the rest of the nights. I started working at eighty-five cents an hour, and I usually worked both Monday and Friday nights, a couple of afternoons after school, and at least a half day on Saturday.

On Wednesdays, after the store closed at six, some of the boys would stay on and restock the shelves for the coming weekend. A semi-truck full of grocery products would arrive at the store at about six, and everyone would help unload the truck and then place the new groceries on the shelves. There were no expiration dates on the groceries at that time so it was necessary to rotate all of the old can goods and boxed foods to the front of the shelves and place the new cans and boxed foods in the back. After a couple of months, I was asked to help on Wednesday night. Working stock meant that I made more money.

At that time each individual item at the store had to be marked with a stamp or a paper tag indicating the price of that item. If there was a price change, each item had to be removed from the shelf, the old price would be taken off, and a new price tag attached. The person at the checkout cash register, usually a woman, typed in the price of each item.

I developed a good relationship with a number of the checkout women, and a couple of them always wanted me to be the bagboy at their register. I could bag groceries as quickly as the checkout could ring up the items. I also became familiar with a number of the customers to the point that I knew which car belonged to which one of them. Quite often a customer would hand me the keys to his car as he paid the bill, and I would take the groceries to the car and hand him the keys as he came out of the store. My use of "Yes ma'am" and "Yes sir" was still with me, and the people I worked with and the customers occasionally would comment on how well-mannered I was.

I enjoyed working at the A&P store, except when I had a toothache, and that happened a lot. My teeth had many cavities, and in the winter, a deep breath of cold air often set off a toothache that would last most of the working day. I could not do much to relieve the pain while I was working, except take an aspirin and try to tough it out until it was time to go home. I started going to see a dentist, Dr. Kelbaugh, and usually when I found out how much more it cost to have a tooth filled rather than pulled, I would opt to have the tooth pulled.

Because I needed to wear a white shirt whenever I worked at the A&P, it became necessary for me to learn how to wash and iron my shirts. I bought three new shirts and started washing two shirts at a time because Mom did not always do the washing for the rest of the family to suit my schedule. I ironed my own shirts because the girls did most of the ironing, and they ironed their own clothes and whatever mom wanted ironed and left my shirt in the basket. We did not have steam irons at the time, so I needed to sprinkle the washed shirt to dampen it. We had a small cork-like sprinkler head that fit into a pop bottle. I would fill the pop bottle with water, insert the sprinkler head, and shake the bottle over the shirt to get it ready to iron. Mom helped me iron the first shirt and from then on, I was on my own.

My hours at the A&P did not always fit with the meal times that were built around Pa's schedule. Lunch was between 12:00-1:00 PM, and supper was at 5:30 PM sharp so Pa could eat and do whatever evening work he had lined up. Sometimes when I got home, there were no leftovers so I soon learned to cook my own meals. Grilled cheese sandwiches, bacon and eggs, and fried bologna sandwiches were my usual meals. But as time went by, I learned to cook other things, and I found that I really liked to cook. In fact, I even began to think about joining the Navy after I graduated where I would apply to become a cook on a ship. Blynn and I started talking about what we were going to do after high school, and we decided that we would join the Navy together.

CHAPTER 28

SENIOR YEAR

1957-58

My Senior Picture

My senior year was my best school year in every way. I had an English Teacher, Miss Malory, who was able to look past my bad spelling and value my ability to write. She even singled out a couple of my writing assignments. I wrote a paper entitled, "My Dad is a Hot Rodder," a description of Pa and his '39 Packard. I also wrote a paper entitled, "My Brother Is an Only Child," the story of my brother, Dan. She read both papers in front of the class.

I signed up for physics in my senior year and was initially told I could not take the class because I did not have enough math credits to qualify. I talked to Mr. Rice, the physics teacher, and he agreed to let me in the class, but he said I had to do well the first quarter or he would drop me from the course.

I was working at the A&P on the Friday night of our first away football game. After work, Blynn and I picked up Addison and decided to drive to Maumee to go to the McDonalds and see if we could hook up with some of our classmates coming home from the game. When we arrived, we did not see anyone we knew so we got a hamburger and started back to BG. On Route 25, coming home, we came up behind the school band bus going back to the high school. We passed the bus, blowing our horn as we went by. I did not think that we did anything wrong, but on Monday when I went to physics class, Mr. Rice started the class by asking me, "Are you the owner of a green '50 Mercury with a raccoon tail on the rear antenna?" Of course he and everyone in the room knew that was my car so I said, "Yes that's my car." He told me that the band bus driver had complained that I was speeding when I passed the band bus on Friday night, and as the student/teacher coordinator, it was his job to talk to me about my driving. He told me to slow down and be careful when I passed the bus in the future.

Physics turned out to be one of my best classes. One of the assignments that first quarter was for the students to research the planet Mars, and then write a paper describing what life on Mars would be like. He selected the best three papers and read them to the class. After reading these papers, he said, "I have one more that I would like to read. This paper did not make the top three because the spelling is so bad, but the content is as good as any of the other three." He then read my paper.

One of our many experiments that year was building a Van Der Graff Machine. A Van Der Graff Machine generates static electricity. When the machine was operating, a person could hold his hand on the top of the machine and become charged with static electricity. This person could then hold his finger near another person and have the electricity jump to the other person, giving that person an electrical shock.

The physics class was a double class with a break between sessions. The hall would then be filled with students changing classes. A bunch of us in the physics class turned on the Van Der Graff Machine during the break and formed a line, holding hands with the first person placing his hand on the machine. The last person in the line stood just outside of the classroom door, and as students passed by, he pointed his finger near someone (usually an underclassman) and gave him an electrical shock. It didn't take long for the passing students to give the physics room a wider berth on their way to the next class.

We also did an experiment where we demonstrated that sound does not travel in a vacuum. We did this by putting a bell in a large glass bottle, sealing the bottle, and then pumping the air out of the glass jar. When we rang the bell in the vacuum, there was no sound. The experiment was successful and ended in time for the class break. During the break, someone reversed the pump from a vacuum setting to a pressure setting, and the pump started pumping air into the jar. As the class was reconvening, the glass bottle exploded, sending flying glass on the students returning to their seats. Winston Richards, a classmate was struck in the forehead and cut to the point that he needed stitches to close up the wound.

Blynn set me up on a blind date with a girl named Lorena Keller who lived in Moline and was a junior at Lake High School. Lorena was short, tiny, and cute, and easy to talk to. On our first date we went to see *Bridge on the River Kwai*, at the Paramount Theater in Toledo. Lorena was the first girl that I dated steady, and the first girl who invited me to dinner with her family. She also asked me to go to church with her one Sunday so we spent a lot of time together while we were dating. I invited Lorena to our house to meet my parents and have a Sunday dinner. I thought that we were getting along quite well, but after a couple of months, she told me that she wanted to date a boy in her class, and I was back to having an occasional date with girls I knew in school.

Jail House Rock, a movie starring Elvis Presley, came out in November, and Blynn became a big fan of Elvis, and he especially liked the title song from the movie. He attached a speaker to the roof outside his bedroom that he could connect to his stereo. I was picking him up every morning for school at about the same time so he knew when to expect me. Each morning, as I turned on to Ordway Avenue and approached Blynn's house, I could hear Elvis belting out *Jail House Rock* on Blynn's roof-mounted speaker. I often wondered why the neighbors didn't call the police because every morning for a couple of months, this was the way Blynn started his day.

On New Year's Eve, Blynn, Addison, John Montgomery, and I spent the evening at Blynn's house. His parents were gone for the evening, and we had the house to ourselves. John brought a bottle of sweet vermouth that he claimed he shoplifted from the A&P store. Addison brought a six pack of beer, Blynn produced a bottle of whiskey that he had taken from his father's liquor supply, and I brought Coke. We started playing poker, and each of them was drinking the alcohol he had brought with exception of Blynn, who was drinking all three. I was getting teased because I was only drinking Coke. I did taste the vermouth that John brought but I could only wonder why anyone would drink it, not realizing that it was actually just the mix, not a drink. At about 11:00 PM, John said he was going home and he left. We continued to play cards, and at one point, Blynn leaned back onto the back legs of his chair as he adjusted the cards in his hand. He started to say, "I'll bet—," but he never finished the sentence. He fell over backwards, landing on the floor.

Addison and I looked at each other and then we looked down at Blynn. He was still sitting on the overturned chair with his legs being the highest position of his body. His hands were lying on his chest, still holding the cards, his eyes were closed, and he was very still. Addison looked up at me and whispered, "He's faking." Just as I whispered back, "I don't think so," Blynn began to throw up. Vomit erupted out of his mouth and ran down his face, under his glasses, and into the recesses of his eyes and ears. He started to choke as Addison and I knelt beside him and rolled his head to the side to clear his mouth. He stopped vomiting, but he was totally passed out.

We managed to get him and the chair back into a sitting position, but he could not sit on the chair without support from one of us. We did not know when his parents would be home so we decided to clean him up and put him to bed. Now in my life, I had seen my share of people who were drunk, my father, both of my grandfathers, and most of my uncles, but this was the first time I had seen someone so drunk that he totally passed out. Carrying a person who has passed out is like carrying someone without a back bone. No matter how Addison and I got hold of him, we were always dragging an arm or a leg or some part of Blynn's body on the floor.

The stairway to the upstairs was also a real challenge. It had a landing and a turn about four steps up, and I thought that we would surely drop Blynn or at least bang his drooping head on one of the steps before we got him upstairs. Once we got him into the bathroom, we took off his clothes and washed him up as best we could, and we put him in his bed. We took his clothes down to the laundry room in the basement and then cleaned up and mopped the kitchen floor. We checked Blynn one last time and left the house.

The next day when I went over to Blynn's house, neither Blynn nor his parents said one word about the night before. Neither did I.

Louise and Larry announced that they were planning to get married once Larry had completed basic training, and a January 18th date was selected. On Sunday afternoon, January 5, we received a phone call telling us that there had been an accident, and Grandma Dickerson had been killed. My Uncle Corkey was driving his 1954 Kiser with Grandma in the backseat and his wife, Eloise, in the front seat. They were driving north and had stopped for the stop sign at Crissey Road and Route 2, but for some reason, Corkey pulled onto Route 2, directly into the path of an oncoming car. He was struck broadside, and Grandma was thrown from the car and killed instantly, and Corkey and Eloise were in the hospital.

Louise suggested that she postpone the wedding, but Mom insisted she go forward with the plans because it was so close to the 18th date. The wedding did go on as planned, and Louise and Larry were married in the old St. Mark's Lutheran Church on South Enterprise Street in Bowling Green. Louise was married in a white lace wedding dress that she bought with help from Mom and Pa.

At this time, Pa was driving the '49 Packard which was a black, four-door sedan. Grandpa Dickerson was also driving a black, four-door, '49 Packard sedan, and shortly before the wedding, Larry bought a black, four-door, '49 Packard sedan. After the wedding was over, Grandpa Dickerson left to drive back to Toledo. He was only gone a short while when we got a phone call from him asking Pa to pick him up out on Route 25. Something was wrong with his car. Pa and I went out to get Grandpa, and when we got to the car, we could not believe the odor that was coming from under the hood.

Pa opened the hood to discover a large slab of Limburger cheese melting on the exhaust manifold and oozing down between the manifold and the engine block. Apparently, one of Larry's friends had mistaken Grandpa's '49 Packard for Larry's '49 Packard and had put the

Limburger on the manifold of the wrong car. As the engine heated up and the cheese began to melt, the smell became so strong that Grandpa thought that there had to be something seriously wrong with his car. It took awhile to get the melted cheese off the manifold, but Grandpa did finally get on his way. He was not very happy when he left because there was still a strong odor. As Louise and Larry drove off on their honeymoon after the wedding reception, they must have felt very lucky the mistake had been made.

January was a unique time for me. The total shock and sadness of Grandma's death and funeral and Mom's uncontrolled grief, followed by the joy and happiness of Louise's wedding was something that I had not experienced. I had been to funerals and weddings before but as a child. This was the first time I had dealt with either as a near adult. It was also the first time a close family member had died, and it was difficult to watch my mother grieving. At times I felt I needed to do more to ease her pain, but as a teenager I did not realize that just an occasional hug would have been the best way to console her.

Louise and Larry moved to Chicago after the honeymoon as Larry was assigned to O'Hare Field Air force Base. I got back to school, and the confusing feeling of January became easier for me to deal with. But it was still sad at times for Mom. She had lost her mother, and to a certain extent, her oldest daughter all in a two-week span.

Blynn's father had a sudden massive heart attack and died that spring. He was only in his fifties, and Blynn and his mother took his death hard. His name was Harold, but everyone called him Shorty, as he was quite short in height, shorter even than his wife. He worked for Fred Uhlman and was in charge of the warehouse for the Uhlman's Store downtown. He liked to bowl, and he had just bought a new 1958 Ford. I did not know Harold all that well. He never seemed to be too interested in me or any of Blynn's friends, and usually, when I was at Blynn's house, he was sitting in front of the TV.

On the other hand, Blynn's mother, Thelma, was been very friendly with Blynn's friends. She seemed to be happy most of the time and wanted to talk to me whenever I was at the house. She liked to bake so there were often cookies on the table, and her peanut butter cookies were my favorite. She also made peanut butter and jelly sandwiches adding a slice of cheese. The first time she offered me one, I thought the combination sounded strange, but I was surprised how good it tasted.

Late in the school year, an experiment in physics class that went awry involved me directly. Each student in the class had the opportunity to do an extra credit project as long as Mr. Rice approved it. At this time, the United States was in a race with the Russians to put a satellite in orbit around the earth, and to do this, there was often a test firing of various rockets by the US Army and Navy, all of which ended in fiery crashes. I had read in a *Popular Mechanics Magazine* article how to build a model of the Snark rocket, one of the rockets under development by the US Military. I got permission from Mr. Rice to build a rocket as an extra credit project. I built the rocket out of basal wood and bought two solid-fuel model rocket engines and attached them to the wings. I then built a catapult out of wood, powering it with rubber bands, all per the instructions in the magazine. I painted the rocket with model airplane dope and attached all of the USA decals suggested in the article and took the finished product to school. It looked quite impressive; the only question was, "Will it fly?"

Mr. Rice arranged for a bus to take the whole class to the City Park where I set up the catapult and the rocket on the fifty yard line of Bud Gallier Field. The class gathered around as I lit the fuses of the solid fuel rocket engines and pulled the lever of the catapult. The rocket flew off the end of the catapult slide and arched gracefully through the air about thirty feet above the ground, soft smoke trailing slowly behind from the rocket engines. Suddenly, the soft smoke became heavy black smoke, and flames could be seen coming from the wing tips of the rocket as it nosed down toward the ground. A moment later, as the Army and Navy rockets had done before, my rocket contacted the earth in a fiery crash. Darrel Habel was in the physics class, and was also on the staff of the *Scarlet Parrot*, the school newspaper. He wrote a tongue in cheek account of the great rocket launch describing in detail the crash of my rocket.

Mr. Helm taught Industrial Arts and in my senior year he showed up at the start of school with one of the first Volkswagen Beetles seen in Bowling Green. He was always one of the first teachers at school every morning, and his new Beetle was one of the first cars parked on South Grove Street. One day, as I was parking on South Grove Street after picking up Blynn, Addison, and Jack, we encountered a number of other boys, all looking at Mr. Helm's Volkswagen. We talked about the car for a moment, and someone said, "I wonder how much it weighs?" Addison said that he bet between all of us, we could pick it up. We all got a hold of it on the bumpers and on the rocker panels and were surprised to find that we could pick it up. So, on the count of three, we all lifted again and we were able to lift, slide, and scoot, until we had the VW sitting on the sidewalk. We did this a couple of times more before there was a general announcement in school that the parking area along South Grove Street was being watched.

The Industrial Arts Class room was usually quite noisy so an air horn was used to signal the start and end of classes. The problem was that the air horn volume was too loud, so a rag had been stuffed in the horn and tape put over the end of the horn to keep the rag in place. One day, someone in the class removed the tape and the rag, and filled the horn with wood chips, and then put the rag back in place. However, the tape was not reattached to the horn. We all enter the classroom and were taking our seats, and Mr. Helm was sitting at his desk, directly below the air horn. When the horn signaled the start of class, a great shower of wood chips spewed out of the horn and drifted down like snowflakes onto Mr. Helm's head. He sat there staring at us as the wood chips settled on his desk. He never said a word. He just stared straight at us. He eventually told us to go to the metal shop and start working on our metal project.

I did quite well in metal shop that year. I learned to weld using electric arc welding equipment, and I was told by Mr. Helm that I was one of the best welders in the class. However, there were a couple of events that happened that still bother me.

We had a session doing copper relief. We were given a thin sheet of copper and we used a sharpened wooden rod to draw in a design or picture on the copper. We then put the copper sheet on a padded surface and rubbed the copper with a rounded wooden rod to raise portions of the design or picture to give a three dimensional image. I did a profile of the actor James Dean that turned out good enough to be put in the Industrial Arts Display Case for viewing along with four other pieces from the class. I received a number of positive comments from classmates who saw the copper relief in the display case. Once the display was over, Mr. Helm took all of the copper reliefs out of the case and put them on a table in the Industrial Arts room and, he told us we could pick them up after school. When I went to get my relief, I found that someone had obviously hit the raised face of James Dean with something and flattened it out. Since there was no way of knowing who had vandalized my copper relief, nothing was ever done about it.

Shortly after this, we had a session on shaping aluminum with a ball peen hammer. I elected to make a fruit bowl and progressed to the point that I had the upper part of the bowl attached to the pedestal, and I was in the process of finishing the edges and buffing out the surface scratches. One day, Mr. Helm announced that he was selecting three of the projects to take to the State Industrial Arts Show in Columbus. He also indicated that he intended to take my bowl and two others that he still needed to select.

The next day, when I came to class, someone had taken my bowl and bent the sides together and totally ruined the bowl. Mr. Helm tried to find out who had done this, but he never did. In my own mind I had a good idea of who the vandal might be. I had had a number of run-ins with a certain classmate beginning in junior high. He had tried to bully me on a number of occasions, and I had basically either ignored him, or just walked away from him. He was harassing me about my bowl being taken to Columbus, and I responded by saying "Gees, Jim. I never knew you cared that much about me, and I appreciate the fact that you are so worried about what I am doing." The other boys in the area started laughing when I said this, which did not go over well with Jim. I guessed that he was responsible for both the copper relief and the bowl, and I considered confronting him about this. But I also knew that he out-weighed me by about fifty pounds and that he would probably kick my ass if I said anything so I let it go.

One local situation during our senior year bothered us all for a couple of months. An unknown assailant had molested a number of college girls in Bowling Green. Everyone in town wondered who this person could be and some started referring to him as, "Chester the Molester." The local police issued a warning about being out late at night, and all of us were concerned about the possibility that one of the high school girls could be attacked. Then, one of my friends and one of the nicest girls in our class did become a victim, and we were shocked and angry. Something like this had never happened before, and it affected all of us. The police did finally catch him and he turned out to be a college student.

During my senior year, I met a few more girls, and I dated a couple of sophomores and juniors as well as a couple of seniors. None of the dates were serious relationships but more about friendship and having a good time together. I took Le Veta Luce to the Homecoming Dance. Le Veta was a friend throughout high school, and we often were at the same parties and dances. She was easy to know and was always fun to be with.

One Friday night after we got off work at the A&P, Blynn and I picked up Addison, and we headed over to Barbara Janzer's house where a bunch of the senior girls were having a slumber party. Addison was dating one of the girls at the party and he wanted to see her for a few minutes. We ended up being asked to come in for something to eat. At that time Barbara Janzer's father was the Mayor of Bowling Green, and here we were at the Mayor's house, crashing a slumber party. We had to leave at midnight, but we had a great time before we left.

I took Sharon McConnell to the Junior Senior Prom. I met Sharon when I was working at Rappaports with her mother Gladys McConnell, and Sharon and I often talked when she would stop in at the store to see her mother. We went to the prom with Jim Berry and his date, Diana Kithcart. The prom theme was "Roman Triumph" and the Rec Hall was decorated with a fountain and a Roman chariot. The dance lasted until midnight and then we all went to the Cla-Zel to watch the movie *That Certain Feeling* with Debbie Reynolds. After a breakfast, the prom broke-up at about 5:30 AM. We all gathered later in the morning and drove to East Harbor. By the end of the day we were exhausted.

In June, I became the first male descendant of my Grandpa Myerholtz's line to graduate from high School. Until then, none of my uncles or my older male cousins had graduated, and they had all quit school to get jobs. It had been my plan to quit school when I became sixteen, but Mom and Pa insisted that I stay in school and graduate, and I was very glad that I had not quit.

We received our senior yearbooks later that summer. As in most senior yearbooks, there was a quote beside the picture of each senior, describing the person. Beside my picture was written, "Have car, will speed." The incident with the band bus was to be with me every time I opened my yearbook.

Chapter 29

WELCOME TO THE REAL WORLD

FALL OF 1958

The New Me

When I graduated, Ed Richard offered me a fulltime job at Averys working with Pa for $1.15 an hour. When I went into the A&P Store to tell Mr. Reed that I was quitting, he said that he was disappointed because he considered me to be one of the best workers in the store and thought I had the potential to be a store manager someday. I thanked him for his kind words and confidence in me, but I had decided to take the job at Averys so I could be working with my dad.

At that point in time, Averys was still the largest supplier of coal in Wood County and most customers were homeowners who lived in rural areas. When Pa started working for Ed Richard in 1951, Averys sold about 120 car loads of coal a year. When I started working in 1958, the business was still selling about 80 loads annually. Coal was delivered to Averys by the Baltimore and Ohio Railroad in coal cars carrying from forty to sixty tons of coal, depending on the type of coal and the size of the car. Hard coal came from Pennsylvania, and most of the large lump coal and other soft coals came from Kentucky. The coal came from the Patsy, Jewel, and Pocahontas mines.

Averys had a series of large overhead storage bins that each held at least one car of coal. Usually three to four cars of coal were delivered to Averys at a time. The cars were put onto the siding on the east side of the coal bins, with one of the cars positioned over the unloading pit.

The pit was located below the train rails and when the pocket of the coal car was opened, the coal in the car fell into the unloading pit. At the bottom of the pit was a steel chute with a sliding steel door. Under the end of the chute, there was a large steel clam shell bucket that held about three quarters of a ton of coal. The sliding steel door was opened to allow coal to flow from the unloading pit into the bucket. When the bucket was full, the sliding door was closed. The bucket was suspended on a cable system that could lift the bucket out of the pit and up in the air about forty feet to the enclosed area above the storage bins.

Once the bucket was lifted into place, the lifting cable brake was put on, and a second cable system would run the bucket sideways over the bins until it was in position above the right bin. The lifting cable was again used to lower the bucket into the bin and when the bottom of the bucket touched the bottom of the bin or the coal in the bin, a trip lever on the bottom of the bucket opened the clam shell and dumped the coal into the bin.

The bucket was returned to the pit to be refilled and the process continued until the coal car was empty. All of the cables were powered by an electric motor with the control of the cables done through a series of hand levers and foot pedals that Pa operated.

When we unloaded coal cars, I usually was responsible for making sure that the coal was flowing out of the car into the unloading pit. Stoker coal was about one square inch in size so it flowed out of the car quite easily. Hard coal was as slick as glass and flowed the easiest of any coal. Cook stove coal was about three square inches in size and, again, flowed out of the car without too much of a problem. Other coals were larger in lump size and most of the soft coals and the large lump coals needed to be poked and prodded with a steel bar to get the coal out of the car pocket.

During the winter, coal cars could freeze solid, and it was necessary to heat the coal car pockets to thaw out the coal. This was usually done by filling a five gallon bucket with gasoline, placing the bucket under the pocket of the car and lighting off the gasoline. No matter what we did to get the coal to flow out of the car, it usually became necessary to get up into the car, and poke the coal from above the open pocket. The problem was that in doing this, I was standing on the coal that I was trying to get out of the car. Once I poked the lump that was plugging up the pocket, the coal I was standing on started to move also, so I had to scramble to keep from going through the open pocket with the coal.

Another problem in winter was that the pit area was usually filled up with ground water, and depending on the temperature, there were a few inches of ice on the water. It was necessary to lower someone into the pit with a rope to break up the ice so the pit could be pumped dry. Once the water was out of the pit, it was necessary to shovel the ice out of the pit and into the bucket to clean up the pit.

When there was an order for coal, a truck was backed under the proper bin and a sliding door was opened to let the coal out of the bin into the dump box of the truck. I soon learned to judge the approximate weight of the coal in the box because people quite often would order coal a ton or two at a time. Once the coal was in the truck, it was normal to raise the box of the truck just a bit and hose down the coal with a water hose. This was done to reduce the amount of dust during the unloading process. By raising the box, the water would run out of the back of the truck and not affect the weight of the coal. The coal was weighed on the truck scale at the office and then delivered.

Averys had a deal where the coal customers could save fifty cents per ton if they filled up their coal bins during the summer months. Ordinarily bins were in the basement of the homes, and summer fill-ups were for stoker coal. Averys had two small dump trucks that were used to haul coal. Both trucks were equipped with a power take-off cable that connected to a portable coal-belt conveyor which was used to convey the coal from the truck into the customer's coal bin. The conveyor was about fifteen feet long and was carried on a rack attached to the side of the truck. The conveyor weighed about 150 pounds, and it had wheels on the drive end.

One person could handle a conveyor by lifting one end at a time off the rack and pushing the conveyor into place on its wheels; however, it was easier to handle with two people. The power take-off cable was connected to the conveyor, and the conveyor belt was controlled by a hand-throttle and an off-and on-lever located at the rear of the truck. The rear tail gate of the truck had a sliding door, operated by a hand lever that let the coal dump onto the conveyor belt as the truck-box was raised. Again, all of this was arranged so that one person could operate the unloading process. When we filled the bins, it was necessary for one person to be on the truck running the conveyor, while another person was in the bin ensuring that the coal was distributed evenly to fill the bin totally. I was usually the one in the bin. As the bin filled up, I would deflect the coal coming off the conveyor with a scoop shovel to fill in the low spaces and, in some cases, shovel coal as fast as I could to try to keep up with the conveyor. In doing this, it was necessary to lie almost flat on top of the coal as the bin filled up until there was very little room between the coal and ceiling of the bin. When the bin became full, I would bang on the end of the conveyor with the shovel, and Pa would stop the conveyor.

One time Pa did not hear me and continued putting more coal into the bin. I ended up buried in coal, except for my head and the hand that was holding the shovel. He finally realized the situation when coal began backing up onto the conveyor, and he stopped the conveyor. Pa had to come down to the bin and help dig me out of the coal.

Some customer's coal bins were in the garage, and some were in a separate building adjacent to the house, so the conveyor could not always be used to unload the coal. Also, some of the larger lump coal could not be conveyed. When this happened, it was necessary to hand shovel the coal off the truck. In the mid 1950s Tennessee Ernie Ford had a record out entitled, "Sixteen Tons," which told the tale of a coal miner who shoveled sixteen tons of coal a day. I soon found that I could also shovel sixteen tons of coal in a day, and I did so on a number of occasions.

Filling coal bins in the summer was hot, dirty work. Between the sweat and the coal dust, my clothes and any exposed skin were usually coal black. I did not wear a hat so my hair was also black from hauling coal. There was a shower at Averys, and I would shower before I went home, but once I was home, I would usually shower again. I found it was almost impossible to wash the coal dust out of an eyelash. The soap would get in my eye long before the coal was gone from my eyelash. I found the only way I could clean them was by using Brylcreem. This was the hair cream that I used to groom my hair, and I would squeeze a little unto a tissue and then rub my eyelashes with the tissue. The Brylcreem absorbed the coal dust and cleaned my eyelashes without burning my eyes.

One day when we were filling coal bins, Pa pulled into the parking lot of the Whitehouse Hamburger restaurant for a cup of coffee and a donut. At that time, the restaurant was owned by Pa's cousin Harry Wentz, and we had stopped at the restaurant a number of times before, but this was the first time that I was totally black with coal dust. I told Pa that I would wait in the truck because I did not want anyone to see me this dirty. Pa responded, "Get your ass out of this truck, and don't you ever be ashamed of dirt from honest work." I went in with Pa and ate a donut.

One day, just after we had unloaded fifty tons of stoker coal into the overhead bin, I backed one of the coal trucks under the bin and opened the sliding door to fill the truck for a coal delivery. As I slid the bin door open, the door and the door slide broke loose from the bottom of the bin and fell into the truck, followed by as much of the fifty tons of coal in the bin as would flow out unto the truck. As the coal poured out, I managed to scramble out from under the bin, and I took up a position in the driveway in front of the truck.

I am not sure how many tons of coal spilled out of the bin, but when the coal finally stopped running, only the hood ornament of the truck was visible. It took Pa and me a couple of days of shoveling with scoop shovels to move all of the coal away from the truck and empty the bin. We repaired the sliding door, and then we had to load the coal into a dump truck, dump the coal into the track hopper, and use the coal bucket to redeposit the coal into the coal bin. During that event, we handled about 100 tons of coal that never left the coal yard.

Nothing about working at Averys was easy. All of the building materials came into the yard either on semi-trucks or railcars and had to be unloaded by hand. Anything that went out of the yard had to be loaded onto the trucks by hand and again, unloaded by hand at the point of delivery. Bagged materials were in either 100 pound, 70 pound, or 50 pound bags. Bagged product was unloaded into a warehouse, reloaded on a truck for delivery and unloaded at the jobsite. All bagged products were handled three times. Bricks were loaded and unloaded with brick tongs that picked up seven bricks at a time. Sometimes the bricks were delivered and unloaded directly at the jobsite so we only handled the brick once. But if the brick was not delivered directly to the site, we unloaded the brick in the yard, reloaded the brick for delivery, and unloaded the brick at the jobsite, handling the bricks three times also. Roofing material was also unloaded into a warehouse, reloaded for delivery, then unloaded at the job site. Concrete blocks were loaded onto the truck by hand and unloaded from the truck by hand. Because the cement surface of the block was very abrasive, I wore gloves whenever I handled it. However, if I handled block most of the day, it would usually wear a hole in at least one or two fingers of the glove. Once there was a hole in the glove, the block would start to wear away the skin on my finger. If I was not careful, by the end of the day the skin on my finger tips would be worn away and I would have very sore fingers. The only item that was loaded by machine was the sand and stone which were loaded into a dump truck with a front end loader.

We worked eight hour weekdays and four hours on Saturday morning, all at straight-time pay. We also made concrete block in the evenings or worked on car repairs. By the end of the week, I was ready for some fun. However, I was still doing the *Sunday Blade* papers every other weekend which did not leave me much free time.

I had not worked at Averys very long when I had a painful accident. I had lifted a 94 pound bag of cement off the loading dock and was in the process of putting it into the trunk of a customer's car. As I was turning slightly to place the bag in the trunk, I got a sharp pain in my back that caused me to crumble to my knees, still holding the bag of cement. I had pulled or dislocated something in my back, and Pa had to help me back onto my feet. I could walk, but only with a great deal of pain.

Pa took me to the emergency room of Wood County Hospital, and after a brief examination, the doctor indicated I had dislocated my back, and that I would need to check into the hospital and be put in traction until my back was back in place. Pa told the doctor that he would prefer to take me to see Dr. Jones, the local chiropractor. Occasionally, Pa had some back problems and whenever this happened, he would go see Dr. Jones, so he was confident the doctor could help me as well. We went to his office in the Wood County Bank building for my first visit to a chiropractor. Dr. Jones checked me over, put some heating pads on my back for a period of time, and massaged my lower back. He then put me into a position lying on my side with one knee drawn up to my chest. He put one hand on my shoulder and one hand on my hip, and pushed each in an opposite direction. I felt something in my back snap, and the pain was gone. He told me to take a day off, but I could go back to work the next day as long as I took it easy. Instead of spending a couple of weeks in traction in the hospital, I was off work only one day.

Once I started working at Averys, Pa informed me that I would have to pay rent to stay at the house. I was making about fifty-five dollars a week from Averys, plus whatever I made delivering the *Sunday Blade*, making block and working on cars, so he felt that it was only fair that I pay ten dollars a week for my rent. I also decided at that time to get a different car. Pa had been driving a Packard for the last five or six years so I decided to look for a Packard. I traded in the Mercury and bought a 1953 Packard four-door sedan. It was a decent car and it had a very smooth ride, but it did not get very good gas mileage.

The Wood County Fair opened the first week of August as usual, and when Jim Berry called me and asked if I would like to double date with Diane and him, I finally decided to ask Gail Nicely for a date. I had a crush on Gail all through junior high and high school, and I had probably danced more dances with her than any other girl in school. I called and asked if she would like to go to the fair, and she immediately said, "Yes." When we got to the fair, the first thing that we did was ride the Ferris wheel. As we were getting off the ride, I took her hand and helped her down the ramp, and I continued to hold her hand as we started to walk away. We took about three steps when she stopped, raised our still clasped hands, and said, "Oh Dave, do we have to do this?" She told me she was dating a guy named, Jerry. They were quite serious about the relationship and were even talking about getting engaged. She said that she felt it was okay to go to the fair with me because we were such good friends, and she knew Jerry would not object to her spending time with a friend like me. All of my hopes of Gail and romance suddenly crashed to the ground, and I let go of her hand and told her I understood. We had a good time that night, but when Jim dropped me off at home, I felt very sad.

My eighteenth birthday was coming up, and I had never had a birthday party, so I decided to give myself one. I rented the City Park Swimming Pool for a two-hour period starting at eight o'clock in the evening, and I invited a number of my friends to the pool including Blynn, Addie, Jim, Jack, Gail, La Veta, Pat, and my sisters. I think that there were about twenty people in all. After we swam, we partied at one of the shelter houses with pop and chips and such. It was a great time.

Shortly after the party, I took a week off from work and went camping at East Harbor State Park with Blynn and Addison. I had camped quite a bit, but neither Blynn nor Addison had done much. I rented a tent and three cots from BG Rental, and I took Pa's white gas stove and lantern. We spent most of our time on the beach that week and met several girls in the process. I did all of the cooking, and one night after a dinner of hot dogs and pork and beans, we were lying on our cots in our underwear, just horsing around and talking. All of a sudden Addison did something that I had never seen done before. In fact, I did not even know that what he had done was possible. Blynn was equally surprised.

Addison was lying on his back on his cot when he calmly raised one of his legs, reached down with a match, and lit off a very loud fart. The flame that shot through the air was totally surprising and amazing. Blynn and I just looked at each other with our mouths wide-open in disbelief. Then the laughter came. Needless to say, this little bit of scientific experimentation was repeated a number of times that night. In fact, I am surprised that we did not burn down the tent, given that we had eaten pork and beans for supper. I tried to imagine if there would have been any way we could pulled off this demonstration in Physics class.

Late in August, Addison left for college in Nebraska. He had won a football scholarship at Dana College in Omaha. Blynn continued to work at the A&P store, and Jim Berry started his college classes at Bowling Green State University. High school life was over, and we were all dealing with a new and different world.

As Thanksgiving approached, I got word from Addison that he would like to come home for the holidays. He would be out of class from Thanksgiving through the New Year, but he did not have the money to buy a bus ticket. I talked to Blynn, and we decided to drive to Omaha and pick him up. I took a couple of days off work, and we left on a Tuesday morning. We drove all day, arriving at Omaha late that evening. I had a toothache the whole day and was not feeling very well when we arrived.

Addison had offered to help out two girls who were looking for a ride to Chicago. We loaded up everyone in the '53 Packard, and I was glad that the car had a trunk large enough to hold four or five suitcases. As we left Omaha, it started to snow, and it snowed all the way to Chicago. When we dropped the girls off, one of them told us her mother had been concerned that two strange boys from Ohio were driving them home. She had instructed her daughter to put an aspirin tablet between her knees and hold it there until she got home. The girl smiled as she thanked us for the ride home, and told us, "My mother thanks you for being such gentlemen." We all chuckled a bit, as we wondered about the point of this suggestion.

It continued snowing, and when we arrived early in the morning of Thanksgiving Day, we had ten inches of snow on the ground. The toothache had also continued all the way to Bowling Green, and after Thanksgiving, I made an appointment with Dr. Huffman, the dentist who made Mom's false teeth.

After an examination, Dr. Huffman offered me two alternatives. One, I could have him pull two teeth and fill about four others, and he would then make four partial bridges to fill in for the teeth that had already been pulled. The second alternative was to pull all of the remaining teeth that I had and make a full set of dentures. We discussed and compared the costs and the long term affects of the two alternatives, and I decided to have him pull my remaining teeth.

He pulled five teeth that day and had me return one day each week until the remaining teeth were extracted. It was necessary for my jaw, gums and mouth to be totally healed before he started measuring and constructing the replacement dentures. So from mid-December to late-February, I did not have a tooth in my head. I was amazed that in that time, my gums and jaw toughened up to the point that I could eat popcorn without any teeth. With no teeth, I did not go out in public much, but I did go to work every day. I tried to keep my mouth closed as much as possible, and I didn't talk very much when I was with anyone other than family.

After New Years, Addison took a bus back to college, and Blynn decided he was going to join the Navy as we had planned. Blynn and Caroline had recently broken-up, and he took the breakup badly and even sent her the 45 RPM record *Return to Me* by Dean Martin. Since I was in the middle of getting the new teeth, I decided not to join up with him.

The new dentures were finally done in March of 1959, and I looked like a different person. I asked Pa to cut my hair differently which he did. I had been wearing a standard ducktail haircut with the hair on the sides of my head cut long enough to be combed to the back of the head to form a ducktail, and the front part of my hair combed back over the top of my head, much like Elvis combed his hair. With my thin face and slightly bucked old teeth, my face had looked quite long and narrow. The new haircut was what we referred to as a Detroit Haircut, where the ducktails on the sides remained, but the hair on the top of my head was a crew cut, with just enough length on the front to form a small curl on my forehead. With my new teeth I smiled a lot more, and with the new haircut my face appeared wider and fuller. I felt so good about how I looked that I went to Jack Weissbrod's studio and had a new photograph taken.

I also decided to change a couple of other things in my life. I had not been totally satisfied with the '53 Packard that I was driving. It was a good-running car, but it just looked like a car that my grandpa would drive, and I needed to have a car that looked more like what a nineteen-year-old, single male with new teeth would drive. So what car did I get? A 1955 Packard Clipper DeLux, painted two-tone blue-and-white, with a matching interior, and the biggest engine in any car to that time, a 352 cubic inch V8. It was a Packard, but it was a good-looking car. It weighed over two tons, but with that engine it could move fast and smooth. When I remember the '55 Packard, I think that it was probably the best-made car I ever owned.

One other thing that I decided to do was start taking guitar lessons. I had tried for a couple of years to learn how to play the guitar on my own with little or no success. I signed up for lessons at Spratt's music shop. Jack Spratt owned and operated a music shop which offered lessons for playing accordion and guitar, but the shop was mostly geared to selling a new accordion or guitar to whoever was taking lessons. I began using the guitar I had received for Christmas three years earlier. It did not take too long for Jack to convince me that this guitar was not the easiest to play or the best sounding guitar available. I ended up buying a Les Paul Gibson Sun Burst, a hollow-bodied electric guitar with an amplifier. It was beautiful and looked a whole lot better than it sounded when I played it.

Pa decided that he wanted to brick the outside of the Lime Street house and we started by putting in a new foundation around the perimeter of the house. As we began laying the brick, Pa decided to replace all of the old windows which meant that as each window was removed, the opening had to be modified to fit the replacement window. In modifying the window opening, it was necessary to cut out or fill in some of the inside walls. Basically, we tore out most of the old inside walls of the house, and the brick job turned into a major modification of the interior, including new kitchen cupboards. We worked all summer and into the winter before the remodeling and brickwork was completed.

Chapter 30

THE ANDERSONS AND A GIRL NAMED VI

1959-1960-1961

My '56 Lincoln in Front of Anderson Home
Left to right: Ray Anderson, me, Troyl Anderson

The Anderson family was living in the old John Goodman house on the corner of Fifth and Elm Street. Edgar and Jessie Anderson moved to BG a few years before from Kentucky with eight kids: three girls and five boys. Sue was a couple of years older than me, Pat was a year younger than me, and Gail was the same age as my brother, Ray. Troyl, Ray, and Howard were all in high school, and there were two other sons, Bucky and Greg who were about the age of my younger brothers.

I had not become good friends with the Anderson boys because they were younger than me, and I had my friends from high school. With Blynn in the Navy, and Addison and Jim in college, I was pretty much on my own. I started playing baseball with the Anderson boys at the Third

Street ball field in the evenings after work, and I soon started going to the drive-in with Troyl, Ray and Howard on the weekends.

One evening I was with the Andersons, and we stopped at Max's Drive-In on North Main Street for a hamburger and Coke. It was located on North Main Street, and a number of girl carhops took orders and then brought the food out to the cars. We went to the drive-in often enough that we knew all of the girls who worked there. This particular night, the girl who came to our car was working her first night as a car hop. We all thought that she was quite cute, and she had a very strong southern accent.

After I took the Andersons home, I drove back to Max's Drive-In and ordered another Coke to have a chance to talk to the new girl. I found out that her name was Violet, but that she liked to be called Vi, and she was living just outside of Custar. I asked her when she would be working again, and she told me the nights that she worked that week. I told her I would see her the next time she was working. Later that week when I went to Max's, I asked her if she would like to go out on a date some night, and she told me that she couldn't because she was dating a boy from Milton Center, a small town not far from Custar.

The next time I came into the drive-in when Vi was working, she took my order, and when she brought me my hamburger, she asked me if I was still interested in having a date. I replied that I certainly was. She said that I could pick her up at her house on Saturday, but she did not have a phone, so if I changed my mind, I would have to tell her at work.

We went to the Portage Drive-in on our first date and talked a lot during the movie, getting to know each other. She had just turned seventeen and was the oldest of four children in the family, having two sisters and a brother. Her family had moved to Ohio from the Huntington, West Virginia area earlier that year, and she was the first one in the family to find a job. Vi told me that she had quit school at the end of her junior year to get a job to help support the family. When I took her home, I asked her out for the following weekend and she said, "Yes."

I started stopping at Max's Drive-in almost every night, either by myself or with one or all of the Anderson boys, and ordered something to eat. This gave me an excuse to see and talk to Vi without getting her into trouble at work. Vi and I started having at least one date a week and sometimes two on the weekend.

One Saturday morning, my sister Caroline asked me if I would pay her to wash my car. She and her friend Paula had spent the night together at our house, and they were looking to earn some money to go to a movie that night. I usually parked my car along the drive on Fifth Street. The problem with this spot was that it was under the cottonwood tree and starlings roosted in the tree at night so often my car was spotted with bird droppings. I had a date with Vi that night so I told Caroline that I would give them two dollars apiece if they did a good job washing it and cleaning the inside.

I went to work with Pa and left the Packard at home. When I came home from work, the Packard was all washed, but it looked like it had developed a skin rash. Little, round, pale blue spots covered the body. It turned out that in her efforts to make sure that she got the car really clean, Caroline used an SOS pad to scrub off the bird droppings. The SOS pads had also scrubbed off the paint surface at each spot, leaving the car with permanent paint damage. I did pay Caroline for the wash job, but I also had to have the car totally repainted.

I used the excuse of repainting to do a few modifications. I removed the front hood ornament and the Packard name and emblems from the trunk. I also installed a choke wire to the locking device in the trunk and made it possible to open the trunk from inside the car. I bought a set of cruiser skirts, a special set designed for the '57 Mercury that were long and white, for the rear wheel wells. The last thing that I did was install one blue light in each of the front wheel wells so that when I turned on the head lights, a blue light would also light up and show a blue glow in each well behind the front tires. I hired a friend, Bill Smith, to repaint the car in a metallic blue-and-snow white, but not in the same pattern as the original factory two-tone. The top and the area under the chrome on the front fenders of the car were painted white, and the rest of the car was painted blue. With the white cruiser skirts on the back of the car, it really looked sharp!

I started spending all of my free time with either the Anderson boys or with Vi. Most every night I was gone from the house, except when I had to help make block or work on a car. Some nights, I would put fifty miles on the car and never leave BG. I just cruised from the A&W Drive-in on the north end of town to the Big Boy or Silver King Drive-in on the south end of town.

I had lost interest in rabbits, and none of my brothers were interested in being responsible for taking over the rabbit business. I did my best to sell off most of them, but I still had about twenty left. The City of Bowling Green had recently opened a new park in a wooded area off Wintergarden Road. I talked to one of the city officials involved with the park and asked him if it would be alright for me to release my remaining rabbits into the new park, and he told me that I could. I loaded up the rabbits in the trunk of my car, and along with the Anderson boys, I drove out to Wintergarden Park. We lifted each of the rabbits out of the trunk and set them on the ground. We watched as they slowly started to explore the wooded area that was now their home. At first they hopped a few feet away, but kept coming back to the area where the car was parked, but soon they began to stray farther and farther away. Eventually, most of the rabbits had disappeared into the woods and we left. A few days later I drove out to Wintergarden Park, parked the car, and took a short walk into the woods. I was surprised to find that a couple of the rabbits came hopping out of the trees and seemed to recognize me. I spent a few minutes petting the rabbits and when I left, I had seen at least a dozen that I had released. Every few days I would stop by the woods to check on the rabbits, and they seemed to be doing well in their new home.

One day as I drove into the woods, I saw a bloody rabbit lying by the side of the drive. I stopped the car and discovered that the rabbit was dead, and it appeared to have beaten to death. As I walked around the area, I discovered one after another, all of the rabbits that I had released into the woods, had been clubbed to death I concluded that a group of kids had probably come across the very tame rabbits and had decided to kill them all. I went home to get a shovel and returned and carefully buried what was left of my rabbits. I felt sad and responsible. I had hoped by releasing them, the rabbits would enjoy a life of freedom after spending most of their lives in a cage, but all I did was get them slaughtered for no good reason.

The trip to Vi's house was about twenty-five miles one way so each week I was putting a couple of hundred miles on the car. When I was driving home from Vi's house, I usually came into Custar and took Route 281 south to Route 25 into Bowling Green. It was midnight or later when I headed home, and usually I was one of a very few cars on Route 281. The Packard was a big heavy car and speed did not seem to change the way it handled. One night I decided to see what it was like to drive 100 miles per hour. The faster I drove, the more the Packard seemed to smooth out, and when I hit 100 miles per hour, I was amazed that it did not seem that fast. It occurred to me that driving that fast was more of an imagined risk than it was a real risk. I found myself driving 100 miles per hour quite often on my way home late at night. That is, until one night when for some reason, I suddenly panicked about the possibility of a crash and killing myself at that speed. It really bothered me, and I found myself driving at about forty miles per hour. I tried to speed up, but each time I got up to about seventy or eighty, I would start to sweat and get really nervous. I began to feel like I did when I was in catechism and thought about going straight to hell. It took me a few weeks of driving slowly to feel alright about driving a normal speed again. I never did drive 100 miles per hour after that.

My sister, Janet, met a boy from Weston, Ohio named Terry Lashaway, and they began dating and soon were going steady. Janet was still in high school, but Terry was out of school and working. Terry had black hair that he combed in ducktails, and he used a great deal of Brylcreem to keep it in place. He was naturally dark skinned, and he looked like he had a summer tan even in the winter. He and Janet seemed to get along well, but Pa, for some reason, did not warm up to Terry very much. Of course, Pa did not easily warm up to any of the boys dating his daughters. Vi and I double dated with Janet and Terry for a few dates, but it was evident to me that Vi preferred not to double date with anyone. She told me that she felt uncomfortable around other people and preferred to be with me alone.

I had tried to double date with Vi and Jim Berry and his date a couple of times, and each time there were problems. For one thing, when we were with another couple or with members of my family, Vi would not eat anything. She would not eat even when she was invited to our house for dinner. She told me that she just did not like to eat in front of others. Most of our dates were at the drive-in theaters or movie theaters, and when we would stop to get a hamburger, she would just have a Coke. It was a bit of a problem for me that Vi was a member of the Jehovah's

Witness Church and could not dance. I had always liked to dance, and it was not unusual for a bunch of the family, aunts, uncles, and cousins to go to a barn dance on a Saturday night.

Late in the spring, Pa decided that he wanted to have his own garage, so we began building one between our house and Grandpa's house. It was a two-bay wide garage and two cars deep so there was room for two cars to be parked in the rear of the garage and still have room to work on two cars in the front part of the garage. We also built a room in the front corner of one side to have a pool room, and the space on the other side was used for a tool bench and tool storage area. We made the building with concrete block which Pa laid, while my brothers and I mixed the mortar and handed the block to him. The building had a flat roof, with a plan for building an apartment at the second level at some point in the future. We poured the concrete floor and started parking the cars in the garage even before it was totally built.

During the summer and before the start of the August coal fill-ups at Averys, it was necessary to do maintenance on the coal unloading equipment which included the cables and pulleys that raised and lowered the coal bucket. The main problem was the pulleys were about fifty feet in the air, suspended from steel beams between the coal bins. The only way to get to the pulleys was by climbing a vertical ladder on the side of the coal bin up to the roof level at the top of the bin, and then climbing a temporary ladder up to the upper roof of the area, where the coal bucket traveled back and forth above the coal bins. At this level we were about fifty feet in the air. Once on this roof, we laid pieces of plywood across the steel beams that supported the lifting equipment to create a work platform above the pulleys. We walked out on this temporary platform above the pulleys and reached down and hoisted the pulleys up to the platform. We then replaced the bearing and lubricated the pulley shafts. We did all of this without any safety equipment or guard rails on the roof or platform. I think that if the coal bins were still standing, my rusted finger prints would still be imprinted in the steel beam, from my death grip the first time I was up there.

One Saturday night when I was doing the *Sunday Blade* papers with Cap, he asked me if I was considering going to college. I told him that I hadn't thought about it that much because I did not consider myself college material, and I didn't think I could afford to go on my own. I told him I knew that my parents could not afford to help me, and my living at home without paying rent would probably be a financial burden for them since there were five other kids at home. He told me that he thought I should go to college, and he offered to help by paying my way to Bowling Green State University. He told me to talk it over with my parents and let him know what I was going to do.

From the first time I brought it up with Mom and Pa, I could tell that Pa was not in favor of the idea. He was very silent while I told them about Cap's offer to pay my way, and the fact that I would need to live at home while I was in college. Pa told me that he and Mom would not be able to help in any way with money, and that I would have to take care of all of my own expenses. In the days after our first conversation, Pa seemed to be upset with me all the time at work and on a number of occasions, he would say things like, "It never hurt me to work for a living" or "I think that I have done alright for only going to the ninth grade at school." He also implied that it would be a problem for Mr. Richard if I quit Averys to go to college. He would always follow up these statements by saying, "But it doesn't matter to me what you do. You need to do what you think you should do."

I know that he told me that it didn't matter to him, but I could tell that it did matter, and it was clear he did not want me to go to college. I wondered if he was concerned about losing the forty dollars a month that I was paying for rent to live at home, or if he was feeling bad that someone else was offering to pay my way when he could not afford to do so. I also wondered if it was the competition thing that Pa seemed to have with me at times, and if he felt that my going to college was going to make me think I was better than him. I knew that my going to college was going to be a real problem for Pa.

I was starting to wonder where my relationship with Vi was going. She was the first girl that I had dated for more than a couple of months. We were seeing each other at least two nights every weekend, sometimes on a Tuesday or Wednesday night, and sometimes on

Sunday. We spent most of this time together alone at a movie or just driving around. We were both experiencing a serious relationship for the first time, and I think that we both were unsure what would happen next, or for that matter where we wanted the relationship to go. My concerns and feelings for Vi played into my struggle to decide what to do about college. In the end, the questions in my mind concerning Pa's negative response and my relationship with Vi made me feel that going to college was not going to work out. I told Cap that I had decided to keep working and not accept his offer to pay my way to college. I could tell that Cap was disappointed in my answer, but he told me if I changed my mind to let him know.

Sometime that winter I had a problem with the transmission on the Packard which Pa and I were able to repair, but it made me worry about keeping the Packard any longer. The Packard Motor Car Company had been bought out by Studebaker in 1956, and that was the last year that a true Packard was made. Packard parts were starting to be hard to find, and Packard dealerships were disappearing. I traded in the Packard for a 1956 Lincoln. Bumper to bumper, the '56 Lincoln was the longest car ever made to that point. I had become accustomed to a big heavy car while driving the Packard, and I thought that the Lincoln would be a good replacement. I was wrong. The Lincoln was a nice enough car to look at, but it did not ride or handle like the Packard. The Lincoln had a four barrel Holly carburetor which would not hold adjustment so I was constantly readjusting it or rebuilding it. The Packard was never good on gas mileage, but the Lincoln was even worse.

In early spring, I drove the Lincoln to Vi's house for the first time. There was a drop in the temperature, enough so that the roads were starting to ice over. I drove up State Route 281 into Custar where there is a bridge at the east end of town. I guess the longer wheel base of the Lincoln was something that I had not adjusted to and when I slowed down for the bridge, the Lincoln went into a skid, and I ended up crossing the bridge backwards. I was very lucky that there were no other cars on the bridge at that time.

Caroline started dating a guy from Tontogany, Bill Asmus, who had graduated from high school in 1956. He was five years older than Caroline, and she was still a junior in high school. This did not sit well with Pa. However, since Bill was driving a 1959 Ford hard-top convertible, I knew he was okay. Bill was farming the Asmus family farm with his dad, and he was also working part-time for a local building contractor, Walt Siders. Pa and I both knew Walt because he bought most of his supplies from Averys, and we would occasionally see Bill when we delivered materials to the jobsite.

Caroline and Janet both had midnight curfews while they were dating. I did not have a curfew, but I did have to wake up Mom to tell her I was home. Caroline would sometimes come into the house after a date and go upstairs to bed, but she would occasionally crawl out the upstairs window onto the roof, drop down to the ground, walk up the street, and talk to Bill, who had quietly driven up near our house. Other times, Bill would drive by our house after dropping Caroline off, and kick his transmission into neutral and rev the engine just enough to make the Ford engine emit a low rumble. This let Caroline know that he was passing the house. Pa did not like this either, to the point that he took a twelve gauge shot gun shell and removed the B-Bs and loaded the shotless shell into his shotgun. When Bill went by the next time and made the engine rumble as he passed, Pa opened the front door of the house and fired the shotless shell into the air. Needless to say, Bill did not engine-rumble by the house again.

Janet decided that she wanted to marry Terry as soon as school was over, and she and Mom started planning for a June wedding. The plan was that she and Terry would move into a house in Weston. Mom and Pa decided to have the reception at the Lime Street house. We all cleaned up the garage so that tables could be set up inside, with the garage doors open to allow for easy movement in and out of the eating area. This was a good plan as it was quite warm the day of the wedding. Janet wore the same wedding dress that Louise had bought for her wedding, and the service took place at St. Mark's Lutheran Church. The reception turned into quite a party with a lot of beer and other liquor available. The problem with this was that Pa had finally quit drinking and had not had a drink of any sort for a couple of years. With all of the beer and all of the male family members and friends drinking and having a good time, Pa gave in to the urge and joined in the liquid refreshments.

Vi was at the wedding with me and I needed to take her home so when we left, the party was going strong. When I got home, I found that Pa, Bill Asmus, and my Uncle Gordon had all had way too much to drink, and they were sleeping it off in the backyard behind the garage. Mom was so upset with Pa that she had gone to bed and left him passed out outside. Pa decided the drinking had not been worth it, and he never fell off the wagon again.

In July, I took a week off work and went camping in the Smoky Mountains with the Anderson boys. We went to Lookout Mountain and Chattanooga, and we were surprised to see how segregated the south still was at that time. Everywhere we went there were signs of "Whites Only." We saw an area in Chattanooga where the public drinking fountains were marked, "Whites Only" and "Blacks Only" with a "Dogs" sign and water dish located directly below the "Black's Only" fountain. We went to see Ruby Falls at Lookout Mountain and saw a "Blacks Only" waiting room where black tourists had to wait until there were enough people to fill an elevator to be able to go down to another waiting room near the viewing area for the falls. Before the Blacks were allowed to go into the viewing area, all Whites had to be taken to the surface to be sure that no Whites were in the viewing area when the Blacks were there. None of us had ever been exposed to this type of segregation before. It was a real eye-opener.

When we camped in the Smokys, we asked if we could go into a remote area for a few days. The park service allowed us to drive into an area normally used by the Boy Scouts. It was very isolated, and we saw more bears than humans while we were camped there. Each evening about the same time, a number of bears would wander through the campground and look into each trash can at the campsite, and then they would continue on down the mountain, barely taking note of us. At times we had as many as six bears within ten to twenty feet of our tent. After leaving the Smokys we drove to Ash Camp, Kentucky where the grandparents of the Anderson's lived. The Anderson Family had lived in this area before moving to Bowling Green, and all of the kids were born here. To get to the grandparent's house, we had to drive off the main road onto a dirt road, and then onto a lane where we drove through the creek twice before arriving at the house. The house itself was built into the side of the hill, with one end of the porch at the same level as the side of the hill while the other end of the porch was about fifteen feet above the side of the same hill. There was electricity in the house but no running water. Water was hauled to the house from a well located near the up-hill end of the house, and an outhouse was located on the downhill end of the house.

We spent a couple of days there. One morning I took a walk by myself down the hill to the creek, and I followed the creek into a small valley. I came across another man there who asked me if I was, "Singin' in the holler?" I was not sure what he was asking me so I said, "No, I'm just taking a walk," to which he said that he was, "Singin' in the holler." I told him good luck and headed back up the hill. When I got back to the house and told the Andersons about the man I had seen, and my confusion about what he was saying, Ray's grandfather explained it to me. Ginseng grew wild in that area, and that the man was looking for some. The locals all referred to it as "seng," and the man was asking in a strong southern accent if I was *sengin*, or *looking for ginseng.*

When I returned from this trip, I went back to work and back to dating Vi. She told me that she was planning to go back to school in September, and that she would be attending McComb High School. I was pleased because a number of times I had suggested that she go back and finish high school. We were getting along well most of the time, but at the same time we were arguing more about little things. A couple of times I left angry, and Vi told me not to come back. But each time I did go back, and we would makeup and things would seem to settle down. I am not sure what caused the final breakup; I do not remember a specific moment when we decided not to see each other again. I do know that before school started in the fall of 1959, we were no longer dating.

It was obvious that the rest of the family, especially Pa, thought that I had made a real mistake by breaking up with Vi. Everyone liked Vi, and they just assumed that at some point we would get married. I had never had this kind of a relationship before, and I admit that marriage was something that Vi and I had talked about, but every time we did, I came away thinking that I was not ready for marriage. I spent my evenings with Ray, Troyl, and Howard, and I was gone from the house almost every night, but I did not start dating anyone else. I just did not have an interest in dating at that time. I wasn't satisfied with the relationship with Vi, but I also did not want to get involved with another relationship.

I started having health issues with my stomach. I went to the see Dr. Rothe, and he put me on a diet and told me to drink milk and lay off the fried foods. I tried to follow his advice, but I was not very good at staying away from hamburgers and French fries. Suddenly some of my favorite foods were giving me a cramp-like pain in my stomach. I had always loved rhubarb and Mom would often cook up rhubarb sauce for dinner, but now I could not eat rhubarb without getting quite sick very quickly. I also liked sliced cucumbers in vinegar, and Grandma usually had a bowl of these in the refrigerator during the summer, but each time I would eat them I would have problems. Sometimes shortly after eating, I would get so nauseated, I would have to pull the car over to the side of the road. I wondered what was wrong and was afraid it might be something serious.

I was also getting sea sick whenever we went fishing in a boat on Lake Erie. Pa, my Uncle Gordon, and I had been going fishing for perch in Lake Erie for a couple of years, and I had never gotten sea sick anytime before, but now I was getting ill whenever I was in a boat and there was any kind of wave action. I figured that it had something to do with the fact that my stomach was upset almost every day, but I kept telling myself that I would get over this if I just drank enough milk.

Ed Richard and Bill Schuler had agreed to split up the business, with Ed taking sole ownership of the coal and supply yard, and Bill taking sole ownership of the vault company. This was done so that either party could retire and sell his business without impacting the partnership. Not long after this took place, Ed told Pa that he was ready to retire and that he was looking for someone to buy the coal and supply company. Pa immediately talked to the bank to see if there was a way for him to buy the business. The bank was willing to discuss it, and Pa asked me if

I were interested in becoming a part owner of Averys if he could work it out with the bank. I told him I was.

Before Pa could get everything lined up to make Ed an offer, Ed informed us that he had sold the business to Newt Simpson, one of the contractors who did business with Averys. I know that Pa was very disappointed that Ed had not given him the opportunity to make an offer to buy Averys. Pa had seen this as a chance to own his own business and be his own boss, and that chance disappeared before he even had the opportunity to pursue the dream. It was the first time that I could remember feeling the hurt and disappointment that Pa was going through. But once Newt took over the business, Pa was the same committed and hard-working employee that he had been with Ed Richard. Pa was always devoted to his job, and he took pride in being the hardest working person that he could be.

One Saturday night, I was at home playing cards with Mom and Pa, and Caroline and Bill came into the house after their date. I can't remember who my partner was, but we were playing euchre which was Pa's favorite card game. He loved to play the 'horse and pepper' version where a player can play the hand alone.

We were playing a hand that Pa said he would play alone, and my partner and I played against him. He had both bowers and two other trump cards with an ace and queen of the same off-suite. He led out all the trump, and then threw down the ace of the off-suit, and I played the ten of the same suite. When he threw down the queen, he threw it down the way he usually threw down the last winning card so that it spun around as it hit the table. At almost the exact same moment, I threw down the king of the suite so it would spin on the table just like his queen was spinning.

He became instantly angry that I had set him and made some comment about the way I had been playing my cards that night, saying that I wasn't a good card player, I was just lucky. I replied, "I might not play that well, but I played well enough to set you."

Pa was shuffling the cards when I said this, and he threw the cards in my face and yelled, "Go to hell!" I didn't know what to say, I just got out of the house as quickly as I could. I drove away wanting to cry but trying not to. I felt at that point like I had no one who cared about me. I had broken up with Vi, I was worried about my stomach problems, and now my dad had just told me to "Go to hell." I drove around town for what seemed like a long time thinking about where I was going to go to spend the night and telling myself there was no way I could go home.

As I pulled up to the stop sign at the intersection of Haskins Road and West Wooster Street, Pa pulled up beside me, rolled down his window, and told me he was sorry and he asked me to come home. It was the first time I could remember that Pa told me he was sorry, and I felt he really meant it. When I got home Mom was in tears and so was I.

The elections of 1960 took place that fall, and for the first time in my life I became interested in the campaign for President. I had been aware of 'Give 'em Hell Harry Truman' in 1948, and I knew that 'We Needed Adlai Badly' in 1952 and again in 1956, but I didn't really know why. I had never been aware of the real issues involved in a presidential election to the point of knowing what all of the fuss was about. With John Kennedy, I actually listened to some of his speeches and read most of the newspaper articles about him and Richard Nixon. I even watched the television debates and felt that there was no question that John Kennedy was the man who would take his place in history as one of our great presidents. I was disappointed that I was only twenty years old, and too young to vote for him.

One day, Vi stopped in to see Mom and told her that she was going to be in the school play. She invited Mom and Pa to come to see the play. She also told Mom to tell me that she would like for me to come. I rode to the McComb High School with Mom and Pa, and we saw Vi perform. She had an acting role in the comedy, and I was surprised and impressed. After the play we all talked a bit, and before we left, I asked Vi if she would like to go out sometime. We made a date for the following weekend, and Vi and I started dating again. We dated the rest of the winter and into the spring, but we found that we were again arguing about little things. I felt that Vi wanted to get married, and I knew that I was not ready for that. My stomach problems kept me on edge, and I was never sure if I would get sick whenever I ate anything. I also was not totally happy with living at home or with my job at Averys so there were other issues that were bothering me. Vi and I broke up again in the spring.

My stomach problems were getting the best of me, so I went to see Dr. Rothe, and he suggested that I needed to have a series of tests to determine what my real problems were. I had never heard of an Upper GI, but I soon learned what it was. I was given a very distasteful and sticky substance to swallow, and the doctor watched on a scope as this mess of goo went down my throat and into my stomach, all the while I was gagging as I tried to swallow it. I had never heard of a Lower GI either, and I soon learned that this test was even more unpleasant. The doctor gave me what seemed like a five gallon enema and told me to hold it while he took a series of X-rays of my stomach and intestines. To take the X-rays, I needed to lie flat on my back with five gallons of liquid trying to find a way out of my body.

After all of this, the doctor told me I had a stomach ulcer just above the duodenum, and that I would need to go on a strict diet and drink plenty of milk. I was also told that after each meal I had to take a spoon full of a liquid, Maalox, to help coat my stomach during digestion. At that time, it was the belief that a stomach ulcer was caused by emotions or nerves so everyone in the family assumed that I had an ulcer because of the problems with my relationship with Vi.

CHAPTER 31

THE CONVERTIBLE

Sketch by David Myerholtz

My '56 Ford in Front of the Cla-Zel

It was the spring of 1961. My cousin, Barbara, was living in Toledo, and she and her brothers and sisters were going to Libby High School. Barb had a boyfriend, Lee Partin, and he had a 1956 Ford Convertible. Barb called Pa and asked him if he would be willing to put a new set of brakes on Lee's convertible, and Pa said that he would if they brought the car to Bowling Green.

As they were driving into Bowling Green, a dump truck stopped in front of Lee and the brakes were in such bad shape that he was unable to stop, and he ran into the rear of the truck. Neither Barb nor Lee was injured, but the Ford convertible was heavily damaged. Both front fenders, the grill, the front bumper and the hood were all damaged as well as the radiator, the engine fan, and some of the other small engine parts in the front of the car. We towed the car to our house, and a couple of days later, Lee's Insurance Company came to the house to make an inspection to determine how to handle the insurance claim. The adjustor decided that the car was damaged beyond repair and it would be cheaper to pay Lee for the total loss of the car.

I asked the adjustor what was going to happen to the car, and he told me it would be sold to a local junkyard and hauled away. I told him that whatever the junkyard was willing to pay for the car, I would match. He agreed, and I bought the wrecked 1956 Ford convertible for $200.00.

Pa and I towed the Ford up to Averys and put it in the front part of the garage in a spot where we could still get a truck or another car in the garage, and I began removing all of the damaged fenders, hood, and such until I had removed the front end back to the doors of the car. I then removed the engine and transmission and started overhauling both of them. I put new brake shoes on all of the wheels and replaced all of the wheel cylinders.

Once the engine and transmission were rebuilt, I reinstalled them and started to rebuild the front part of the body. I bought new fenders and a new grill, and I bought a used hood and bumper from a junkyard. Other parts for the body and the engine were either purchased as new or as used, depending on the cost. I removed the hood ornament and all of the Ford emblems from the hood, the body, and the trunk and filled in the holes. I spray-painted a coat of primer paint on the body.

During the crash, the padding on the dash was split, so I removed it and installed a new padding. The Ford was originally painted pink-and-black with a black-and-white interior, and I bought a set of custom-made black and white seat covers and recovered all of the seats. I removed the original taillights and modified the mounting to accept the taillight lenses from a 1961 Ford taillight. I hired my friend Bill Smith to paint the car with Ford White paint above the side chrome trim and a Ford Metallic Blue below the side trim. After it was painted, I took the Ford to the Hoffsis Upholstery Shop in Portage, Ohio, and they installed a new, white convertible top.

I then took the Ford to a custom paint shop in Cygnet Ohio, and had them add a little pin-striping to the rear fenders, write the name *Li'l Darling* on each side of the rear fenders just above the chrome and in front of the taillight mounting, and detail *Dave* on the dash just below the radio. I added a new set of white-wall tires and a set of white cruiser fender skirts, and I was ready to take her out on the road. I was the proud owner of a totally rebuilt 1956 Ford convertible.

Shortly after the Ford was completed, I sold the Lincoln and decided to start dating again. I had a few dates with a couple of different girls, but I did not develop any kind of a real relationship. I also started bowling in a bowling league with Caroline's boyfriend, Bill Asmus. Caroline and Bill were getting serious and they were talking about a wedding when she graduated in June.

Caroline had given Bill her class ring, and he wore it on the little finger of his left hand. One day when Bill was working on his father's farm, he was on top of a truck load of sugar beets, rearranging the beets to make sure that they would stay on the truck during the ride to the sugar mill. He leaned over and put his hand on the top of the sideboard of the truck to steady himself as he jumped down from the top of the truck. The ring caught on the edge of the sideboard while Bill was on his way to the ground. The weight of Bill's body basically pulled off most of his little finger. He was taken to Wood County Hospital where they cut off what was left of his finger.

I was still spending most of my free time with Ray, Troyl, and Howard, and I met a number of the girls that they knew from high school. Ray was dating a girl named Jerrie Potter, so I met and came to know her through Ray. Shortly after we met, Jerrie decided to give me a nickname that I did not particularly like, but she seemed to think that it was appropriate. My hair was straw-colored, but not truly blond. I did not wear a hat, and during the summer, the sun would bleach out my hair to the point that it got quite light in color and became more of a true blond shade. I also wore my hair a little long on the sides of my head and when I rode in my convertible with the top down, wind blew from the back of the car to the front of the car and my longer hair would usually be blowing forward. Jerrie decided that a good nickname for me was Goldilocks. Fortunately, she was the only one who liked this nickname or called me by it, so it didn't stick.

Jerrie introduced me to Linda, who lived with her mother in an apartment on South Main Street and was in Jerrie's class. Often I would end up with Jerrie, Ray, Troyl, Howard, and Linda, and we would cruise around Bowling Green in the convertible. One night we were all sitting around in Linda's front yard when Ray and Jerrie had an argument about something. Jerrie came over to me and asked if I would take her away from the house for awhile to let her get herself back together.

As we were walking to the convertible, she asked me if she could drive my car. Up to this point, no girl had been behind the wheel of my convertible, but I thought that it would help her feel better so I said "Yes." We drove around town for about fifteen minutes and talked, until she felt better and wanted to go back to talk with Ray. A fire hydrant stood just off the curb in front of Linda's house. As Jerrie pulled the convertible up to the curb to park, she snagged the right front fender on the large nut holding the cap on the front of the fire hydrant and ripped a hole in the fender from the wheel opening almost back to the door. Jerrie was upset, and I struggled to control my anger, but I did not make an issue of it. I replaced the fender and took the car back to Bill Smith for a repaint and a few days later I was back on the road.

I spent some time with Linda, but it was strictly as friends. She had recently broken up from a long relationship and I was not seriously looking for a relationship. Linda had a different way of looking at things and sometimes I was not sure that I totally understood her reasoning or her mood, but she was usually fun to be with, and we both understood that there were no strings attached.

One day Linda and I were driving to Port Clinton to spend a Saturday afternoon with Jerrie Potter who was staying at her parent's vacation home. As we were driving along at about sixty miles an hour, we had a disagreement about something, and Linda became upset. She reached over to the car keys, pulled them out of the key slot, and threw the keys into the ditch. I stopped the car as quickly as I could and walked back up the road to where I thought we were when she threw the keys. After a bit of searching, I was able to find them in the ditch, and we continued our trip. Linda never mentioned the incident and acted as if nothing had happened. Like I said, I did not always understand Linda.

Another girl that I met through Ray and Jerrie was Tammy, who was also in Jerrie's class in high school. I dated Tammy off and on at the end of school and into the summer a bit, but again, it was more as a friend than as a serious relationship.

The good news was that I seemed to be doing better with my diet, and I was not having all of the problems that I had been having with my stomach. The time I spent working on the convertible took my mind off the situations I had been worried about, and I know I was paying better attention to what I was eating. I was also involved with another project that occupied some of my time; I was making a ring.

My Uncle Harmie made a ring, and when he showed it to me, I immediately wanted to make one for myself. He was involved with a project at LOF that included a certain kind of steel nut and bolt. The nuts and bolts were made of a special cadmium stainless steel which would not rust, and when polished, gave a high luster to the steel surface. Harmie had made his ring from one of the nuts, and when I said I wanted to make one for myself, he gave me one of the special nuts.

I first bored out the threads to make the hole the size of my finger. I then started grinding off five of the six flat surfaces of the hex-head nut, leaving one of the flats for the ring surface. Once I had ground the nut into a circular shape with one flat surface, I smoothed and polished the ring with emery cloth. I had not purchased a class ring when I was in high school because of the cost and I had never had a ring until I made this one. It was very special to me.

Caroline and Bill were planning a summer wedding. I was somewhat surprised when Bill Asmus ask me to be the best man, but I felt good that Bill considered me to be that kind of friend. Bill and I had been bowling and hunting together, and we spent a lot of time with Pa. But all of this had taken place after he met Caroline.

The wedding was held in St. Paul's Lutheran Church in Haskins with the reception at the American Legion Hall in Tontogany. Caroline wore the same dress that Louise and Janet had worn for their weddings. I went to the wedding stag and because of my stomach problems and my diet, I was not drinking anything alcoholic. Almost everyone else at the wedding was drinking, including a married woman that I had never met before that night. I did not know her name, but everyone called her Cookie. I had just finished dancing with Louise when I was grabbed by the arm by Cookie and she told me that she had the next dance. As we were dancing, she asked me if I was interested in stepping outside to get a little fresh air. I'm not sure what I said at that point, but she made it quite clear that she thought that we could have a better time in the parking lot than we could on the dance floor. I joked about her suggestion as the dance was ending, and I led her off the floor and over to the table where her husband was sitting. A little later, I was beginning to get a little warm so I went into the coat room to hang up my Tux jacket, and as I started to leave, Cookie came into the room and closed the door. She put her arms around my neck and told me that she was going to have a good time that night one way or another. I told her that I did not think that her husband would agree that this was a good time. She said that he was so drunk he would not know. I pulled away from her and said that I would know, and she needed to find someone else to have a good time with. I avoided the coat room and any other tight space the rest of the night, and I made sure that I always had a dance partner.

I met a girl named Evelyn just before the end of the school year. She was also in the same class as Jerrie and some of the other girls that I had been dating or seeing. I had talked to her a few times during the early summer, and I had occasionally been able to pick her up after a movie or when I saw her downtown. We would get a burger or just ride around town for a bit, but she always seemed to have other plans whenever I would ask her out. I kept asking, and it was mid-summer before we actually had a date. About a week later I left on vacation with the Anderson boys.

We drove down to see the Anderson's grandparents in Kentucky and spent a few days there. We than drove over to Front Royal, Virginia and onto the Blue Ridge Parkway and followed it to the Smoky Mountains where we camped for a few days.

Two things had a real effect on me on this trip. First, I had just bought a new camera, and I was taking pictures of everything. One day as we were driving on the Blue Ridge Parkway, we spotted a small heard of deer feeding on the hillside above the road. I pulled over at a scenic view parking area and walked back up the road to where the deer were feeding. I decided to see if I could sneak up the hill undetected to get a close-up shot of the deer. I checked the wind and started making my way as quietly as I could, keeping myself downwind of the deer. I moved very slowly and whenever a deer would look up at me, I would stand still and wait until the deer started feeding. Then I would carefully move again. After about twenty minutes, I found myself less than ten feet from the nearest deer. I took a number of pictures, and I sat there for a few minutes, just watching. Every now and then, a deer would stop and look directly at me for a few seconds but then go back to eating the grass. I had never been this close to an animal in the wild, and I had never been able to sit and watch a wild animal just being a wild animal. After awhile I slowly moved away down the hill and the deer went on feeding. Afterwards, I could not get the image of those very large, brown eyes out of my mind. Moving up the hill, taking pictures, and just sitting and watching the deer, was a far more exciting experience than I ever had when I was hunting. Being almost face-to-face with a wild animal in his world and looking into his eyes, I knew that I could never shoot a wild animal again.

We drove most of this trip with the convertible top down. Driving through the mountains with the blue skies and the green tree canopies overhead, and just being able to see in any direction without any obstruction from the car roof and door frames, made every view spectacular. I had really enjoyed having a convertible, but after the drive on the Blue Ridge Parkway, I loved having a convertible.

When I got back from vacation, I called Evelyn and asked her for a date, and she told me she was dating someone else. Whenever I would see her, she was always very friendly and she flirted around with me, but try as I would, she was always busy when I asked her for a date.

Chapter 32

A NEW GIRL IN TOWN

FALL OF '61

Christmas 1961
Nancy and me

I turned twenty-one on August 12, 1961 and I was not dating anyone. I was working at Averys in a job that I did not want to do for the rest of my life and I had an ulcer. My life was about to change. Just before Labor Day, I was driving on South Church Street making a delivery in an Averys pick-up truck, when I saw Jerrie walking up the street with a girl that I did not recognize.

I pulled over to the curb and rolled down the window to talk to Jerrie. She was now a junior and still dating Ray who had graduated in June. She introduced me to the girl she was with and told me that Nancy had just moved to Bowling Green from Okemos, Michigan.

A week or so later Ray and I were driving around one evening, and we saw Jerrie and Nancy walking downtown. We picked them up and Ray got in the back seat with Jerrie and Nancy sat in the front with me. We went to the Big Boy and had burgers and just sat and talked. I noticed that Nancy was attractive, tall, slender, and easy to talk with, but I was still trying to get a date with Evelyn and not thinking of finding someone else. However, at some point Ray and I made plans to drive Jerrie and Nancy to Friday night's football game at Norwalk.

That Friday, I took my brother Ray with me as one of the boys for the first time. Ray was a freshman that year, and I thought he was old enough to run around with the Andersons and me. We picked up Ray, Troyl, and Howard, and then Jerrie at her house. She directed us to Nancy's house on South Church Street and we left for the game.

Nancy sat in the backseat with my brother Ray, Troyl, and Howard, and Jerrie, Ray and I sat in the front. It was the first time that Nancy had met Howard, Troyl and my brother Ray, but she seemed quite at ease with all of them. At the game, she sat beside Jerrie and Howard so I did not have a chance to talk to her. After the game, it was apparent that Howard had a crush on Nancy and I thought Nancy liked him too.

One day the following week, I saw Jerrie when she was alone, and she told me that there was someone who would like to have a date with me, and I immediately asked "Is it Nancy?" and she answered "Yes." I had been thinking about asking her for a date, but I also knew that Howard was talking about doing the same thing, and I did not want to get in his way. Knowing that Nancy was interested in me made it easier to tell Howard that I was going to ask her out. On Tuesday, Nancy and Jerrie skipped Rec Hall and we all rode around. I asked her for a date the following Saturday, and she said, "Yes."

On Friday, the four of us, Jerrie, Ray, Nancy, and I went to the football game and then bowling. On Saturday, I took Nancy to the Valentine Theater in Toledo for our first date, and we saw the movie, *Fanny*. During the next week, I saw Nancy several times. She and Jerrie stopped up at Averys one evening and on Thursday night, they came to the bowling alley where we were bowling in tournaments. On Saturday we had our second date; we saw the movie, *Come September* and went bowling afterwards. The following week, we saw each other Tuesday night, went to the game on Friday night, and Saturday there was a hayride party at the Anderson's for Ray Anderson's birthday. With each date I knew that I was feeling more and more comfortable being with Nancy, and the relationship seemed easy and natural and on the night of the hayride, I gave her the record, *Don't Blame Me* by the Everly Brothers. To me it was not love at first sight, but it was very close to that. We were seeing each other two to three times a week, and when I was not with her, or talking to her on the phone, I was thinking about her. On October 10, I asked Nancy not to date anyone else, and she agreed.

I had met Nancy's parents on our first date when I picked her up at her house. Her father, Ed, had taken a job as Manager of the Massey Ferguson Farm Implement Store which was located just north of town on Route 25. Ed seemed friendly enough when I first met him, but we only talked briefly. Her mother, Margaret, was a teacher and I don't recall her smiling or saying much to me that first meeting. I remember that I felt she was a little cool about my dating her daughter.

I always tried to be very friendly and polite, and I called them Mr. or Mrs. Miller whenever I spoke to them. I was hoping to show her parents that I was okay and that given the chance, they might find me to be someone they could trust and grow to like. Ed did warm up a bit and was more inclined to talk to me when I was there to pick up Nancy, and I got to the point that I called him Ed. But Margaret did not warm up and spoke to me only on occasion. I continued to call her Mrs. Miller as she seemed to prefer that formality.

I also met the rest of the Miller family. Nancy's sister, Sue, was one year younger than Nancy. Nancy and Sue did not look like they were sisters. Nancy was tall with dark brown hair and a slim face. She looked very much like her father's side of the family, including a dimple in her chin. Sue was shorter, with very blond hair and a round face, and she looked very much like her mother. Larry, who was in my brother Ray's freshman class, was the oldest son, and he looked like his dad. Bill was the youngest son, and like Sue, resembled his mother's side of the family. Bill was quite tall; in fact, he was taller than me, and he was only twelve years old and in the same grade as my brother, Art. Ann was the youngest member of the family. She was five years old and a very cute little girl.

On October 12, as I was driving down Main Street, I saw Evelyn walking on the sidewalk, and she waved at me. I drove around the block and pulled up to the curb beside her, and we started talking. We decide to go get a Coke and continued to talk. She told me that she would very much like to date me and that she hoped that I still wanted to date her. We drove over to the city park and parked.

After I took Evelyn home, I could only think of Nancy and how badly I had just screwed up. I did not sleep well that night and the next day, it was obvious that Nancy knew what had happened the night before. We talked about what I had done, and she was hurt and disappointed. I told Nancy that I now knew how much I really wanted to be with her. I asked her to forgive me and she did, and we agreed that we were committed to each other and would not date anyone else. I took my handmade ring into Klever's Jewelry Store to have it initialed, and gave it to Nancy the next day. Nancy gave me her Okemos class ring, and I wore it on the little finger of my left hand, despite what had happened to Bill Asmus's finger when he wore my sister's ring.

Nancy's parents were not pleased that she was dating me. They did not like the fact that I was over twenty-one or the fact that I had not gone to college. They did not like it that we were seeing each other a couple of times a week, and that I was the first and only boy Nancy had dated since moving to Bowling Green. They thought that she was limiting herself socially by not seeing high school boys. They finally told Nancy that she could have only one date a week with me and that she needed to see other boys and do other school-related activities. Nancy and I continued to date that one official time a week with me picking her up at her house and talking briefly to her parents. But during the rest of the week we managed to find ways to see each other. Tuesday night was still Rec Hall night at the High School and Nancy would usually go with Jerrie or with her sister, Sue. I would show up, sometimes with Ray Anderson and sometimes by myself, and Nancy and I would go out for a Coke, or we would all ride around in the convertible until it was time for Nancy to be home when the Rec Hall closed at 9:00 PM.

I would park the car on South Church Street and walk Nancy part of the way home, stopping under the Maple tree in front of the Shuck House on the corner of South Church and Pearl Streets to have a goodnight kiss. Nancy would walk the rest of the way home, and I would go back to my car and wait until she was in the house, and then I would drive slowly passed the house, put the Ford in neutral, and rev the engine slightly as a final goodnight as I went by. Every Thursday night I bowled with Bill Asmus in the Industrial League at The Al-Mar Bowling Alley. Al Stevens had sold the bowling alley to Bob and Ann Brim, and they kept the name Al-Mar Lanes. Our leagues started at 6:30 PM, and we were done before the next league started at 9:00. Quite often Nancy would show up at the bowling alley, either with Jerrie or Sue or by herself, and watch part of the games. When the bowling was over, we would go somewhere for a short period of time before I would again walk her part way home for our goodnight kiss under the Maple tree, and then I would drive by her house for the engine-rev final goodnight. I often wondered if her parents ever connected the fact that shortly after the time Nancy came into the house on a weekday night, a car would go by the house and rev its engine.

We would see each other when and wherever we could. Nancy would call me to meet her somewhere, or she would be with Jerrie and they would stop by my house or even come up to Averys if I was working that night with Pa. I was amazed that her parents did not seem to question where she was or what she was doing. On a couple of occasions we were driving down Main Street in Bowling Green with the top down on the convertible, and we passed Nancy's dad driving somewhere, and he never seemed to notice us. We were supposed to be having only one date a week, and we were seeing each other about four times a week. Our relationship soon became serious, and we started talking about marriage by early November.

I was finally invited to Nancy's house for Sunday dinner one day. I can't remember what the occasion was, I only know that it was the first time that I was invited, and everyone seemed to be in a very good mood especially when it was time for dessert. Nancy said with a great deal of excitement in her voice that they were having a family favorite for dessert, rhubarb pie. Now remember, at this time I had an ulcer and I have already shared that the one thing that made me very sick very quickly was rhubarb! However, I knew I had to eat a piece of pie. I could feel the sweat running down the back of my neck as I took the first bite. I slowly finished eating every bite of the pie, and once we were finished eating, I suggested to Nancy that we take a walk. As it turned out I was okay, but I can remember saying to Nancy as we left the house, "If you ever have any doubts about my loving you, just remember that I ate a piece of rhubarb pie for you."

Early in December, Nancy's parents discovered that we were going steady. Up to this point, she had not mentioned it to them and wore my ring on a chain as a necklace often hidden beneath her clothes. They were very upset and told her to give the ring back, get her ring back, and never date me again. Nancy agreed to exchange back the rings, but she also told her parents that we would find a way to see each other if they forbid it. Nancy gave me two little angora octopuses, one was white and one was blue. Strings of angora yarn covered small rubber balls and the tentacles were made by braiding the yarn. It was something girls were doing and guys attached them to their rearview mirrors. She put an heirloom topaz ring around the neck of the octopus since I had to give back her class ring, and we continued to see each other whenever we could.

When Christmastime came, my parents invited Nancy to our family gathering and they gave her a pair of red gloves. I gave Nancy a very large stuffed dog and a picture of myself. On the back of the picture I had written words from the record I had given her early in October, "Don't blame me, for falling in love with you." Nancy and I started 1962 together and committed to each other.

CHAPTER 33

I CAN'T FIND A PULSE!

1962

Grandma and Grandpa Myerholtz's 50th Anniversary

Back Row Left to Right: Esty, Irene, Pa, Anna Mae, Harmie

Front Row; Left to Right: Gusty, Lois, Grandpa,
Grandma, Bob, Carrie

One late winter day after the first of the year, Larry and Louise were visiting. Pa and I were delivering coal to a customer, and Larry had elected to go with Pa and me on the coal delivery. There was about a foot of snow on the ground as Pa and I started to take the coal conveyor off the truck. I had the front end of the conveyor, and Pa had just bent over to lift the heavy end of the conveyor off the carrier. All at once, we were all startled when a large collie dog came running up and mounted Pa from behind and started humping away.

At this point Pa was standing bent over in a foot of snow holding at least ninety pounds of conveyor in his hands, and a dog was locked onto his waist with his front legs and getting as much traction as he could with his back legs to accomplish his goal. Pa tried to shake off the dog, and I was trying as hard as I could to hold my end of the conveyor and keep my footing in the snow, all the while laughing at the site in front of me. Larry had actually fallen down in the snow laughing as hard as he could while telling Pa, "Just stick him on the end of the conveyor and let him ride it out."

Pa was finally able to set down his end of the conveyor and get the dog off him. But the minute that Pa tried to pick up the conveyor again, the dog nailed him again. The owner of the dog finally came out and took the dog into the house, chuckling as he tried to apologize to Pa. I can't remember ever witnessing such a funny scene, even in the movies, as that day when a collie dog got amorous with Pa.

Nancy and I were dating and seeing each other as much as we could with her parents still trying to limit the amount of time that we spent together. We quite often had to sneak a time together and sometimes our meeting only lasted a few minutes, but we both seemed to need that few minutes to get through the rest of the day. When spring came Nancy bought matching short sleeve shirts for us. One day Nancy's sister, Sue, decided to wear Nancy's new shirt to school. This did not sit well with Nancy. I only heard what she told me, but Sue learned that the one article of Nancy's clothing that she could not wear was the "Her" shirt.

In late spring, I took Nancy fishing with me and the Anderson boys at Wier's Rapids on the Maumee River. Nancy had never been fishing before, and she seemed quite eager to learn how to cast a fishing rod. I stood behind her and held the back of her hand as she held the fishing rod and brought it back over her shoulder. I told her to bring her arm back a bit farther, and then flip the rod forward from the elbow and cast the line out in front of her. She followed my directions quite closely and snapped her arm forward to cast out the line. The problem was that when she brought her arm a little farther backwards, she ended up with the fishing line and the fish hook dangling quite close to the back of my neck as I was standing behind her. When she did move her arm forward, the hook embedded itself in the skin on the back of my neck. Between Nancy and Ray, they were able to get the hook out of my neck without doing too much damage. I told Nancy that she had successfully hooked and caught me so she had to keep me.

One Saturday night I took Nancy square dancing with other members of my family. My family had been square dancing for quite a number of years and square dancing was part of every family party and wedding. When I say "my family," I am referring to my immediate family as well as aunts, uncles, and cousins. We would usually have at least one square and sometimes two squares or eight couples. Nancy had square danced in school activities, but she had never experienced square dancing with the Myerholtz Family. A number of the men in the family liked to swing their partner off her feet, and since Nancy was new to the group she spent more time hanging on for dear life as they all tried to swing her off her feet.

In one particular square dance, the Myerholtz men always did some improvising to the standard calls of the dance. The caller would call out "All four men in the center back to back, and the ladies walk around the outside track." When this was called and all of the men were standing back to back, one or two of the Myerholtz men would poke or pinch the behind of the person standing behind them and before too long, every man was either poking or pinching or trying to avoid such touching so that there was a bit of chaos while the ladies walked around the outside track. Nancy, who had led a rather sheltered life, did not know quite what to make of all of this, but she did enjoy the dancing and she was a really good square dancer. Nancy and I danced most every dance that was played, whether it was a square dance, a jitter-bug or slow-dance. But I liked it best when we were slow dancing. We were close in height so we fit together nicely. We seemed to flow easily as we danced around the floor.

As mentioned earlier, Nancy had made two octopuses that were hanging from my car rearview mirror. The octopus that held her ring disappeared in March. We had parked on Main Street across from the Cla-Zel with the top of my convertible down. While we were gone from the car someone ripped her octopus off the rearview mirror and took it and her grandmother's heirloom ring with it. She was very upset about it, and so was I but there was nothing we could do.

When school ended in June, Nancy was going to Alpena, Michigan with some of her friends from Okemos High School. We talked about the possibility of me driving up to Alpena to visit during the time that she would be there. Her parents heard about our plan and made it clear that I was not to get even close to Alpena so I didn't. But I did send her a letter each day, and we had a couple of phone calls while she was there.

One evening Vi stopped by our house. When she arrived, she said that she wanted to see Mom so I went out to the garage to the pool room and started playing pool. I was there about fifteen minutes when Vi came into the room and told me that she had stopped to invite Mom and Pa to her wedding later that summer. She said that she would like to invite me also. I told her that I did not think that was a good idea. I was sure that her future husband would not approve since I didn't think I would be happy about my future wife asking her old boy friend to our wedding. I told her that I hoped she would be very happy and wished her good luck with the rest of her life. We said good-bye and she left.

That summer was typical for most of June and July as I was playing soft ball in the church league for St. Marks, I was seeing Nancy as much as I could, and we spent a lot of the time at the Portage Drive-in. When I wasn't with Nancy, I was with the Anderson boys. My Grandma and Grandpa Myerholtz were planning their fiftieth anniversary for August 16th and a full blown Myerholtz Family reunion was being planned for the weekend of that week. I was looking forward to seeing all of my cousins. I had not seen a number of them in years since they had married and were living in other parts of the country.

In a two-day period near the end of July, a number of things happened to me that may or may not have had a bearing on what resulted in a major health crisis for me. First of all, one evening when I was at Nancy's house, I was eating potato chips and got one of them caught in my throat and I began to choke a bit. After a few minutes, I seemed to be fine. The next event occurred the following morning. I was working at Averys, and Pa and I were doing some repair to the roof of the overhead coal bins. I was using a pulley and a rope to haul roofing material up to the top of the coal bin when I lost my grip on the rope and the roofing started to fall back. As I regained my grip, the weight of the falling roofing jerked me off my feet momentarily, but my weight eventually allowed me to regain control of the rope and the roofing. The last event happened later in the day. I had to go into Toledo to pick up a load of plaster and other building materials, and as I was coming home, a sudden thunder storm blew in. I had to pull over to the side of the road and put a canvas on the load to keep it from getting wet. As I was trying to tie down the canvas on the truck, a strong gust of wind hit the canvas, and it lifted me off the ground and slammed me into the side of the truck as I held on to the canvas. When I got back to Averys, it was just about quitting time, and I remember that I told Pa I might have pulled something in my shoulder because I was feeling some pain there.

After supper I was in a great deal of pain, and Pa finally took me out to the emergency room at Wood County Hospital to have my shoulder examined. The doctor in the emergency room told me that I appeared to have some pleurisy in my left lung, and he suggested that I go home and put a heating pad on my back and I should be fine in a couple of days. I tried to go to bed with a heating pad, but whenever I lay down flat on the bed, the pain in my chest became almost unbearable. I finally got to sleep by sitting upright in the recliner in the living room. I slept off-and-on until about 6:00 AM. I was feeling very weak and as I staggered into Mom and Pa's bedroom to get to the bathroom, I passed out and fell onto the end of their bed. The next thing I can remember is being loaded into an ambulance with Mom crying and Pa telling the driver what had happened. In the ambulance, I took out my teeth because my stomach was so upset and I worried I would be sick and an oxygen mask was placed over my mouth.

As we came into the emergency room, the first person that I saw was a friend of mine named Grace who was a nurse in training at the hospital. She came over to me and started to take my pulse. I heard her say to the head nurse who was also working on me, "I can't find a pulse, I can't find a pulse." I wanted to tell her that I could hear her and reassure her that I was alive, but I had the oxygen mask on, and I could not talk. The nurses finally decided that I did have a pulse and took me up for X-rays. Later in the day, Dr. Janney came into the room where Mom and I were and he told us that my left lung had collapsed and that it had a tear in the lining. I had bled into the lung, and he indicated that they were going to tap my lung and drain off the blood and fluid. Then they would re-inflate the lung.

After my lung had been drained, trying to re-inflate it was accomplished by having me blow into a machine and having the machine blow into my mouth. The lung did not inflate, and I was in Wood County Hospital for almost a week with a collapsed lung. I was getting shots for the pain, and I was barely eating anything and nothing that they did seemed to help.

When I am sick, I look really bad. The main problem is I am pale anyway, and I tend to lose most of what color I have and end up with a gray, corpse-like cast to my skin. Also, this time, I had to be hooked up to oxygen, so I could not have my teeth in my mouth which made my face look sunken. So everyone that came to see me in the hospital left with the impression that I really looked awful. Even Nancy could not hide the concern on her face when she saw me for the first time. I remember that when Ray and Troyl came to see me, Troyl cried. He thought that I was dead or at least near death.

Dr. Janney eventually told Mom that he had called in a lung specialist from Toledo to come and examine me for a second opinion, and he felt I would probably be transferred to a Toledo Hospital for surgery to remove my left lung.

Dr. Hal McClain, the lung specialist, had an impressive appearance. When he arrived, I was flat on my back in a hospital bed. I looked up to see a seven-foot-tall doctor dressed in hospital white, towering above me. He was overpowering. He reviewed the X-rays and examined me. He then told Mom and me that he did not know what we had been told to this point, but he was going to have me transferred to St. Vincent Hospital in Toledo. I would not lose my lung, and he assured us that he would have me back on my feet in a couple of weeks. He left, ducking his head as he walked through the doorway and out of the room.

Later that day, I took an ambulance ride to St. Vincent Hospital. I was glad Dr. McClain was going to be able to save my lung, but I was not prepared for what I had to go through to make that happen. A tube was inserted into my lung, and I was given a shot for pain as well as a local anesthetic. Then an air pump of some sort was hooked to the tube in my lung. When the pump was turned on, the lung was pressurized and depressurized to simulate breathing. The initial pain was almost more than I could bear, and the rapid rate of the simulated breathing was hard for me to keep up with. I felt like I was gasping for a breath that would never come. I looked at Mom who was holding my hand through all of this, and the tears were streaming down her face.

After a short time that seemed like forever, the pain started to ease as did the breathing, and I settled into the rhythm of the machine. Dr. McCain told me that one of the reasons this was so painful was the fact that the lung had been deflated for more than a week, and the tissue had temporarily lost some flexibility. After a couple of days, I was breathing on my own, and my lung seemed to be functioning fine. When I came into the hospital I weighed just about 150 pounds and I now weighed 118 pounds. I was just skin and bones when I returned home. I spent a total of two weeks in St. Vincent Hospital before they let me go home.

Nancy came everyday to visit me when I was in Wood County Hospital even though her parents had told her not to come. One reason they gave was that they were concerned that I might have a serious lung disease. However, when I was transferred to Toledo, they did let her come with Mom and Pa a couple of times.

One of my biggest disappointments was missing the fiftieth anniversary of my grandparents and the reunion of all of my cousins. I believe they were all there. However, Nancy was able to get away long enough to attend the main party for a little while and meet some of my relatives.

Once I was home, I had to rest most of the time, and little by little I started to get some exercise. I had to eat and eat to try to get my weight back. I started walking down Lime Street to Wooster Street, and I would stop at the Dairy Queen to get a double chocolate milk shake as part of my weight therapy. The best part of this was that Bill Asmus's sister, June, worked at the Dairy Queen, and when I would give her a $1.00 for a fifty-cent milk shake, she would give me four quarters in change. Nancy came almost daily after school to see me before she would go home, and once I was strong enough, we started going out again.

It was the middle of October when Dr. McClain said I could go back to work and continue my normal life. I asked him if he had any thought about what might have caused the collapse of my lung, and I reminded him of the events that had happened in the days beforehand. He told me those things might have contributed to my problem, but he believed that it was a classic spontaneous pneumothorax which meant the lung just collapsed on its own without any direct cause. But he did indicate that he had written the collapse up as a work-related injury so Ohio Workmen Compensation would pay for the hospital and the doctor, and I would get some portion of my pay. I asked him what I needed to do to ensure that it didn't happen again, and he told me that since I was a non-smoker, I did not have to worry about anything with my lung. He said that I should just live my normal life and I would be fine. As I was leaving his office, he said, "Oh by the way, you will never be drafted."

Chapter 34
UNCLE SAM WANTS YOU?

Nancy, Me, and Sue in Front of '56 Ford Convertible
at Ohio Caverns

(Ray Anderson was taking the picture)

All through November and December, I ate to gain weight and slowly got myself back in working shape. I was also seeing and spending as much time with Nancy as I could. On Christmas Eve we celebrated Christmas at my house, and I gave Nancy a musical jewelry box and necklace with a small pearl and a smaller diamond in a half-moon white-gold setting. Then we went to the Christmas Eve service at St. Mark's. Nancy's parents were making more of an effort with us, and we spent part of Christmas evening playing bridge with them.

June Asmus and Tom Nicely were married December 28 and Nancy and I attended the wedding together. June wore the same bridal gown that all of my sisters had worn. When it came time to throw the bridal bouquet, June took one look behind her to see where Nancy was standing and then tossed the bouquet over her shoulder directly at Nancy who willingly caught it. We began seriously talking about getting married after she graduated in June.

I got a letter from Uncle Sam indicating that I was to report for a draft physical in mid-January. At that time the draft was in place because the situation in Vietnam was heating up and the government was starting to build up the military. On the morning that I was to report for my physical, the temperature was twenty-three below zero. I got up early to catch the bus that was scheduled to leave Bowling Green for Fort Hayes in Columbus, Ohio at 7:00 AM. Pa also got up to go to work that morning and his '56 Dodge would not start. My Ford would and Pa drove my car to work and dropped me off at the bus station where a charter bus was waiting to take a group of us to Fort Hayes to keep our date with Uncle Sam.

Fort Hayes was basically a large barn-like building with very high ceilings and very poor insulation. Spending most of the day in my underwear left me chilled to the bone, as it must have every other twenty-one and twenty-two year old young man who was there. I was amazed at the number of individuals who seemed to have no idea why they were there or what was expected of them. A number of young men had to have assistance during the written exam because they were limited in their ability to read. One of the men sitting next to me was completing his medical history which included checking off certain diseases and health problems. He did not know whether or not he had had one of the diseases and called the sergeant over to ask him what it was. The sergeant came over and looked at the word that the young man was pointing to and replied, "That's Syphilis. If you had it, you would know it."

I completed all of the tests and examinations and had my quick exit discussion with one of the sergeants. He told me that it appeared I had passed all of the tests with flying colors and since I would be twenty-three-years-old on my next birthday, it was his opinion that I would probably get a draft notice in the next few months. All the way home, I wondered about the statement Dr. McClain had made indicating that I would never be drafted because it appeared at that point, I was going to get a draft notice quite soon.

I went back to work the next day trying to figure out what I would do if I were drafted. At one point I had given strong consideration to joining the Navy with Blynn, and I had even thought that if I joined the Navy, I would sign up to become a cook. That no longer appeared to be an option. I realized that with my ulcer I usually got quite seasick whenever I was on Lake Erie, and I knew the ocean would probably not be much better. A couple of weeks later, I did get a letter from the Army, stating that I was unacceptable for the draft. Dr. McClain had been right.

The cold weather in late January produced a lot of snow, and one Thursday evening, school was canceled for the next day because of the deep snow and the drifting on country roads. Nancy and Sue did not need to worry about school the next day, and came up to the bowling alley. When bowling was over, we decided to drive out into the country to look at the snowdrifts.

Ray had just bought a new 1962 Mercury Comet, and he drove west out of town on Route 6 and turned onto Mitchell Road. Route 6 had recently been plowed so driving on it was not too bad. Mitchell Road had not been plowed, and Ray had gone about a quarter of a mile when he hit a snowdrift that threw snow up over the hood and onto the top of the car. Ray could not get the car to go forwards or backwards so we got out to see what could be done to get us out of the snowdrift.

The drift was deep enough that when we hit it with the front of the car, the snow pack under the car actually lifted one of the tires up off the road surface. The snow around the car was deep enough that we had to push snow with the door to get out of the car. The wind was blowing at such a rate that it was impossible to see more than fifteen to twenty feet, and the temperature was approaching zero. None of us were dressed to be out in this weather, and both Nancy and Sue were wearing tennis shoes.

I told the girls to get back in the car, and I had Ray open the trunk of the car. I got the tire iron out of the trunk, and I removed a wheel cover from each of the back wheels. I handed one of the wheel covers to Ray and told him to start digging the snow away from the back wheels of the car. I did the same with the front wheels. After about fifteen minutes of digging, we had a short area around each tire cleared.

Ray, Nancy and I got into the snow bank at the front of the car and started pushing the car backwards as Sue drove the car in reverse. We started to move slowly and then a little faster. We kept backing up the quarter of a mile to Route 6, digging out snow and pushing when we needed to, and we did make it back.

When Nancy, Ray, and I climbed back into the car, we were all cold to the bone, and Nancy's feet were so cold that she was almost in tears. I took off her shoes and socks and rubbed her feet, and then I pulled up the back of my coat and shirt and told her to put her feet against my back to warm them up. After the feeling began to return to her feet, I again told her that if she ever doubted that I loved her, just remember that I had let her put her ice cold feet on my warm back. We decided that it was not a good idea to check for any more snowdrifts, and we all went home.

A couple of weeks later, the weather was the cause of another situation that was probably even more dangerous than getting stranded in a snow bank. Nancy and I usually spent a part of most dates parked somewhere, and one of the places that we parked was Averys. There was a gate on the front entrance off West Wooster Street that was closed at night, but the back entrance off Gorrel Avenue was always opened, and we could drive into the supply yard and be totally alone. One night, a freezing rain was falling, and when we got to Averys, I backed the convertible under one of the coal bins to get out of weather. The coal bins were closed in on three sides, and the only opening was the one that we backed into so the car was also closed in on three sides. To have heat, I kept the engine running. I was sitting behind the steering wheel and leaning against the door, and Nancy was leaning against my chest as we talked. I noticed that I was beginning to get sleepy, but I just thought that I was tired. When I noticed that Nancy seemed to be drifting off to sleep, I suggested that I take her home because I was afraid that we would fall asleep and we would be late getting her home.

Driving home, it suddenly occurred to me that with the car running in the tight space under the coal bin, we had accumulated engine exhaust in that area. With a convertible, there were plenty of spaces where the exhaust was able to get into the car. I realized we had not been just sleepy; we were being overcome with carbon monoxide.

The next morning, I woke up with a terrible headache. I called Nancy and found out that she too had a terrible headache, and we agreed we had been very lucky. We also concluded that we would never park under the coal bin again.

In March, I received a call one day from Ike Luce asking that I come to see him in the hospital. Ike owned and operated the Bee Gee Rental Company, and I had been renting tents and camping equipment from him whenever I did any camping and I had known him for a number of years. Ike had been involved in an automobile accident in which both of his legs were broken in a number of places, and he was in the hospital having various surgeries to repair them. When I went to see him, he totally surprised me by asking if I would be interested in coming to work for him. He explained that he would be in the hospital for a number of weeks, and after that it would be a number of months of rehabilitation and therapy before he would be able to return to work. His wife, Marian, and his son, Larry, would not be able to run the business by themselves, so he wanted to hire me to run the rental in his absence. He made me an offer, and I told him that I needed to think it over, and I would get back to him in a couple of days.

I was not happy working at Averys. The work was very demanding physically and working with Pa on a daily basis could also be difficult. I knew that it was not the job that I wanted to have for the rest of my life. Actually, I had been looking for a job elsewhere. Nancy and I were going to get married soon, and I wanted to have a different job with the possibility of making more money. Shortly before the call from Ike, I had applied for a job with the City of Bowling Green as a meter reader in the electric department. At the interview for the job, I was told that the main reason they were not going to hire me was the fact that I was single, and the city preferred that the job go to a married man to avoid problems associated with a single man going house to house.

I told Mom and Pa about the job offer from Ike, and I could tell right away that Pa did not think that I should take the job. He asked me if I had considered what would happen when Ike came back to work and there was not enough work at the rental for two people. He also inferred that I owed something to Newt Simpson for the job that I had at Averys, and he suggested that I would be putting Newt in a difficult spot to replace me. I don't know what it was about my leaving Averys that made Pa upset, but it seemed like it was the same discussion that Pa and I had when we talked about my going to college. I went to see Ike at the end of the week and told him that I would take the job. I gave Newt my two-week notice, and started working at the rental on April 1.

My job at Bee Gee Rental included opening the Rental Office every morning at 8:00 AM, running the business on a daily basis, signing out the rental equipment, keeping the rental records, collecting the rental fees, and doing any cleaning and maintenance of the equipment that was required. I also locked up the rental at the end of the day. Marian, Ike's wife, would come over whenever she could and help with the customers, but she had a number of other things that occupied her time. With Ike still in the hospital she spent time there daily. Also her elderly parents lived in the house next door so she spent time with them.

Ike and Marian had three children, Larry, Mary Lou, and Chester. Larry and Mary Lou were both considered retarded at that time, and Chester was attending Bowling Green State University. Chester would show up at the rental occasionally. Mary Lou was living at a home for individuals with learning disabilities, and Larry was my age and living with his parents. He had obvious learning and communication problems, but he worked at the rental each day, and he also had a number of lawns in the area that he mowed during the summer and fall. Larry would usually come over to the rental about 9:00 AM, and depending on his mowing schedule, he would look to me to give him something to do.

Working at the rental turned out to require less physical work than Averys, but it also turned out to be more stressful in other ways. Working with Pa could cause me stress depending on his mood, but working everyday with Larry, who was mentally challenged, had its own kind of stress. In addition, Marian was quite high strung and nervous. The good thing was that most days, I was totally in charge of my schedule, and for the first time, I was not doing only manual labor. I had direct contact with the customers, and I had a say in what needed to be done to keep the business going and profitable.

Another advantage to working at the rental was that some of the equipment was rented with an operator, and I was the operator. Pa always said, "You learn by doing," and I soon learned to operate a power trowel, a jack hammer, a motorized compactor, a floor sander and all of the rest of the power equipment that we rented. I even cut down a couple of trees with a chain saw. I enjoyed operating all of this equipment, but I have to say that the jack hammer was my least favorite. At 150 pounds, handling a 90 pound jack hammer on concrete was not something I wanted to do on a daily basis.

Shortly after I started working at Bee Gee Rental, a house on West Wooster Street just across the street from Averys was for sale by auction to settle an estate. Pa made a bid of $8,000 for the house, and it turned out that he was the high bidder. His plan was to remodel the house and then sell it and make a profit. We started the remodeling by digging a small basement under the house to install a new forced-air furnace to replace the individual gas heaters that were located throughout the house.

CHAPTER 35

WILL YOU MARRY ME?

Nancy's Graduation Reception
316 South Church Street

As Nancy's graduation grew nearer, we talked more about what we wanted our future to be, and that future included getting married sooner rather than later. We both knew that her parents would not give their consent, and in Ohio, she needed to be twenty-one to get married without parental consent. The only thing that I could think to do was to talk to Nancy's father.

On June 4, I called Ed at his office and asked if I could stop by and talk with him. He was too busy that day, but he agreed to see me the next day. I had been to the Massy Ferguson Store a number of times before so

I was familiar with the layout and where Ed's office was, and I made sure that I showed up on time. I was as nervous as I had ever been in my life as I entered Ed's office and after the "Hello" and "How are you?" I got right to the point.

In the strongest and most direct-sounding voice that I could muster, I told Ed that I was in love with his daughter, and I was asking for his permission to marry her. His response was "No." He would not give his permission. He went on to explain that although he felt that I was a good person, he did not see much of a future for me. He said that without a college education, he felt that my future was very limited. He said that he and Nancy's mother very much wanted her to go to college, and they felt it would be a problem if Nancy and I continued to be serious about each other. We talked about a number of things that concerned him about our relationship. But bottom line, he reaffirmed that he would not give me his permission, and that until Nancy was over twenty-one, she would have to go along with his decision.

I told him I understood what he was saying, but I did not agree with his opinion of my future. I also explained that just because he and Nancy's mother were opposed to our marriage, did not mean that we would not be married. I left thinking it was clear that Nancy and I were not going to be able to have the wedding that we had hoped for, and we would probably have to elope.

Nancy and I talked about my meeting with her father, and she reassured me she wanted to get married. Later that week I went to Toledo, to the Keiden's Jewelry Store and bought a small Keepsake diamond engagement ring and wedding band.

On June 7, 1963, I attended the BG Class of '63 graduation ceremony held in the High School Auditorium and watched as Nancy walked across the stage and received her diploma. After the ceremony, I met her about half way down the left hand aisle of the auditorium, and I pulled the box containing the engagement ring from my pocket, and I asked, "Will you marry me?" and Nancy said, "Yes."

The reaction wasn't nearly as romantic and positive when her parents discovered that I had given her an engagement ring. A few days later, they gave Nancy permission to wear the ring, but when it came time for the Bartter Family Reunion on July 7, her mother insisted that she attend and not wear the ring or tell anyone she was engaged. Nancy went to the reunion, but she refused to take off the ring. Her Uncle Chuck saw it and immediately let everyone know that he had seen it.

At some point Nancy and her mother had a conversation, and her mother made an offer to give her $10,000 if she waited to get married until after she graduated from college. Nancy and I talked about this offer, and I told Nancy that in my opinion, her parents were betting $10,000 that Nancy would meet someone else at college. We decided that we would not wait, and we would go forward with our plans to elope.

Nancy and I began planning for how, where and when we were going to elope. We decided that we would go to Monroe, Michigan to get married because a marriage license could be obtained there at age eighteen without a parent's consent.

CHAPTER 36
THE SUMMER OF '63

Pa was driving a '59 Oldsmobile, the current, "Best car on the road," and he and Mom decided to take a vacation, and Pa wanted to do some work on the car before they left. One night Pa, my brothers, Ray and Dan, and I took the Olds up to Averys to get the car ready for the road. Nancy showed up shortly after we began working on the car. Ray was changing the oil and greasing the front end, and I was packing the front wheel bearings and checking the front brake. Dan and Pa were replacing a universal joint on the drive shaft. I had jacked up the front of the car and put two car jack stands under the bumper to support the front of the car. The car was resting on the jack stands and the floor jack was still in place under the front frame of the car. I then removed the two front wheels of the car. Ray found that the floor jack was in the way of his access to the oil filter so he took the jack out from under the car, leaving the front of the car supported only on the car jack stands. I was sitting on a stool by the left front wheel checking the brake, Ray was under the front of the car working on the oil filter, and Dan and Pa were disconnecting the drive shaft.

At this point, the car was in park and could not move. The front of the car was supported on the jack stands, and as it happened, the rear tires were sitting on the edge of the hot water pipe floor trench. When Pa disconnected the drive shaft, the transmission park was no longer connected to the back wheels, and the back wheels were free to roll forward because the floor trench was at a slightly lower level than the rest of the floor. I was just getting up off the stool when the car started to roll forward, and the jack stands under the front bumper started to tip forward with the movement of the car. I felt the car moving against my leg as I stood up, and I immediately grabbed the front bumper with both hands and put my butt against the bumper. I started to push backwards to stop the movement to the car and yelled for everyone to get out from under the car.

Ray was able to roll out immediately. However, the forward movement of the car and the tipping of the car stands had dropped the car frame just enough that both Pa and Dan were pinned between the frame and the floor and neither of them could move. Ray grabbed the floor jack and pushed it under the car frame and started jacking up the front end. Dan was the first to get free, and as he came out from under the car. He grabbed Pa by the legs and started pulling him out from under the car. By this time Ray had jacked up the car to the point that Pa was free, and I was able to let go of the bumper. I had a deep imprint of the edge of the bumper across the palms of both hands, and in a couple of places, the edge of the bumper had cut the skin.

While we were all trying to catch our breath and discussing what had happened, we were also thinking about what could have been the outcome if I had not been able to hold the car from moving forward or if the jack stands had tipped over. At the moment the car started moving, Ray was directly beneath the engine and with both front wheels off the car, the entire weight would have fallen on him. Also, both Dan and Pa had been pinned momentarily by the frame when the car moved slightly forward. Again, if the car had fallen off the car stands, I thought that it was possible that all three of them could have been killed. Slowly, the beating in our chests returned to normal, and we went back to work, making sure that both the jack stands and the floor jack were in place, and that both back wheels were blocked to ensure that the car did not roll forwards or backwards.

The work on the house on Wooster Street was going quite well, and Pa, Bill Asmus, Larry Noon, my brothers, and I were all spending a number of evenings and weekends working on the basement and remodeling the house. It went so well, that Mom and Pa decided not to sell the house when it was finished but to move into it themselves. They planned to either rent or sell the house on Lime Street. I immediately offered to rent the house from them and they agreed.

By July, Nancy and I started accumulating furniture. We went to the Roth Furniture Store and bought a new couch, an easy chair, two end tables, a coffee table, and a bedroom suite. I also went into Toledo to Tiedtke's and bought a new chrome kitchen set which included a table and four chairs, for the dining room. We bought a used stove from Aunt Kate and also purchased a used refrigerator. Nancy and I were now set up for our first home.

In early August, Mom and Pa and my three brothers moved out of the Lime Street House, and I stayed and lived there briefly as a bachelor. I started repainting all of the walls and fixing any little problem that I could see. I also took home a carpet cleaner from Bee Gee Rental and cleaned all of the carpets. Nancy helped whenever she could.

On August 8, Nancy and I took a trip up to Monroe, Michigan. We got our blood tests and applied for a marriage license at the Monroe County Courthouse. Then we went to the Trinity Lutheran Church where we made arrangements with Pastor Fehner to be married in the church at 7:00 PM on August 31, 1963. Pastor Fehner appeared to be nearing retirement age and spoke about the importance of our decision to elope. Although it was obvious that he did not approve of our marriage without parental consent, he agreed that he would reserve the church for that night, and he would perform the wedding ceremony. All we had to do was wait for the next three weeks to go by.

CHAPTER 37

WHAT ARE YOU DOING SATURDAY NIGHT?

Our Wedding: August 31, 1963

Trinity Lutheran Church in Monroe, Michigan
Caroline and Bill were Our Witnesses

The plan was for me to pick up Nancy for our Saturday night date with the premise that we were going out to dinner and to Toledo to see the movie, *Lawrence of Arabia*. After we left Nancy's house, we would meet Caroline and Bill, and Nancy would ride to Monroe with them. This way, I could not be accused of taking Nancy across a state line. A number of our friends were planning to follow us to the church. Caroline and Bill were going to be our witnesses, and my sister, Janet, and her husband, Terry, were also planning to attend, as was Nancy's sister, Sue, and her boyfriend John Caldwell.

The closer that we got to our wedding date, the more people there were who knew we were planning to elope. I wondered how Nancy's mother and father had not heard about it. I told my parents about our plans and invited them to go with us to the church. Mom and Pa decided it was best that they not attend to avoid any future problems with Nancy's parents.

I made arrangements with Ike Luce to take off the first week of September so that we could have a short honeymoon, and I made a reservation at the Commodore Perry Hotel for our wedding night. My Aunt Juanita was working at the Edison Restaurant in Toledo, and she suggested that we come there after the service for sandwiches. She assured me that we could bring a cake to the restaurant, and the restaurant would provide plates and forks for us to serve the cake.

I went to the J.C. Penny Store in Bowling Green and bought a navy blue suit, my first new suit ever. Nancy had told me that she had a new white dress and a vale which she had packed in a bag and taken out of her house so that she could change at the church. Nancy wrote a letter to her parents explaining about our marriage and Sue agreed to give it to them when she returned after the wedding.

I washed and cleaned out the convertible and put my tent, two sleeping bags, and my camping gear in the trunk. Nancy had never tent-camped before and for some reason, I thought it might be fun to camp one night of our honeymoon. I then packed my bag, put on my new blue suit, and left the house. I stopped by Mom and Pa's house to give them a hug on my way to Nancy's house.

When I rang the bell at Nancy's, Ed answered the door and we sat in the living room and talked as we waited for Nancy to come downstairs. There was a brief silence, and then Ed said, "I hear that this is a very special night tonight." I almost fell off my chair as I wondered what he had heard and what he meant by that statement. I must have taken a few seconds to respond because Ed continued by saying, "I mean dinner and going to see *Lawrence of Arabia.*" Relieved, I quickly answered," Yes, it is a special night." Fortunately, Nancy came into the room about this time and we said good-bye and left. We met Caroline and Bill as planned, Nancy moved into their car, and we all headed for Monroe.

Our little car caravan included me in the lead, followed by Caroline, Bill and Nancy in Bill's car, Ray, Troyl, and Howard in Ray's car, and friends, Bob Moreland and Sue Boyer in Bob's car. Janet and Terry were running late and planned to meet us in Monroe. Nancy's sister, Sue, and her boyfriend, John Caldwell, were also planning to meet us in Monroe.

We arrived at the church shortly before seven. Janet and Terry had gotten a speeding ticket on the way so Terry was not happy. Sue and John were nowhere to be seen as we all went into the church. Nancy changed into her white dress, and we were ready to walk up to the altar. Pastor Fehner used the standard Lutheran Sacrament of Marriage, and after Nancy tried to put my ring on my right-hand, we finally got it right, and we both said, "I do." Pastor Fehner pronounced us Man and Wife, and we kissed.

Outside the church, we stopped for a quick wedding picture, and then we all started back to Toledo to the Edison Club for a reception. Sue and John were still missing which worried Nancy. However, as we drove out of town after the wedding, we saw Sue and John driving into town, and we all pulled into a parking lot. We got out to talk and see what had happened, and found out that John had taken a wrong turn. We all climbed back into our cars to head for Toledo, and as we pulled out of the parking lot, a police car with flashing red lights pulled up in front of us blocking us in the parking lot. Many thoughts ran through my mind at this point, and I fully expected to see Ed step out of the police car and personally arrest me for kidnapping his daughter.

As it turned out, the police had noticed the large group of kids in the parking lot and all of the Ohio license plates. When we started to pull out, we were exiting from the "Entrance Only" drive. They used that mistake as an excuse to stop us, mainly to see what we were up to. I explained that we had just gotten married, and they gave us their congratulations and allowed us to leave.

CHAPTER 38

WHAT ARE YOU DOING THE REST OF YOUR LIFE?

After Our Wedding

On August 12, I had turned twenty-three years old. I had survived my childhood and a part of my young adulthood. I had grown up financially poor in a large family that was far from poor in character or values. I had taken on bits and pieces of most of the people that had come in and out of my life to this point. I was a product of the past that I have just shared with you. I knew at that time I was not satisfied with my job, and I couldn't help but agree with Nancy's dad, that my financial future might be limited.

I knew that I had an ulcer that was still giving me problems, and at some point I needed to do something about it besides drink Maalox and milk to treat it. I knew that we had to face Nancy's parents and find out what our marriage might mean to our relationship with them, and how that would affect our relationship with each other. I knew that there would be rumors about how and why we eloped. Some people would assume that Nancy was pregnant and we had to get married. They would soon find out they were wrong. I knew that Nancy was registered for college and wanted to go, and that subject would come up soon with fall semester beginning shortly. I knew that we both wanted children, and we had talked about this whenever we were planning our future. And I wondered what Nancy would say when I suggested that we camp out a night on our honeymoon. Finally, I knew that returning from our honeymoon, Nancy and I had many unknowns and challenges to face.

But at that moment, as we drove from Monroe to Toledo, all I cared about was that I had just married the person who was going to share the rest of her life with me, and we were very much in love. I knew that we were not riding off into the sunset on a white horse, but we were going toward ever after in my '56 Ford Convertible . . . together.

ACKNOWLEDGEMENTS

What started out as an attempt to pass on some memories to my grandchildren turned into almost two years of revisiting my past not only in my memory but also through trips to the various places and houses that were a part of my childhood. In the process I met and talked with family members and also current owners of the properties. I visited such places as the Woodville Ohio Historical Society, the Bowling Green City Municipal Building, the Wood County Court House, the Bowling Green City Library, and other locations that are mentioned in the book as I tried to verify dates and details.

All of the people who appear in the writings are real, and all of the events took place as I have described to the best of my memory. However the chronological order of some events may be less than totally accurate. I know that individuals who were a part of these writings may have a different memory of some events and my only comment is these are my memories.

There are many people that I would like to thank for their interest, comments, assistance, and patience with me during this writing.

At the top of my list is my mother[2] who was an important resource for helping me with time frames and details about various events. My brothers Ray, Dan, and Art, and my sisters[3], Janet and Caroline, gave me their memories and interpretations of shared experiences. A number of aunts, uncles and cousins also helped me, especially Marie, Laura, Pug, Uncle Bob Myerholtz, and Aunt Juanita. Friends[4] Jim Berry and Addison Adkins were available and willing to discuss our high school adventures and verify dates and details.

---

[2]   Myron Myerholtz, my father, is deceased
[3]   My sister Louise Noon is deceased
[4]   Blynn Gauze is deceased

To my very large Myerholtz and Dickerson families, I can only say thank you for being such an influence on my life, and for being such a varied and colorful family not only to be a part of but also to write about.

To my son Eric, who assisted with the editing, and his wife Linda, and grandchildren Elizabeth, Emily, and David; and to my son Matthew, his wife Laura, and grandchildren Leah, and Ben, I say thank you for continually adding joy and love and memories to my life.

Finally, to my wife Nancy, thank you for working with me to polish and edit the many drafts of my story and for avoiding the temptation to correct or censor too much. During the final review of this book we observed the fiftieth anniversary of our first date and our forty-eighth wedding anniversary. Thank you for all of those years, the memories that we have made, and the memories that we well share tomorrow. I love you, always and forever!

CPSIA information can be obtained at www.ICGtesting.com
Printed in the USA
BVOW022253081211

277790BV00006B/10/P